Asian American Literary Studies

Introducing Ethnic Studies

General Editor: Robert Con Davis-Undiano

Titles in the series:

Native American Studies
Clara Sue Kidwell and Alan Velie

Asian American Literary Studies
Edited by Guiyou Huang

Forthcoming:

Introducing the Arab World
Edited by Mohja Kahf

Asian American Literary Studies

Edited and with an introduction by Guiyou Huang

Edinburgh University Press

© in this edition, Edinburgh University Press, 2005.
© in the individual contributions is retained by the authors

Edinburgh University Press Ltd
22 George Square, Edinburgh

Typeset in Monotype Ehrhardt
by Servis Filmsetting Ltd, Manchester, and
printed and bound in Great Britain by
MPG Books Ltd, Bodmin, Cornwall

A CIP record for this book is available from the British Library

ISBN 0 7486 2012 5 (hardback)
ISBN 0 7486 2013 3 (paperback)

The right of the contributors
to be identified as authors of this work
has been asserted in accordance with
the Copyright, Designs and Patents Act 1988.

Contents

Acknowledgments

This book owes its existence to the vigorous research and writing of the contributors. Special thanks are due to Robert Con Davis-Undiano, Neustadt Professor of Comparative Literature at the University of Oklahoma and General Editor of Edinburgh's *Introducing Ethnic Studies Series*, for his confidence and support. Jackie Jones, Deputy Chief Executive and Head of Publishing at Edinburgh University Press, deserves kudos for her professional guidance and enthusiasm for the project. Fiona Wade did an excellent job of copy-editing the typescript, and Robert Swanson provided a thorough index. I also owe a debt of gratitude to James Dale, Carol Macdonald, and Anna Somerville, all of Edinburgh University Press, who contributed to the shape of the book in one way or another. Most importantly, my wife Yufeng Qian and my four-year-old son George Ian supported the project with love, understanding, and patience every step of the way; to them I owe an eternal debt.

Series Editor's Foreword

The series "Introducing Ethnic Studies" provides an important tool for students and researchers in the study of ethnicity. With volumes now available on Native-American Studies and Asian-American literary studies, the series will still include volumes on Arabic, Latino, Judaic, and African-American studies. Building on the critique of ethnicity and ethnic affiliation gaining momentum over the last thirty years, this series is dedicated to evaluating available resources concerning cutting-edge issues and future trends in prominent areas of ethnic studies. The goal of this series is to enhance the ability of students and scholars to do independent inquiry in a university course or in research.

Except for the first volume – *Native American Studies*, co-written by Clara Sue Kidwell and Alan R. Velie – the books in this series are multi-authored collections containing specially commissioned essays. In its own way, each of the books demonstrates the rise of ethnic studies as intrinsically interdisciplinary. That is, all of these books will tend to cycle through literary study, history, sociology, philosophy, art, and law so as to enable the connections and relationships necessary for understanding ethnicity in any form it may be expressed. The volumes in this series will demonstrate the tendency in ethnic studies to inquire in at least two domains at once, often literature and history, art and sociology, or philosophy and religion.

The current volume on Asian-American culture emphasizes literary studies instead of a more diverse approach in order to satisfy a particular lack in its field of inquiry – the lack of a clear scholarly map in Asian-American literary studies. In this collection, literature and history and literature and culture are prominent as couplings for most of the contributions. These chapters show that modern scholarship finds new ways to demonstrate that all knowledge is at some level interdisciplinary. The style of interdisciplinary inquiry in ethnic studies – even in this volume on literary studies – emphasizes the drama of inquiry playing out across disciplines. Moreover, as the study of ethnicity in any area will tend to map a circuitous path through all human endeavors, we glimpse through this volume the broad perspective that cuts across nationalities and cultural identities, the perspective necessary to capture the history and development of ethnic studies.

The volume on Asian-American studies also foregrounds a key issue pertinent to all ethnic study, an issue clearly evident in the volumes of this series. Does the study of ethnicity necessarily need to advance, or champion, the *cause* of that culture? Or do the requirements of scholarly inquiry demand totally dispassionate observation and analysis of a culture? There are strong arguments both ways, and good and effective scholarship exists along a line of possibility extending between these two extremes. Every ethnic studies scholar at some point takes a stand somewhere along this line. The choice of the scholars in *Asian American Literary Studies*, as with the other volumes of this series, is to invest in the integrity of dispassionate scholarship as a strategy for advancing the cause of Asian-American culture as a body of knowledge. This "solution" is a choice to be at the same time engaged and analytical, the best of both extremes. The effectiveness and power of this volume, as will be the case with all the volumes in the series, will be proven by how well it opens doors for students and scholars alike.

Introduction: Global and Interdisciplinary Perspectives on Asian American Literary Studies

Guiyou Huang

The label "Asian American" has gained a relatively stable currency within the academe, though the newer and more inclusive "Asian Pacific American" has also garnered significant political and academic recognition and broadens the field to include Asian Canadians and Pacific Islanders. In *Asian American Literary Studies*, "Asian American" applies to the generally accepted designations for descendants from China, Japan, Korea, and the Philippines – the populations that were recognized first in the 1970s as Asian American, and to populations with ethnic ancestries in South and Southeast Asian countries, including Burma, India, Malaysia, Pakistan, Sri Lanka, and Vietnam, to register the heterogeneity of ethnic groups and the diversity of their originary cultures. But even these names do not holistically reflect the complexity of the racial and ethnic composition of North America. Canadian Asians, albeit occupying a different nation-space, are considered under the Asian American category, with "American" implying "North American." Thus, "Asian American" as used in this book straddles both United States and Canadian borders, and encompasses East, South, and Southeast Asians, as well as Pacific Islanders, particularly Hawaiians.

In the latter half of twentieth-century Asian America, a few landmark publishing events laid the groundwork – and one may even say ground rules – for the establishment and development of Asian American literature: few would argue that Frank Chin et al's *The Big Aiiieeeee!*, Maxine Hong Kingston's *The Woman Warrior*, Amy Tan's *The Joy Luck Club*, Joy Kogawa's *Obasan*, and Bharati Mukherjee's *Jasmine* – all published in the 1970s and 1980s – brought Asian American literary writing to an unprecedented level of visibility that made impossible a continued marginalization of this emerging ethnic literature. A single most important gauge of the healthy development of a literature is a clear and strong presence of critics, and by that standard, Asian American literature has clinched an impressive success in both the sheer volume of its productions in all genres – short fiction, poetry, drama, autobiography, novels, and anthologies – and in the critical literature that has grown with it. Since Elaine Kim's 1982 study, *Asian American Literature*, critical works on this branch of American literature have flourished and the trend is showing no signs of waning. The United States, especially its academic institutions on the west coast and on a smaller scale in the northeast, has given progressive attention to the rise of Asian American literature by publishing a considerable number of monographs and reference volumes to facilitate teaching and research. The impact of the rise of Asian American literary studies has made itself felt in many Asian and European countries as well, which further attests to the popular and critical demand for studies in the field. The current volume is a literature- and culture-based collection that cuts across various disciplines: social and political thought, film, sociology, history, linguistics, gender studies, popular culture, and literature (autobiography, novel, drama, and literary history), and consists of ten original essays, thematically divided into three sections, that represent scholars from Germany, Japan, Singapore, Spain, and the United States, covering a diverse range of interdisciplinary topics and multiple global perspectives in contemporary Asian American literary studies.

Section I, "Perspectives on Literature and History," examines the intersections of literature and history in varied manifestations: national histories, family history, and life stories. In the opening chapter, "Asian American Literary History: War, Memory, and Representation," Gayle Sato probes the impact of Asian/American wars on Asian American writers and the vital role that the memory of war plays in the production of Asian American literary works. Sato investigates the relationships between two histories that are central to an understanding of ethnicity and American culture: an international history of wars between the US and Asia, and a domestic history of Asian American cultural formation. These wars include the Asia Pacific War, the Korean War, the Vietnam War, and the Cold War, of which Sato focuses on the Asia Pacific War and the Vietnam War by considering the Vietnamese American Andrew Pham's memoir *Catfish and Mandala*, the Korean/ German American Nora Okja Keller's novel *Comfort Woman*, the Korean American Chang-rae Lee's novel *A Gesture Life*, and the Japanese American Karen Tei Yamashita's novel *Tropic of Orange*.

War provides the subject or impetus for a striking proportion of Asian American literary works in the second half of the twentieth century. Intertextual study of literature and war is not only demanded by the intrinsic themes and politics of Asian American literary texts, but by the failure of literary studies to incorporate Asian American writing into their definitions and analysis of "modern" culture. Sato draws on recent works on memory, narrative, and war in the fields of cultural studies, history, and psychology, such as Lisa Lowe's *Immigrant Acts*, Caroline Chung Simpson's *An Absent Presence*, Marita Sturken's *Tangled Memories*, Anne Anlin Cheng's *The Melancholy of Race*, and Yoshikuni Igarashi's *Bodies of Memory*. Using literary texts to identify and explore the implications of different representational practices, psychological paradigms, or political interventions, Sato organizes her chapter around aesthetic and political issues such as representational strategies, the politics of grief, memory and post-memory, redress and other forms of political intervention, and transnational narratives in which Asian Americans find themselves occupying multiple and often conflicting roles in the processes of remembering and forgetting Asian/American wars.

In Chapter 2, "The Self in the Text versus the Self as Text: Asian American Autobiographical Strategies," Rocío Davis turns to the function of the self in the life writings of some Asian American autobiographers: the Chinese American Kingston's *The Woman Warrior* and *Tripmaster Monkey*, the Sri Lankan Canadian Michael Ondaatje's *Running in the Family*, the Pakistani American Sara Suleri's memoir *Meatless Days* and, under the name of Sara Suleri Goodyear, her *Boys Will Be Boys*, the Korean American autobiographer Helie Lee's *Still Life with Rice*, along with two co-authored autobiographies, Clark Blaise and Bharati Mukherjee's *Days and Nights in Calcutta*, and May-lee Chai and Winberg Chai's *The Girl From Purple Mountain*. Cruising through these texts, Davis examines autobiographical strategies that Asian American writers employ to chart the itineraries of subject dialogue and positionality.

Davis first considers the use of the short story cycle as an autobiographical strategy that emphasizes the constructedness of ethnic identity formation and representation. The story cycle reflects the narrator's process of memory as non-lineal, associative, non-temporal, fragmented, and incomplete, making structure and content mutually reinforcing. The organization of the discrete narratives becomes the author's attempt to control a series of fundamental memories, to define their meaning and significance with regard to her own formation, subverting the dictates of causality. Davis points out that the forms of relational autobiography have become increasingly common in Asian American women's writing. The figure of the narrator is now a composite built up from the accounts of the other characters, and the autobiographical self has to be found obliquely, in relation to the characters in the text: the authors "decenter" themselves and substitute in their place discrete personalities, each bearing a profound psychological and emotional relationship to the narrator that serves to unify the text. Davis also identifies the rewriting of the inherited scripts of the autobiography of childhood as a strategy, arguing that Asian American writers challenge the accepted form and revise the traditional representation of issues in new ways. Collaborative writing is yet another strategy that challenges the fundamental paradigm of the unified self of traditional autobiography, as well as the concept of the monologic voice. Davis addresses the narrative approaches employed in collaborative texts as a discursive means toward proposing a particular socio-political or personal agenda, within the multilayered context of Asian American writing; she demonstrates how the plural position of these writers, performed through their dialogic life-writing exercise, reflects the shifting boundaries of memory, transcultural positioning, and representation.

Cheng Lok Chua's "Asian Americans Imagining Burma: Chang-rae Lee's *A Gesture Life* and Wendy Law-Yone's *Irrawaddy Tango*" focuses on Burma as a location of the fictive imagination that plays a notably important role in the two novels. Chua argues that although Lee imagines a Burma of the past (during the Japanese Occupation of the 1940s) and Law-Yone projects a Burma of the future (as the fictional state of "Daya"), both writers imagine it as a land of extremes, the extreme being a location beyond measure. In Lee's novel, Burma represents the geographical and cultural extreme of Japanese imperialism, and in Law-Yone's work, the socio-political excess of state-sponsored military coercion. Burma is such an extreme that it is almost beyond the remembering for Lee's narrator-protagonist who nearly burns down his prized American home inadvertently when memories of his Burmese days return to him. And the Burmese military dictatorship is so extreme that it is beyond the usual mimetic telling for Law-Yone, who sets her novel in a nonexistent dystopia in order to censure its continuing existence. This experience of extremism, emblematized by Burma, acts as a catalyst for the revelation of a profound human truth in each work – in Lee's, the road through Burma leads to the truth about an individual human psyche while in Law-Yone's, the path back to Burma leads to the truth about a human society and polity.

Section II, "Perspectives on Gender Roles and Representation," focuses on gender issues, a hotly debated topic among Asian American writers and scholars in the last quarter of the twentieth century. In "Globalization, Masculinity, and the Changing Stakes of Hollywood Cinema for Asian American Studies," Karen Fang looks into the impact of globalization on the film industry's representation of Asians and Asian Americans in mainstream and independent films. Reviewing a number of recent movies such as *Better Luck Tomorrow*, *The Guru*, *The Joy Luck Club*, and more generally, *The Matrix*, *Charlie's Angels*, *Pearl Harbor*, and *The Phantom Menace*, Fang considers the entertainment season of 2002–3 a turning point in the history of Asian Americans in American media and popular culture. Not only did it witness the release of Justin Lin's *Better Luck Tomorrow*, a critically acclaimed independent film that was picked up by MTV Films for national release, but it also included *The Guru*, a lightweight romance which conducted a smart critique of stereotypes of Asian masculinity. Fang explores the advantages of these 2002–3 releases, highlighting the important cultural work those films initiate as well as illustrating why earlier releases from the 1990s – including the optimistic possibilities of *Mulan* and *Joy Luck Club* – failed to culminate in the success that finally arrived after the millennium.

The issues that Fang's work addresses include the integration of ethnic Asian actors for roles which either render race irrelevant or which make aspects of the ethnic culture or appearance desirable, fashionable objects; the specific attacks on longstanding stereotypes of Asian Americans; the expansion of the notion of "Asian American" to include any combination of East-West hybridization and the theoretical analogues drawn with other oppressed groups; and the permeation of these theories of ethnic identity in popular culture, such as more general-interest movies like *The Phantom Menace*. Grounded in the context of globalization, in which the worldwide consolidation of culture and media enabled both the diffusion of alternative forms of entertainment as well as the audience tastes that support them, Fang's chapter makes a case for entertainment media as the single most important arena of cultural critique and ethnic empowerment, not only because popular entertainment is a major source of racist perception and self-identity, but also because the very superficial qualities of media which reduces to stereotype can also be asserted for ethnic reinvention.

In "Gender Negotiations and the Asian American Literary Imagination," Wenxin Li examines Kingston's *The Woman Warrior*, *China Men*, and *Tripmaster Monkey*, and John Okada's *No-No Boy* for their exploration of gender crossings toward an alternative articulation of Asian American consciousness, arguing that Asian American men and women should strive to go beyond the confines of binary oppositions of gender as the defining model for articulating Asian American subjectivity. Li points out that gender strife has dominated the critical discourse in Asian American literature since the 1970s, known as the "gender wars" between ethnic nationalists and feminists surrounding the publication of *Aiiieeeee!* and *The Woman Warrior*, and that much of Asian American critical discourse has been propelled by the debates between these opposing camps on a number of issues concerning the formation of an Asian American identity, such as race, culture, and gender.

Li builds his argument on recent developments in gender theory that have repeatedly challenged the early model of antagonism between feminism and masculinity as being simplistic and restricting. Critical race theories and queer theories have prompted scholars to go beyond the traditional model of binary oppositions of men versus women, heterosexual versus homosexual, white versus black, among others, recognizing that in addition to the apparent antagonisms there also exist unexpected dependencies among the opposing pairs: while each has its own particular interests and negotiates its position in relation to the dominant political, economic, and cultural forces, they cannot expect to eradicate or replace their opponents. Despite the inevitable gaps between their perceived goals and objectives, Li argues, they can actually learn from each other in terms of strategies for the collective advancement of their causes.

In "Long a Mystery and Forever a Memory: God vs. Goddess in the Ethnic Novel," Guiyou Huang approaches the Asian American novel from the vantage point of Amy Tan's critique of patriarchy that utilizes the metaphor of God and Goddess in the novelist's depiction of the battle for equality, happiness, and freedom in *The Kitchen God's Wife*. Hawthorne's romance *The Scarlet Letter*, among other mainstream works, provides a historical and literary pre-text for Tan's novel and paves the ground for a critique of the function of oppressive patriarchy. Tan appropriates Chinese culture and her own familial past for her fiction, but she also hearkens back to a mainstream literary icon – the fountainhead of American fiction – to establish intercultural and intertextual links between a most canonized mid-nineteenth-century male writer and herself, a late twentieth-century ethnic female novelist. More importantly, Huang probes Tan's presentation of gender roles through her understanding and articulation of the religiosity of Chinese and American life metaphorized in the Christian God and the godly figure of Confucius.

Tamara Silvia Wagner's chapter, "Realigning and Reassigning Cultural Values: Occidentalist Stereotyping and Representations of the Multiethnic Family in Asian American Women Writers," investigates the repercussions of Kingston's *Woman Warrior* on the fiction of subsequent women writers, the international popularity of Tan's *The Joy Luck Club*, and the redeployments of recurring themes and plot development in more recent novels such as Fae Myenne Ng's *Bone*. Wagner analyzes the increasing popularity of two-plot novels that connect cultural clashes not only to generation conflicts but also to gender issues by juxtaposing the "exotic" past of an earlier generation, typically the mother or mother-surrogate, with predominantly sentimental, though frequently comical, representations of cross-cultural relationships and family structures in contemporary America.

Wagner points out that Tan's later novels – most notably *The Kitchen God's Wife* and *The Hundred Secret Senses* – are seen to transcend occidentalist and orientalist ways of stereotyping, leading the genre to new heights, as an almost self-parodying irony circumvents much of the criticized sentimentality. This new development is juxtaposed with the two editions of Shirley Geok-lin Lim's *Among the White Moon Faces*, published as *An Asian American Memoir of Homelands* in New York and as *Memoirs of a Nonya Feminist* in Singapore. Wagner also examines Lim's novel *Joss & Gold* and Hwee Hwee Tan's *Mammon Inc.*, arguing that it is the selling of authenticity and marginality as a consumer product that is at once self-ironically re-examined and reissued in recent fiction such as *The Hundred Secret Senses* and *The Bonesetter's Daughter*. As both orientalist and occidentalist preconceptions are exposed as discursively constituted conceptualizations, the value and composition of authenticity are drawn into question, dismissing the easy polarization that structures earlier variations on the themes of cross-cultural conflicts within the family and the burdens as well as potentials of cultural hybridity. Building on studies of hybridity and orientalism as well as on more recent interest in occidentalism as a revisionist, but equally polarized counterpart to orientalism, Wagner provides an overview of the developments and potentials of an important subgenre of Asian American writing.

Section III, "Perspectives on Language and Culture," explores how culture and language contribute to the perception and formation of the ethnic and cultural identity. The complexity of identity politics for second-generation Indian Americans is the concern of Vincent Melomo's chapter, "'I Love My India': Indian American Students Performing Identity and Creating Culture on Stage." Based on theory in anthropology and sociology

on identity in late modernity and cultural models, Melomo draws on observations and interview data that he collected while conducting ethnographic
fieldwork on the children of Indian immigrants in North Carolina in the late
1990s. Little work has been done on the struggle of second-generation
Indian Americans to resolve conflicts faced in adolescence. The cultural programs, put on by Indian or South Asian student organizations, are key sites
for the creation of ethnic culture and identity in the US, and have been
largely overlooked by scholars. Discussing the content, structure, and
meaning of several of the programs he observed, Melomo interprets the cultural programs as public performances of ethnic/cultural/national identities that intersect with racial, class and gender ones.

These programs include performances based on classical Indian dance
and music forms, regional or folk dances, movie-songs and dances, hybrid
music and dance forms, fashion shows, and skits. The performances represent different regions, time periods, styles, and ideas of the "traditional"
and the "modern." Melomo considers how these elements are combined in
the programs to construct a more distinctly second-generation ethnic identity. Although cultural programs are designed primarily just to entertain,
through the use of skits the second generation often addresses issues and
concerns that are more directly relevant to their daily lives, providing
models for identity and behavior. The skits may challenge the normative
behavior expected by their parents, while also struggling to negotiate a compromise. Melomo addresses how the second generation uses these skits to
explore pressures for educational success, and concerns about marriage and
gender – key concerns following from struggles with their parents' immigrant dream. Melomo's contribution to an understanding of these immigrant issues is significant for its focus on cultural programs, which are
important sites for the construction and performance of identity and community for young Indian Americans and many other Asian American
groups.

In "Speaking Outside of the Standard: Local Literature of Hawai'i,"
Amy Nishimura examines a communal language: Pidgin – Hawaiian Creole
English – developed by ethnic peoples who all worked under oppressive
conditions in the early 1900s Hawaii to communicate with one another.
Nishimura looks into works written in Pidgin by local Hawaiian writers,
especially Lois-Ann Yamanaka's *Wild Meat and the Bully Burgers* and *Blu's
Hanging*, Zamora Linmark's *Rolling the R's*, Lisa Linn Kanae's *Sista
Tongue*, and Milton Murayama's *All I Asking for Is My Body*, to demon-
strate that this hybrid language is representative of a polyvocal society, a

society that continues to negotiate what it means to be a "Local" person who lives in Hawaii. Nishimura analyzes how writers dispel notions that speaking/writing in forms other than Standard English is "fractured," "broken," or "incoherent," arguing that the organic inception of Pidgin has become a marker of Local identity, yet despite its working-class and cultural heritage, stigmas against Pidgin remain.

Nishimura discusses the consequences of policies such as those by the Hawaii State School Board on the use of Pidgin by reading narratives that focus on themes of self-hatred and isolation. Imposed standards left people feeling inadequate and incompetent about their scholastic potential; however, current work of local authors undoes some of the misguided notions about Pidgin, which ethnic writers of Hawaii use in their narratives to portray life in plantation camps, laborers' desire to go "home," the displacement and isolation that workers felt, assimilation in a new society, and exploitation of plantation owners. Nishimura's work adds considerably to the ongoing discussion about the distinctions between Native Hawaiian literature and settler, not immigrant, literature.

Christiane Schlote, on the other hand, focuses her attention on dramatic literature in "Staging Heterogeneity: Contemporary Asian American Drama," considering issues of pan-ethnicity, identity politics, community, and gender relations in three plays written by Asian American writers: Velina Hasu Houston's *Tea*, Jeannie Barroga's *Walls*, and Elizabeth Wong's *Kimchee and Chitlins*. Schlote shows that these playwrights' attempts to construct visions of Asian American identities go beyond narrow and presumably "representative" definitions. She observes that while the development of Asian American theatre in general has been strongly influenced by women playwrights, directors, and theatre managers, it is still often mainly identified with the pioneering works of Frank Chin, David Henry Hwang, or Philip Kan Gotanda. However, in the wake of reconceptualizations of such slippery terms as Asian American identity and Asian American community, there has been a call within Asian American Studies for an increased awareness of the heterogeneous nature of Asian American groups.

Asian American playwrights – women playwrights in particular – have long pointed out that the category of Asian American is strongly divided along national, ethnic, socio-economic, sexual, and religious lines. But not only have they emphasized the need to challenge cultural and sexual stereotypes of Asian Americans as imposed on them by the Anglo-American mainstream, they have also stressed the need to complement specifically gendered theatrical representations by Chin and others. Schlote situates the plays within the context of the development of Asian American theatre (exemplified, for example, in the work of the New York-based Pan Asian Repertory Theatre and Ma-Yi Theater Ensemble) and analyzes them within the broader framework of Asian American cultural studies.

Asian American Literary Studies is meant for specialized studies and for student use in the high school and university classroom. The teacher and the student will do well with this book by taking advantage of the depth and breadth of the subjects included. Regardless of the approaches and focuses adopted by the contributors, the reader will be sure to find five intrinsically connected topics that run across all sections of the book: gender roles (in Fang, Huang, Li, Schlote, Wagner), stereotyping (in Fang, Nishimura, Wagner), identity politics (in Davis, Fang, Li, Melomo, Nishimura, Schlote), the intersections of literature, history, family, and the self (Sato, Davis, Chua, Huang), and the impact of wars on Asian American culture and literature (Sato, Huang, Chua, Schlote, Fang). Indeed, none of these vital issues stands alone and makes critical, cultural, or political sense absent a larger, interdisciplinary context. While the chapters do not reference one another due to their synchronous presence in this volume, they illuminate each other by providing a cultural and intellectual nexus that intertextualizes all, in the sense that each piece presents ideas and issues that are the enlargements of other, related themes and topics. The interplay of these subjects is apparent in all ten chapters that explore fictions, autobiographies, sociological issues, films, drama, performance, dialects, politics, and history.

It is also noteworthy that some Asian American writers figure prominently in the critical discourses of Asian American cultural and literary studies. Figures like Maxine Hong Kingston and Amy Tan – both of whom achieved notoriety in the 1970s and late 1980s respectively – continue to be popular subjects of critical inquiry in the twenty-first century. Kingston's name, along with her work, is a point of reference in almost every chapter. Sato refers to Kingston's representation of the Vietnam War; Davis cites Kingston's autobiographical strategies as innovative and unconventional; Li analyzes the polemical debate between Kingston and Frank Chin over the "real" and the "fake" in Asian American literary writing; and Wagner considers Kingston's *The Woman Warrior* in connection with the representations of the multiethnic family in Asian American women's writing. Tan's work has likewise garnered a considerable amount of interest from the contributors represented here. While Huang focuses on Tan's second novel *The Kitchen God's Wife*, Wagner looks into her *Joy Luck Club*, *The Hundred*

Secret Senses, and *The Bonesetter's Daughter*; in fact Tan's work takes a central place in Wagner's chapter. Fang, on the other hand, deals with the movie version of *Joy Luck Club* in her study of Hollywood films.

South and Southeast Asian American literature emerged in the past decade, accompanied by the publications of numerous immigrant and war narratives by Vietnamese and Burmese American writers, and is represented by Chua's chapter that considers two novels that both concern Burma. Two other pieces in this book are unique: Melomo's "I Love My India" and Nishimura's "Speaking Outside of the Standard." The former undertakes a sociological study of cultural programs performed by second-generation Indians as expressions of their definition and articulation of their bifurcated identity; the latter, on the other hand, offers a socio-linguistic analysis of the role of a Local dialect – Hawaii Creole English – in the life of Local people and in the writing of Hawaiian writers. Together, the ten essays in *Asian American Literary Studies* provide a considerable array of global and inter-disciplinary perspectives on the intersections of literary, political, cultural, historical, and social issues cutting across the broad discipline of Asian American Studies, be it in the form of a novel, an autobiography, a stage performance, a film, a play, or a form of a language.

Perspectives on Literature and History

CHAPTER I

Asian American Literary History: War, Memory, and Representation

Gayle K. Sato

I. CULTURAL REENACTMENT OF US WARS IN ASIA

How does Asian America remember America's wars in Asia, and how do Asian American writers represent this memory? The importance of the question for Asian American cultural studies can be glimpsed in the recent burgeoning of Vietnamese American writing and translations of Vietnamese literature, revised histories and oral histories of Japanese Americans and World War II, multidisciplinary studies of comfort women following upon the first public testimonies by survivors in 1991, reexaminations of the Asia Pacific War, and a remarkable proliferation of interest in memory work, particularly in the areas of trauma, mourning, the various media, artifacts, and sites through which public memory is inscribed and transmitted, and the relationship between these forms of cultural memory and the production of historical knowledge and collective identity.[1] The importance of the question was precisely articulated by an Asian American critic in the mid-nineties; in *Immigrant Acts*, Lisa Lowe argues that the (ongoing) history of Asian immigration is one wherein "the American *citizen* has been defined over against the Asian *immigrant*, legally, economically, and culturally," and that this citizen-immigrant binary is inseparable from "crises of national identity that occurred in periods of US war in Asia – with the Philippines (1898–1910), against Japan (1941–45), in Korea (1950–3), and in Vietnam."[2] Among Asian American writers, the question was already being framed in equally explicit ways by the 1980s, as illustrated by the following excerpt from a chapter in Kingston's *China Men* that narrates her pacifist brother's dilemma during the Vietnam War in the context of her own memories of World War II, the Korean War, the Cold War, and the anti-war movement of the seventies:

> For the Korean War, we wore dog tags and had Preparedness Drill in the school basement. We had to fill out a form for what to engrave on the dog tags . . . our dog tags had O for religion and O for race because neither black nor white. Mine also had O for blood type. Some kids said O was for "Oriental," but I knew it was for "Other" because the Filipinos, the Gypsies, and the Hawaiian boy were O's. Zero was also the name of the Japanese fighter plane, so we had better watch our step. . . . "The War," I wrote in a composition, which the teacher corrected, "Which war?" There was more than one.[3]

There indeed has been more than one war of consequence for Asian Americans, but young Maxine's memories also tell the truth: that a continuous history of American wars in Asia and their profound, cumulative effect on Asian American life can in fact be signified as a singular entity, "the War." A quarter century after the publication of *China Men*, the presence of war in Asian American writing is even more pronounced, a situation that calls for a more deliberate reading of this literary history as a form of cultural memory and counter-memory of twentieth-century wars in Asia.

Three novels and one memoir have been selected to serve as examples of approaching Asian American literature through such a framework. Authored by a third-generation Japanese American, two first-generation Korean Americans, and a Vietnamese American who entered the United States as a refugee, these reenactments of home/fronts in the Asia Pacific War and the Vietnam War reflect different gendered, generational, and politico-geographical perspectives. Andrew Pham's *Catfish and Mandala* narrates his family's escape from Vietnam by enfolding it within two other "survival" stories: that of Pham's elder sister, a battered teenage runaway, transsexual, and suicide, and the author's solo bicycle journey through Vietnam to come to terms with her death. Nora Okja Keller's novel *Comfort Woman* depicts a woman's struggle to resist death and insanity through identification with another comfort woman who was brutally murdered for disobedience, and through a tape that she prepares for her daughter to discover upon her death, on which she reveals the past and reclaims her Korean name and the names and lives of other comfort women. Chang-rae Lee's novel, *A Gesture Life*, depicts a contrastive resistance through the story of a Korean man raised in Japan and sent to the Burmese front as a medic, where he betrays a Korean comfort woman by refusing her request to kill her. He spends the rest of his life reenacting that betrayal through the pursuit of model-minority assimilation in the United States, which becomes a giant screen memory[4] when he attempts to narrate and justify his past. In Karen Tei Yamashita's novel, *Tropic of Orange*, a former internee at Manzanar Relocation Center stages an epic reenactment of the internment. After suffering a nervous breakdown, he exchanges the life of a surgeon for that of a homeless freeway conductor by the name of Manzanar Murakami. His desire for spectacular visibility and panoramic, extravagant vision speak eloquently of the psychological imprisonment still in effect decades after the war's end.

"Reenactment," in its clinical psychoanalytic sense, refers to a trauma survivor's unavoidable repetition of a traumatic experience. The subject is unable to occupy a point of view outside the event because its overwhelming nature resists narrativization; thus it can only be repeated.[5] While this traumatic model of blocked narration has proved illuminating in analyses of literature's memory work,[6] I would like to explore the implications of media critic Marita Sturken's definition of "cultural reenactment," which shifts the emphasis from narrative obstruction to narrative production, and to narratives that inscribe and rescript popular memory of events that prove especially disruptive to national identity. Building on the premise that "memory is a narrative rather than a replica of an experience that can be retrieved and relived," Sturken examines the Vietnam War and the AIDS epidemic as key examples of processes through which national memory, often centered around traumatic events, is created, sustained, and altered through narrative reenactment.[7] Though focused on the role of objects (such as the body, the AIDS quilt, the Vietnam Veterans Memorial) and camera images ("photographic, cinematic, televisual, documentary, docudrama"), Sturken's deployment of "cultural reenactment" as narrative scripting and rescripting is useful for reading the representation of memory in literary texts. Sturken writes: "Though the still photographic image is crucial to memory, and memory and history are often evoked by flashes of images, it could also be argued that memory most often takes the form of cultural reenactment, the retelling of the past in order to create narratives of closure and to promote processes of healing."[8] The question of healing in particular, as both psychological recuperation and political rectification, is especially significant in Asian America's cultural reenactment of America's wars in Asia.

Anne Anlin Cheng insists on an important distinction between grievance and grief in Asian American narratives of racial and cultural identity. She asserts that an identity politics focused on defining damage or attaining reparations in purely economic or socio-political terms fails to address the psychological processes of identity formation which underlie and sustain racial stereotypes, racial fantasies, and racial wounding. Working against "a contemporary American attachment to progress and healing," Cheng turns to literature in order to examine what it means, instead, "to *grieve*."[9] Kathleen Woodward also urges the development of a theory of grief to provide a vocabulary for understanding mourning not as a task to be completed and put aside, but as "sustainable grief," which holds on to emotional pain rather than following the conventional wisdom of learning to get over it.[10] Sturken's discussion of the Vietnam Veterans Memorial as a site of mourning where personal and national memory merge and a healing narrative can be constructed illustrates the psychological and political recuperation enabled through "sustained grief." However, this example also raises the question of Asian American participation, the extent to which such nationally constructed sites of mourning encompass the specific histories that underlie Asian American grief. Although no "technology of memory," including war memorials, embodies a single, simple point of view – the cultural memory produced at the Vietnam Veterans Memorial, Sturken points out, ranges from "reclamation of concepts of sacrifice and honor to profound opposition to the codes of war" – it is clear that American war memorials are not understood as embracing a collective or critical Asian American memory of American wars in Asia.[11] Japanese American "relocation," Korean American "resistance" (against postwar Japanese, Korean, and US history), and Vietnamese American "survival" are but three traumatic war memories that are not visibly accommodated at American war memorials.

If literary reenactments of Asian/American wars provide alternative sites for sustained grieving through narrative representation, these reenactments do eventually point to the question of grievance. In each of the four works selected for discussion, grievance is represented through testimony, a telling of and listening to lost histories in which survivors address the deceased and the deceased address survivors. Pham's memoir bears witness to his sister's life and death, Keller's Akiko records her history on tape, Lee's Hata offers a veiled confession, and Yamashita's Manzanar places his traumatic amnesia on display for all to witness. Although none of these speakers is able to directly address or get a response from the family members for whom they struggle to testify, and the narratives thus remain haunted by their respec-

tive histories of unspoken apology and unresolved injustice, this haunted-
ness itself comprises a critical and moving representation of Asian American
memory and the possibilities of political intervention.

In Field's discussion of the history of Japan's apologies to former colonies, testimony bears a crucial relationship to both grief and remorse, grievance and restitution, the linked conditions whereby victims seek and
perpetrators offer a genuine apology:

> Testimony and apology are dialogical processes: both parties speak,
> and both must listen. To listen and to watch – acts of witnessing –
> are emblems of our willingness to care. We need to be prepared to
> extend our imagination to fragmentary testimonies, to barely
> distinguishable testimonies, to testimonies that never reached us
> because their utterers perished first and because their locus, in terms
> of political geography, didn't matter enough. Testimony mediated
> by art is effective in developing our affective readiness to mourn the
> loss of and the pain inflicted upon lives that never impressed their
> uniqueness upon us.[12]

The artistic mediation Field refers to is a documentary film on Holocaust
survivors, but Asian American literature's reenactment of losses and suffering that have been erased or ignored in official and popular history is also a
powerful medium for the transmission of testimony.

II. JAPANESE AMERICAN MEMORY: THE
REENACTMENT OF RELOCATION IN KAREN TEI
YAMASHITA'S *TROPIC OF ORANGE*

During the season of *obon* in August 1943, a traditional Japanese summer
festival that celebrates the annual return of the spirits of the dead to their
natal homes, internees at Manzanar Relocation Center erected a 15-foot
stone monument in the camp's cemetery. An article in the camp newspaper,
The Manzanar Free Press, noted that many graves remained unmarked
because families had no money or access to materials for the construction
of headstones. The internee who supervised the construction of the monument noted quietly that it was made to last.[13] Engraved only with the three
Japanese characters for the word "cenotaph," the Manzanar monument was
probably first seen by outsiders through the now famous photo in Ansel

Adams's *Born Free and Equal*, his privately-funded, critical witnessing of the mass imprisonment of Japanese Americans during World War II.[14]

> The Manzanar monument symbolizes Japanese American losses during World War II and the community's postwar history of mourning. Pilgrimages to Manzanar and other Relocation Center sites have been held since the 1970s; they have become annual or biannual events organized and attended mainly by Japanese Americans, their extended family, and others involved in the Japanese American community, in groups averaging a couple to several hundred.[15] . . . Compared to the U.S.S. Arizona Memorial at Pearl Harbor, which saw more than eighteen million visitors between 1980 and 1997 alone, the Manzanar site today remains almost as invisible as it was in 1943, a symbol of the "absent presence" of Japanese Americans in official and popular constructions of national identity and history.[16]

Sturken employs the term "absent presence" in her essay on Japanese American reenactment of internment, which discusses Rea Tajiri's video documentary *History and Memory: For Akiko and Takashige* (1991) and its relationship to wartime and postwar Hollywood movies about World War II, especially one that was singled out by Tajiri herself. Sturken writes: "In *History and Memory*, Tajiri notes that the 1954 film *Bad Day at Black Rock*, directed by John Sturges, perhaps most powerfully reenacts the absent presence of the Japanese American internment,"[17] which Sturken calls "a historical event that has spoken its presence through its absent representation."[18] Caroline Chung Simpson redeploys Sturken's "absent presence" in her book about the representation of Japanese Americans during the Cold War era, a period in which, she writes, "the potential of interned Japanese Americans' presence in the body politic to disturb the problems of American identity remained a perpetual threat, an irrepressible part of the negotiation between the needs of national history and the 'incommensurabilities' of racial memory."[19] In Simpson's study, "absent presence" names the manipulated erasure of Japanese Americans from official history and public memory in the interests of maintaining America's image as the world's leading democracy.

Whereas Sturken's article examines Japanese American memory of the internment on the occasion of the fiftieth anniversary of the end of World War II, Simpson is concerned with dominant and popular memory of internment during a period prior to the Asian American movement whose cultural politics undergird Tajiri's documentary. The 1970s thus mark a border between the domains of these two studies, a time when important political and social gains were won by disenfranchised groups but counter-measures to contain such activism also arose. One such strategy was "model minority" identity, a discourse and practice of rewarding Asians for giving up a political agenda in exchange for socio-economic promotion above other racial groups. This strategy proved effective with Japanese Americans, particularly after the trauma of Relocation and the necessity of reestablishing economic security in the immediate postwar years. But as Tajiri's 1991 videotape demonstrates, the effects of constructing Japanese America as an "absent presence" did not stop with the end of the Cold War, nor with the redress movement two decades later. Here *Tropic of Orange* serves as an example of a recent Japanese American writer's response to a continuing history of managed invisibility.

The plot of *Tropic of Orange* covers just one week, but its framework and elaboration are epic in style and global in scope. There are two main events. One is a traffic accident on the Harbor Freeway caused by a driver who loses control after biting into an orange containing lethal concentrations of smuggled cocaine. Colossal gridlock develops, drivers abandon their cars, and the homeless, unable to resist the lure of all that prime hardware and real estate suddenly vacated, move in and build up a lively, enterprising, democratic community. The state decides to clear them off the freeway with gunfire. The other key event is a relocation of the Tropic of Cancer, which begins to move when an orange from a tree growing exactly at the latitude of the Tropic of Cancer falls to the ground, is entangled with the Tropic, and gets carried to Los Angeles by Arcangel, a divine being disguised as a poor street performer from South America. He is scheduled to fight Supernafta in a pro-wrestling match in Los Angeles, which is being billed as a fight to the death between South and North America. Supernafta is mortal but equipped with the latest in high-tech weaponry. As the freeway crisis develops, Arcangel travels north on foot with the magic orange, accompanied by a growing crowd of supporters and the warping and desta-bilizing of normally fixed axes of time and space.

Almost every Japanese American writer (who identifies as such) has penned something on the internment, a fact that has led me elsewhere to give the name "writing relocation" to the history of Japanese American lit-erature.[20] It wasn't until the 1980s, however, that narrative reenactments of relocation came of age, most notably through Canadian writer Joy Kogawa's groundbreaking novel *Obasan*, and in the United States, Lawson Inada's "The Rhythm of Tradition," a long poem dedicated to Toshio Mori and John Okada. Much has been written about this literary front of the redress campaigns and need not be reviewed here.[21] Rather, I would like to propose that we view *Tropic of Orange* as initiating a post-redress form of Japanese American memory, marked by a broadening of the geo-political terrain where reenactment of relocation occurs, and a development of the psychological terrain of reenactment's memory work.

Manzanar calls himself "the first sansei born in captivity," a point that underscores several things.[22] Regardless of the fact that this information cannot be verified in the novel, it suggests, first and foremost, that Manzanar associates his identity and personal history with the internment, second, that he represents the last generation of Japanese Americans who actually experienced the camps, and third, that he adopts homelessness either during the height of the redress campaign or well after its successful completion, which implies that the official apology and symbolic monetary restitution did not answer to the needs that compel him to exchange scalpel for baton.[23] Emi, the only other individualized Japanese American character and Manzanar's granddaughter, is a smart, stylish, politicized fifth-generation Japanese American with a high-visibility career as the producer of a television news program. The only thing she can't handle is serious talk about her personal identity as a Japanese American, suggesting that she has not gotten over her grandfather's unexplained sudden disappearance from her life when she was nine. Her family has hidden the truth from her, just as second-generation Japanese Americans dealt with the original trauma of relocation through silence. Manzanar's silent and silenced disappearance from Emi's life is a reenactment of relocation on several levels: as a mimetic recreation of the likewise inadequately explained, astonishingly quick disappearance of 120,000 Japanese Americans in 1942, as a traumatic reenactment or manifestation of the continuing legacy of the mass uprooting and dispossession, as a repudiation of the model minority solution to unresolved grievance, and as a reflection of the price of refusing to grieve, to verbalize pain, humiliation, anger, and sorrow. In other words, as "the oldest sansei born in captivity," Manzanar is created as a quintessential embodiment of Japanese America's "mournful reference point," as the internment is referred to in the conclusion of *Personal Justice Denied*, the official report of the Commission on Wartime Relocation and Internment of Citizens.[24] Further, by placing Manzanar's amnesia in the context of his relationshp to Emi, the novel underscores the issue of Japanese American "post-memory," defined by Marianne Hirsch in reference to the Holocaust as the memory of a traumatic event that is not directly experienced but inherited by children of survivors, whose lives also come to be defined by the trauma via indirect memory.[25] Though Emi finally recognizes the crazy freeway conductor as her long-lost grandfather when the traffic accident brings her news crew to his vicinity, she is extremely reluctant to meet him and is murdered before making up her mind to do so.

We are told that Manzanar viscerally registered every shot that was fired. The first shot that mortally wounded Emi "penetrated Manzanar's very being with a vengeance he did not understand."[26] Every subsequent shot he "clothed . . . in desperation with pain and more pain. Great shuddering sobs welled from within."[27] Such receptivity reiterates his voluntary relocation into the homeless community, which is part of Yamashita's re-scripting of Japanese American memory of relocation to underscore its connections to a broader American counter-memory of Asian/American wars. Half of the homeless community are veterans; when the first shot is fired, targeting and killing Emi not only because she represents an uncooperative news station but because she is female and Asian, these homeless veterans "suddenly returned to familiar scenes of fear and bloodshed, jumping into the foliage, cowering behind jeeps, lugging knives and rifles, carefully surveying the fray from that big ditch."[28] Within the first few minutes of the attack, Manzanar's inability to see what is happening because of deliberate camouflaging techniques invokes the strategy through which the Gulf War was carefully staged and "screened" through government control of televised images of the war: "A rainbow of putrid green gas and red, white, and blue smoke hid the fray from discerning eyes, muffled the shrieking and wailing. Lines of cars along the slow lanes south and north exploded into flames, golden clouds of boiling petroleum rising in two great walls, further obscuring the deed."[29] In the end, it is an African American Vietnam vet named Buzzworm who tries to get Emi to Manzanar before she dies. Yamashita's description of the helicopter's circling and hovering, the swirling air currents and noise that drown out human voices so that Buzzworm has to mouth his final message to Manzanar, enfold an iconic image of the Vietnam War into a reenactment of relocation. The freeway slaughter also evokes the 1992 Los Angeles Riots, which are referenced quite deliberately at the beginning and end of Manzanar's seven-day symphony. At the moment Manzanar witnesses the car collision that sets off the freeway crisis, he thinks about Rodney King and wonders if perhaps someone is recording everything on video. In her final moments Emi tells Buzzworm, "Who'd a thought you and I'd get this close? . . . If we can jus' get along, maybe all our problems will go away."[30] The accumulation of references to wars abroad and at home suggests that reenactment of Japanese American relocation must situate itself within a larger history of international and domestic violence in order to maintain its function as a critical cultural politics.

Re-situation means an expanded vision of coalition politics in which Japanese American grievance addresses the larger context in which events like internment are produced and covered up. The kind of grief work necessary to articulate and act upon such a reformulation of grievance is represented above all in the way Manzanar's last moments as a conductor merge into Emi's death. Almost immediately after Manzanar has dropped his arms because the city's music has turned to gunfire, he must raise them again to receive Emi from Buzzworm. This exchange of baton for body at the moment when Manzanar recovers "the full range of memories"[31] and reenters his personal history as Emi's grandfather is emblematic of what sansei filmmaker Stephen Okazaki has called the "unfinished business" of relocation in his film about Fred Korematsu, Gordon Hirabayashi, and Minoru Yasui.[32] Emi's body is an emblem of "unfinished business" because she was lost to Manzanar not just minutes earlier but years ago, when he disappeared even though "he hadn't *meant* to leave her, or anyone else."[33] There is also unfinished business in the sense of Emi's disrupted political work, that is, her collaboration with Buzzworm to use "breaking news coverage" as a means of witnessing the homeless occupation of the freeway as a counter-narrative of official American history. Thus, Manzanar's receipt of Emi's body signifies a revitalized politics of grief and grievance, a new ability to confront and express racial wounding and a broadened formulation of political activism. Emi's body is emblematic of the burden that post-redress Japanese America must carry into the future, which threatens to become dominated by solutions to grievance of the sort enacted on the freeway.

III. KOREAN AMERICAN MEMORY: THE REENACTMENT OF RESISTANCE IN NORA OKJA KELLER'S *COMFORT WOMAN* AND CHANG-RAE LEE'S *A GESTURE LIFE*

Comfort Woman and *A Gesture Life* are the first female- and male-authored fictional representations of comfort women by Americans to reach a national and international audience.[34] In the 1997 special issue of *positions*, "The comfort women: colonialism, war, and sex," much attention is given to the masculinist and patriarchal underpinnings of Japan's former colonial apparatus and the state apparatus of both postwar Japan and postcolonial Korea. Hyunah Yang, for example, points to the problematic nature of relying on Japanese military and government documents to unearth the history of comfort women or to provide the concepts through which history and compensation should be articulated. Hyun Sook Kim, examining Japanese and Korean textbooks, finds a "leveling effect" in Japanese textbooks; by implying that all Asian nations had their share of suffering, Japan's specific role in producing much of that suffering is erased. Korean textbooks, on the other hand, promote a "hypernationalist" history that erases differences between the experiences of Korean men and women in favor of a collective, unified national memory of suffering. Given these limitations of official histories and the fact that Japanese government and military documents comprise most of the available records of comfort women, their personal testimonies are viewed as crucial to any attempt at rectifying history or providing just compensation. Further, as filmmaker Dai Sil Kim-Gibson cautions, testimonies should be used to understand comfort women as individual and historically complete beings; already by 1997, their identities were being reduced to a formulaic story of atrocity limited to the war front.

The following discussion examines the testimonial nature of *Comfort Woman* and *A Gesture Life* in terms of two kinds of "resisting memory," a metaphor meant to capture the manner in which these novels are plotted as narratives of incremental remembering and confessing, but with different motivations and results. Keller's protagonist is a Korean comfort woman whom we know only as Akiko, the name given to her at the comfort station, and Lee's narrator is an ethnic Korean conscripted into the Japanese army and stationed in Burma, whose name, Franklin Hata, encapsulates his history as a colonized Japanese subject who emigrated to the US after the war.[35] For Akiko, a Korean woman abducted from her homeland, "resisting memory" is a form of confrontation and critique. For Franklin, a colonized Korean raised in Japan, first by his biological parents in a Korean ghetto and later by a Japanese couple who adopt him and give him a more privileged life, "resisting memory" is a form of avoidance and acquiescence.

The passages quoted below describe the killing of Induk and Kkutaeh. These are the original sites of traumatic memory for Akiko and Franklin, respectively, where they witness a comfort woman's resistance and must determine their stance toward the scene.

All through the night she talked, reclaiming her Korean name, reciting her family genealogy, even chanting the recipes her mother had passed on to her. Just before daybreak, they took her out of her stall and into the woods, where we couldn't hear her anymore. They brought her back skewered from her vagina to her mouth, like a pig ready for roasting. A lesson, they told the rest of us, warning us into silence.[36]

I could not feel my hands as they gathered, nor could I feel the weight of such remains. And I could not sense that other, tiny, elfin form I eventually discovered, miraculously whole, I could not see the figured legs and feet, the utter, blessed digitation of the hands. Nor could I see the face, the perfected cheek and brow. Its pristine sleep still unbroken, undisturbed. And I could not know what I was doing, or remember any part.[37]

Akiko interprets the crying of frogs on the night of Induk's killing as the extension of her voice and thus an affirmation of her refusal to be silent. Whereas other comfort women believe that Induk snapped, Akiko insists Induk chose death in order to explicitly repudiate her subjugation. Thus, although Akiko must take Induk's place (that night she is given Induk's clothes and Japanese name, Akiko), her statement that "the corpse they brought back wasn't Induk . . . it was me"[38] is not an expression of defeat but an act of identification that will later enable Akiko's own resistance. The narration of Kkutaeh's death is quite different. Whereas Induk's death is experienced like an ambush and anchors Akiko's remembering, the telling of Kkutaeh's death is continuously delayed and evades Franklin's remembering. When the moment of telling finally arrives, her body, in contrast to the uncompromising wholeness and witnessing of Induk's corpse, is nowhere to be seen. There is no possibility of Franklin identifying her corpse with his living body, because it no longer exists. Contrary to Akiko's visceral inhabitation of Induk's corpse, Franklin gathers body parts while unable to see, hear, smell, or feel anything. The silence blanketing this scene, presented like a silent film, is the inverse of the frog chorus mourning Induk's death. Franklin chooses to live in this silence ever after.

In *Comfort Woman*, the rupturing and relinquishing of subjectivity that forms the basis for identification with a murdered comfort woman leads to a rupturing of official history, represented by daughter Beccah's discovery of Akiko's tape-recorded testimonial of the past, which leads Beccah through an experience of dislocation, horror, remorse, anger, grief, and eventually a re-identification with her mother as a grown daughter and Korean American woman. Testimony and witnessing are built into the structure of *Comfort Woman* through its unfolding as a juxtaposition of two personal histories, one narrated by Akiko and the other by Beccah in alternating chapters. Neither woman's narrative follows chronological order, but both Akiko's and Beccah's first chapters narrate the moment when personal history is ruptured. For Akiko this is the psychic death incurred by the first rape, and for Beccah it is Akiko's actual death. At the end of this series of alternating chapters, titled simply "Akiko" or "Beccah," the cumulative, separately narrated histories of mother and daughter are brought together in the discovery of the tapes and reemerge as an intertwined history of a mother's testimonial and a daughter's witnessing.

In *A Gesture Life*, historical intervention is impossible because Franklin fears, above all, any rupturing of his subjectivity. Preservation of the self requires a preservation of official history, represented by Franklin's memory replacing Kkutaeh's and his refusal to disclose the past to Sunny, his adopted daughter, even when she discovers and questions him about the black silk flag, a symbol of Kkutaeh's and his own subjugation which he has brought back from the front and kept hidden in his house all these years. Of course, to the extent that Kkutaeh's words, actions, and figure are fleshed out within Franklin's memory, a limited form of testimonial can be said to occur in *A Gesture Life*, but one that essentially reiterates the formulaic story of rape and death at the front, thus re-objectifying Kkutaeh as a comfort woman and creating a story that can be inserted unproblematically into an official history of war with its "inevitable suffering." The non-disruptive character of Franklin's testimonial and witnessing is represented as a function of his lifelong pursuit of cultural assimilation. At each stage of his identity formation, from birth and childhood in a Korean ghetto through adoption into a Japanese family and the formation of a melancholic colonized subjectivity followed by resettlement in the United States as a Japanese immigrant, Franklin succeeds outwardly in suppressing all traces of his Korean race and ethnicity, but while this acquisition of Japanese self-hood can be performed successfully enough in life, it cannot be narrated. As Franklin, now in his seventies, attempts to give an account of his life, it becomes clear that narrative performance cannot suppress the memory of a Korean past as effectively as his life constructed out of gestures. We witness Franklin's magnificent but doomed attempt to create a narrative that will contain yet hide the memory and meaning of Kkutaeh as perfectly as his magnificent house conceals yet enshrines the black flag that embodies her historical existence.

At the front, Franklin insisted on relating to Kkutaeh as a Korean male – sexually, romantically, and with a desire to protect and save her that betrays a dangerous naïveté about the limits of his masculine agency. As Hyun Sook Kim has observed, comfort women have been marginalized from postwar Korean history because their bodies represent "the inability of Korean men to protect the lives and bodies of their own wives, daughters, and sisters."[39] Franklin resists knowing what Kkutaeh understands from the start: that the relationship he desires with her and eventually forces upon her – he rapes her although it is not narrated as a rape, and later insists on examining her to ascertain the truth of her denial that she is pregnant – makes his behavior complicitous with the colonial apparatus of Imperial Japan. Kkutaeh, like Induk, chooses death over submission, and asks Franklin to kill her, as she is unable to do it herself and would prefer to die by his hand than a Japanese soldier's. He cannot bring himself to do it, but it is not the first time he is faced with a crisis of resistance. He admits to having vowed revenge upon detractors many times, but to never having once "attempted to mark them."[40] Kkutaeh's eventual death-inducing attack on a soldier is described as a "marking" of his face, and prior to this, whereas Franklin plotted to kill Captain Ono by slitting his throat with a scalpel, Kkutaeh actually accomplished it.[41] By thus enacting Franklin's fantasy of resistance, Kkutaeh reenacts Franklin's history of emasculation. The only action left for him, as Kkutaeh's would-be protector and future husband, is to gather her body parts without "remembering any part" of it, a phrase that underscores the inseparability of Kkutaeh's dismemberment and Franklin's disremembering.

The defining characteristic of Franklin's postwar memory is resistance to acknowledging Kkutaeh's death as a repudiation of Korea's submission to Imperial Japan and women's submission to men. Near the end of the novel, Franklin makes the shocking disclosure that Kkutaeh's ghost has been visiting him every night in his American home, at which point we must stop, backpedal, and try to grasp the meaning of her absent presence throughout the novel. We learn that he embraces Kkutaeh every night, a reenactment of his rape that has evolved into a fantasy of sexual gratification and dependable companionship. Then as now, he desires Kkutaeh's body only if it is emptied of meaning as a political agent. We also learn that Kkutaeh makes her appearance the same way every night, asking each time that Franklin take her away from this house. Thus, despite Franklin's description of their relationship as the amiable familiarity of old lovers, the sameness and repetition of the visits and the startling disclosure of their existence through a single instantiation of them suggest pathological rather than therapeutic reenactment. *A Gesture Life* reenacts the production of a colonized subjectivity; it reenacts resistance to the alternative formulation of Korean subjectivity embodied by Kkutaeh's transgression.[42]

IV. VIETNAMESE AMERICAN MEMORY: THE REENACTMENT OF SURVIVAL IN ANDREW PHAM'S *CATFISH AND MANDALA*

The meaning of surviving a war is a central theme in narrative and cinematic representations of the Vietnam War and critical studies of these representations. In *Fourteen Landing Zones*, Don Ringnalda argues that the truth about the Vietnam War cannot be apprehended through mimetic representations of battle scenes, and Kali Tal takes issue with critics who read war as metaphor instead of attending to differences between nonveteran and veteran authors. Ringnalda contrasts the graphic visualization of combat scenes in cinematic or literary narratives, whose unavoidable appeal to voyeuristic appetites is seen as undermining the effects of any critical examination of the war, with the prop-poor, blatant stylization of stage dramas that enables audiences to examine their own violence and their "duplicity and complicity" with "home-front epistemology."[43] Tal points to the necessity of reading veteran-authored narratives through the framework of trauma, which focuses on the "author-survivor" whose retelling of the war involves "the necessary rebuilding of shattered personal myths."[44] Sturken's analysis of Vietnam docudrama also calls attention to the limitations of particular representational choices. Surveying two decades of movies about Vietnam from the late seventies through the mid-nineties, Sturken observes that through an absence of male Vietnamese protagonists and the use of Vietnam as mere prop or background for dramatizing a battle among Americans over the meaning and execution of the war, these movies rescript master narratives of American innocence and masculinity that date from an earlier generation of Hollywood representations of World War II.[45]

More explicitly than the other works discussed in this chapter, *Catfish and Mandala* references central themes in dominant literary or cinematic representations of the war it remembers, but Pham's treatment of these issues expresses a diasporic Vietnamese perspective. For example, Pham's memoir is a work of mourning, but there is no mention of the Vietnam Veterans Memorial that dominates the history and narratives of mourning Vietnam in American culture. Further, the memoir is told through a masculine persona and literary style evident in male writing about war from Ernest Hemingway to Michael Herr, but the author's point of view emphasizes his experience of the Asian male's emasculation within dominant American constructions of masculinity and his ambivalence regarding privileges inherited, rather than earned, as the eldest son in a Vietnamese family. A tendency toward violent behavior, trouble with relationships, and reluctance to express emotions are central issues that link Vietnamese and American patriarchal systems. Finally, if cultural reenactments of the Vietnam War can be divided into three basic areas of concern – leaving Vietnam (inflected variously as withdrawal, abandonment, escape, exile, release), re/entry into the US (questions of reintegration for veterans; resettlement, immigration, assimilation for Vietnamese), and return to postwar Vietnam (pilgrimages to the Vietnam Veterans Memorial, to Vietnam) – Pham's narrative can be said to complicate a dominant narrative of the war in all three areas through its diasporic perspective.[46]

Catfish and Mandala reenacts three phases of escape, immigration, and return through survival stories that foreground different members of the author's family. The narrative of escape belongs mainly to Pham's parents, the narrative of immigration centers on Pham's elder sister, and the narrative of return is the author's story. Further, three kinds of memory weave themselves into and around this tripartite division of the memoir into different historical periods and points of view: "pre-memory," consisting of Pham's parents' experiences and his own earliest memories that are vivid but fragmented and not understood; Pham's more "reliable" memories of his childhood in South Vietnam; and memories of life in the United States since age ten. The memory structure of *Catfish and Mandala* thus resembles a braid: drawing on different kinds of memory, Pham plaits the stories of three phases of survival and their three protagonists so that they twist into each other. The point of view shifts constantly between past and present, but the three major narrative strands move forward together: Pham's bicycle journey (the "two-wheeled voyage" indicated in the title), the escape from South Vietnam, and postwar resettlement in the US all begin together and are braided into a larger narrative of survival.

Escape is remembered through episodes of Mr Pham's survival at a prison camp, where inmates spent their days as human mine detectors and the nights waiting in fear for their names to be called and, if lucky, waiting for the shots to ring out that meant execution. Here, as on the boat barely able to hold seventeen people, and during the year and a half at an Indonesian refugee camp, survival is a harrowing experience of being able to do nothing except wait for time to pass while imagining death. The second narrative strand, immigration, is reenacted as cultural survival. The Phams are sponsored by the First Baptist Church of Shreveport, Louisiana but escape to California at the first opportunity, where they are forced to settle in a multi-racial ghetto next to the city dump in San Jose but find it preferable to being the only Asian family in town. At this point, Pham's fourteen-year-old sister Chi throws out her dresses and manages to fool teachers into believing she is a boy. When Mr Pham decides to cane her into proper behavior, school officials have him arrested for abuse and Chi runs away to prevent her father from being prosecuted. After fourteen years of silence, she returns to them at age "thirty-one, a postoperative transsexual" who had changed her name to Minh, and one year later, hangs herself in her grandmother's bedroom, fulfilling the predictions made by a Buddhist priest at her birth.[47] Whereas the narrative of escaping Vietnam is dominated by Pham's resilient, resourceful parents, survivors par excellence, the narrative of cultural assimilation is dominated by Chi, whom Pham remembers as being completely at home in her body and the world while in Vietnam, but who struggled desperately to find her footing in America and gave up after spending nearly half her lifetime in the attempt. Chi's suicide propels Pham away from home and back to Vietnam, a voyage whose goal is to confront his complicity in Chi's "fate" and try to make sense of a family's "survival" that revolves around a suicide.

Cycling gives Pham the survival story that he needs – a struggle that reenacts the others but belongs to him alone. The beginning and end of the journey are punctuated, respectively, by encounters with Tyle, an American veteran living alone in the Mexican desert, who begs Pham to apologize to the Vietnamese for him, and Tu, a one-legged North Vietnamese veteran who has returned to his natal village, who says there is nothing to forgive. Pham moves between their different perspectives on surviving the Vietnam/American war by visiting with cousins he once played with, the neighborhood where he lived before the fall of Saigon, the beach at Phan Thiet where his family made their escape, Minh Luong Prison where Pham watched his father work the minefields, and finally Hanoi, the paternal natal home and breeding ground for a legacy of violence passed from Grandpa Pham to his son and grandchildren.

Pham's survival is also more than a pilgrimage to landmarks of familial, cultural, and national history. It is a story of atonement and enlightenment through pure physical suffering and endurance, which is represented through pervasive imagery of excrement, blood, filth, defecation, vomiting, gagging, and gutting. During his first weeks in the country, Pham's cousins treat him to an expensive evening at Snake Village, where the bartender brings a live cobra to the table and proceeds to remove its tiny beating heart, which is then plunked into a glass of rice wine, and Pham must swallow it down before the heart stops beating.[48] The ride from Ho Chi Minh City to Hanoi creates a new war inside Pham's body: "I feel dry, scooped out." "I am ... spewing my innards into the toilet." "With them shoving gizzards, intestines, livers, and hearts at me as though I've never seen such delicacies before, I succumb to the peer pressure and swallow . . . snails, goat testicles, fish heads, goat blood pudding."[49] Pham never stops retching or running for the toilet, but he swallows the food because (he says) this is how Vietnamese men bond and how a pampered, Americanized Viet Kieu (overseas Vietnamese) is tested. So Pham becomes a big eater, like Brave Orchid in Kingston's *The Woman Warrior*, a survivor by virtue of necessitous eating.[50] Near the end of the memoir in a chapter called "Fever-Ride," which at first appears to be about nothing in particular, the cycling itself – the war within Pham's body – finally becomes a topic in its own right. The chapter ends with Pham's unexpected yet in retrospect inevitable assertion that the punishing bicycle ride has been his reenactment of survival: "I take the medication. Because I am angry, angry at the weakness of my body, angry at everything, I get on my bike and leave town. To hell with dysentery and fever. I am a survivor."[51]

After this point, the memoir is not focused on cycling. The remaining seven chapters and epilogue bring the narrative back to Chi, an absent presence within the family yet the central figure in its history and memory of survival. In the end, Pham's survival means recovering the memory of Chi's entire life so that she can be represented for a wholeness that once was and perhaps was not fated to be destroyed despite the birth fortune that predicted her loneliness and suicide. In the final chapter, Pham stops a few miles outside of Phan Thiet, the starting point for his family's collective history of Vietnamese/American survival and the maternal natal home where Chi recovered the first time she was severely beaten by her father. In Phan Thiet Chi's body mended and flourished. Pham recalls a tall, strong, athletic sister at home with herself and the world: "she owned the village the way it owned her, and she shared it generously with me, something I, the spoiled first son, never expected."[52] With these memories restored, what remains is for Pham to grasp the possibilities of mending and flourishing contained in his own story of survival, which apparently he does before leaving the vicinity of Phan Thiet:

> I remember the joy of our being near each other. I know my love for her now. Refelt my love for her then and all the love I felt for her in the between years. It isn't forgiveness I seek. All my sins, my sorrows, but a drop of ink in this blue vastness. And my standing here and all the roads opening before me are not my tribute to Chi but her gifts to me.[53]

Even in memory, Chi gives unstintingly to her brother. Her gift to him, as he comprehends it, is forgiveness that would have been too self-centered for him to request, as it could only have reenacted his failure to anchor her to this world as she had done for him at crucial moments in their past; it was Chi who ran back for him on the night of their escape after he tripped, panicked, and lay thrashing blindly in the sand. "Blue-Peace," as this chapter is called, is the mandala Pham acquires through reenactment of survival, the *nuoc* that he has been searching for although this word does not appear in the memoir. *Nuoc* as water, writes Huynh Sanh Thong, has come to designate "the homeland, the country, the nation."[54]

At the end of a journey marked by constant ingesting and expelling of innards and blood, lungs filled with dust and toxic fumes, a body "dry, scooped out," Pham discovers water. This replenishing *nuoc* is a counterpoint to the cumulative imagery of "filth" through which survival is figured, not erasing but balancing and coexisting with it in the manner of "rain and drought, plenty and famine, peace and war," like the two wheels of a bicycle. This *nuoc* is figured not only by the ocean's capacity to encompass and dissolve all tears, but by the water of the catfish pond (where catfish feed on human excrement and recycle it into another meal), the catfish "clay-pot" (comfort food and survival food from Pham's childhood), the incomparable star-fruit from Grandma Le's tree in Phan Thiet, and Coca-Cola, a ubiquitous luxury item in postwar Vietnam that literally fuels Pham's cycling (two or three cans per day for eight months). For Viet Kieu, perhaps one measure of surviving the Vietnam War is their sense of being in possession of *nuoc*. The memoir's concluding sentences seem to point toward the healing function of Pham's reenactment of survival. Describing the buzz in the airplane just before it lands at San Francisco, he shares in the excitement of his fellow Vietnamese passengers entering the US for the first time by recalling his own fear and giddiness at the start of his bicycle journey from the same port. This merging of forward and backward perspectives, positioned simultaneously in Vietnam and the US, enables his remark, in Vietnamese, to the fellow immigrant sitting next to him: "Yes Brother . . . Welcome home."[55]

V. ASIAN AMERICAN LITERATURE AND CULTURAL MEMORY

Jonathan Crewe notes that despite the growing importance of memory as a topic in literary and cultural studies, "literature – and consequently literary history – remains curiously underestimated in prevailing discourses of cultural memory. That deficiency . . . remains evident even when, for example, emergent genres of testimonial fiction and postcolonial writing are recognized as important bearers and construction sites of cultural memory."[56] This certainly seems to be the case for Asian American literature and literary history. In this chapter, I have tried to demonstrate that cultural memory is a crucial area of investigation for Asian American literature particularly because of its relationship to twentieth-century wars in Asia. "Relocation," "resistance," and "survival" are forms of cultural memory that address the entanglement of US history with the histories of various Asian nations, through wars that continue to have a profound impact on the everyday lives of Asians in America. The clearest example of home front hostilities is probably the discursive formulation of Asia's economic power as "warlike aggression." The murder of Vincent Chin in 1982 during a wave of "Japan-bashing" and references to a "second" Pearl Harbor (a theme developed in Perry Miyake's novel *21st Century Manzanar*) is only the most infamous example of a pervasive, persistent construction and conflation of Asia and Asian Americans as "foreign threats." Such explosive expressions of anti-Asian hostility, moreover, represent only half the picture, the other half being what Monique Truong calls the "everyday discourtesy that comes with being Asian American." Her example is an incident in a subway train where a white man passed up a seat only to get angry when her sister occupied it and angrier still when she offered to give it up, causing him to remark, "No, that's alright. I know you don't have chairs where you come from."[57] Asian American writers represent and reveal the relationships between everyday and explosive forms of racial warfare against Asian Americans; they also remember acts of war between and within Asian nations. Literary reenactments of "relocation," "resistance," and "survival" are the bearers and construction sites of Asian American cultural memory. Literary criticism must do its part to enable the testimony and counter-memory articulated at these sites to perform their political and psychological work.

NOTES

Parts of this chapter were originally presented as "Mourning Manzanar: the politics and psychology of cultural identity in Japanese American literature," on 10 April 2003 at the University of Hawai'i-Manoa, where I spent a sabbatical year from 2002–3. I would like to thank the English Department for their support, particularly Cristina Bacchilega, Marie Hara, Marke Heberle, Craig Howes, Ruth Hsu, and Susan Schultz; I also thank Karen Tei Yamashita for extended conversations during a visit to the University of Hawai'i in December, 2002.

1. To highlight just a few titles in each category: for Vietnamese American writing or translations of Vietnamese literature, see Cao, *Monkey Bridge*, Dinh, *Fake House: Stories*, Le, *The Gangster We Are All Looking For*, Ninh, *The Sorrow of War*, and Truong, *The Book of Salt*. On Japanese Americans and World War II, see Hirabayashi, *The Politics of Fieldwork*, Inada et al., *Only What We Could Carry*, Okihiro and Myers, *Whispered Silences*, Takezawa, *Breaking the Silence*, and Taylor, *Jewel of the Desert*. On comfort women, see Choi, "The comfort women," Hicks, *The Comfort Women*, Howard, *True Stories*, and Stetz and Oh, *Legacies of the Comfort Women*. On memory in relationship to literature, history, and twentieth-century wars in Asia, see Barlow, "War memorial," Field, *In the Realm*, Igarashi, *Bodies of Memory*, Simpson, *An Absent Presence*, and Sturken, *Tangled Memories*.
2. Lowe, *Immigrant Acts*, 4–5.
3. Kingston, *China Men*, 275–76.
4. I thank Yukiko Terazawa for pointing out that Franklin's narrative operates like a Freudian screen hiding the past from himself and others. She develops this idea in her unpublished paper, "Obliteration and Rearticulation through Screen Narratives: Chang-rae Lee's *A Gesture Life*."
5. See van der Kolk and van der Hart, "The intrusive past."
6. See, for example, Felman, "Education and crisis," and Kacandes, "Narrative witnessing."
7. Sturken, *Tangled Memories*, 7.
8. Ibid. 24.
9. Cheng, *Melancholy of Race*, 7.
10. Woodward, "Grief-work," 100.
11. Sturken, *Tangled Memories*, 7.
12. Field, "War and apology," 36.
13. See Iritani and Iritani, *Ten Visits*.
14. Adams, *Born Free and Equal*.
15. The first pilgrimage, held in 1978, made history as the largest voluntary gathering of

Japanese American bodies since Pearl Harbor. Robert Shimabukuro explains, "the constitutionally guaranteed right of assembly had been suspended since December 1941 . . . the Day of Remembrance (as the pilgrimage was called) made Japanese Americans realize that they had been internalizing the ban for 37 years." See Shimabukuro, *Born in Seattle*, 49.

16. See White, "Moving history," 741.
17. Sturken, "Absent images," 696.
18. Ibid. 689.
19. Simpson, *Absent Presence*, 11.
20. Sato, "Lawson Inada's poetics of relocation."
21. On Canadian redress, see Miki and Kobayashi, *Justice in Our Time*, and Miki, *Broken Entries*. On American redress, see Commission on Wartime Relocation and Internment of Civilians, *Personal Justice Denied*, and Daniels et al., *Japanese Americans*. On *Obasan*, see Sato, "Momotaro's exile," and Cheung, *Articulate Silences*. On Inada, see Sato, "Lawson Inada's poetics of relocation."
22. Yamashita, *Tropic of Orange*, 108.
23. Even if Manzanar was born before 1942, the year Manzanar Relocation Center opened, the earliest possible year of his nervous breakdown would be around 1981, when the Commission on Wartime Relocation and Internment of Civilians heard testimony from hundreds of former internees in nine cities across the US. However, internal evidence suggests that Manzanar's breakdown probably occurs in the 1990s, and thus well after the Civil Liberties Act of 1988 was signed into law by President Reagan, mandating symbolic redress payments for an estimated 80,000 eligible persons and bringing a twenty-year redress movement to a successful conclusion. See Shimabukuro, *Born in Seattle*, 72–73, 109.
24. CWRIC, *Personal Justice Denied*, 301.
25. Hirsch, "Family pictures," 8.
26. Yamashita, *Tropic of Orange*, 240.
27. Ibid. 240.
28. Ibid. 240.
29. Ibid. 240–41.
30. Ibid. 253.
31. Ibid. 257.
32. Korematsu, Hirabayashi, and Yasui challenged the legality of military curfew and exclusion orders in 1942, procedures that prepared the way for internment. That same year, they received criminal convictions that were upheld at the Supreme Court. In 1983, they filed a legal petition to have their convictions vacated based on evidence that there had been withholding of evidence and submission of false evidence at the Supreme Court trials in 1942. They won the case in 1988, the same year President Reagan signed into law the redress bill that included a national apology. See Irons, *Justice Delayed*, 3, 46.
33. Yamashita, *Tropic of Orange*, 257.
34. Therese Park's *A Gift of the Emperor*, a novel about a comfort woman in Palau, was published in 1997 by Spinster's Ink. See Park, "To give a voice."
35. Names are a key issue in the experience and representation of comfort women and

colonized Koreans. For a concise history of imperial Japan's comfort woman system, current redress movements, and differences in terminology for "comfort woman," see Soh, "Prostitutes versus sex slaves."

36. Keller, *Comfort Woman*, 21.
37. Lee, *A Gesture Life*, 305.
38. Keller, *Comfort Woman*, 21.
39. Kim, "History and memory," 94.
40. Lee, *A Gesture Life*, 263.
41. Ibid. 303.
42. Elsewhere I discuss the relationship of "resisting memory" to contrasting modes of "ritual housekeeping." See Sato, "Nora Okja Keller's *Comfort Woman* and Chang-rae Lee's *A Gesture Life*."
43. Ringnalda, "Doing it wrong," 73–74.
44. Tal, "Speaking the language of pain," 226.
45. Sturken, *Tangled Memories*, 85–121.
46. Viet Thanh Nguyen stresses that Vietnamese, like Filipinos, do not fit easily into a dominant Asian American paradigm of immigration based on the experience of Chinese and Japanese: "In most examples of Vietnamese American literature, issues of racial discrimination and identity, which prevail in early Japanese and Chinese American literature, are relatively muted; instead, the dominant issues are labor, family fragmentation or alienation, nostalgia, the problem of memory and historical reconstruction, exile, loss, postwar trauma, and so on." See Nguyen, 73.
47. Pham, *Catfish and Mandala*, 295.
48. Ibid. 83.
49. Ibid. 122, 185, 209.
50. See Chapter 1 of Wong, *Reading Asian American Literature*, 18–76.
51. Pham, *Catfish and Mandala*, 307.
52. Ibid. 54.
53. Ibid. 338.
54. Thong, "Live by water," vii.
55. Pham, *Catfish and Mandala*, 342.
56. Crewe, "Recalling Adamastor," 76.
57. Truong, "Into thin air," 54.

WORKS CITED

Adams, Ansel. *Born Free and Equal: Photographs of the Loyal Japanese Americans at Manzanar Relocation Center, Inyo County, California*. New York: US Camera, 1944.
Barlow, Tani E., ed. "War memorial." special issue of *positions* 5.3 (1997).
Cao, Lan. *Monkey Bridge*. New York: Penguin, 1997.
Cheng, Anne Anlin. *The Melancholy of Race: Psychoanalysis, Assimilation, and Hidden Grief*. Oxford: Oxford University Press, 2001.
Cheung, King-Kok. *Articulate Silences: Hisaye Yamamoto, Maxine Hong Kingston, Joy Kogawa*. Ithaca: Cornell University Press, 1993.

Choi, Chungmoo, guest ed. "The comfort women: colonialism, war, and sex." special issue of *positions* 5.1 (1997).

Commission on Wartime Relocation and Internment of Civilians. *Personal Justice Denied: Report of the Commission on Wartime Relocation and Internment of Civilians*, Tetsuden Kashima (foreword), 1982–3. Seattle: University of Washington Press, 1997.

Crewe, Jonathan. "Recalling Adamastor: literature as cultural memory in 'white' South Africa." *Acts of Memory: Cultural Recall in the Present*. Eds. Mieke Bal, Jonathan Crewe, and Leo Spitzer. Hanover, NH: University Press of New England, 1999. 75–86.

Daniels, Roger, Sandra C. Taylor, and Harry H. L. Kitano, eds. *Japanese Americans: From Relocation to Redress*. Salt Lake City: University of Utah Press, 1986.

Dinh, Linh. *Fake House: Stories*. New York: Seven Stories Press, 2000.

Felman, Shoshana. "Education and crisis, or the vicissitudes of teaching." *Trauma: Explorations in Memory*. Ed. Cathy Caruth. Baltimore: Johns Hopkins University Press, 1995. 13–60.

Field, Norma. *In the Realm of a Dying Emperor: A Portrait of Japan at Century's End*. New York: Pantheon, 1991.

Field, Norma. "War and apology: Japan, Asia, the fiftieth, and after." *positions* 5.1 (1997): 1–49.

Hicks, George. *The Comfort Women: Japan's Brutal Regime of Enforced Prostitution in the Second World War*. New York: Norton, 1995.

Hirabayashi, Lane Ryo. *The Politics of Fieldwork: Research in an American Concentration Camp*. Tucson: University of Arizona Press, 1999.

Hirsch, Marianne. "Family pictures: Maus, mourning, and post-memory." *Discourse* 15.2 (1992–93): 3–29.

Howard, Keith. *True Stories of the Korean Comfort Women*, trans. Young Joo Lee. London: Cassell, 1995.

Igarashi, Yoshikuni. *Bodies of Memory: Narratives of War in Postwar Japanese Culture, 1945–1970*. Princeton: Princeton University Press, 2000.

Inada, Lawson Fusao, Patricia Wakida, and William Hohri, eds. *Only What We Could Carry: The Japanese American Internment Experience*. Berkeley: Heyday Books, 2000.

Iritani, Frank, and Joanne Iritani. *Ten Visits*. San Mateo, CA: Japanese American Curriculum Project, 1994.

Irons, Peter, ed. *Justice Delayed: The Record of the Japanese American Internment Cases*. Middletown, CT: Wesleyan University Press, 1989.

Kacandes, Irene. "Narrative witnessing as memory work: reading Gertrude Kolmar's *A Jewish Mother*." *Acts of Memory: Cultural Recall in the Present*. Eds. Mieke Bal, Jonathan Crewe, and Leo Spitzer. Hanover, NH: University Press of New England, 1999.

Keller, Nora Okja. *Comfort Woman*. New York: Viking Penguin, 1997.

Kim, Hyun Sook. "History and memory: the 'comfort women' controversy." *positions* 5.1 (1997): 73–106.

Kim-Gibson, Dai Sil. "They are our grandmas." *positions* 5.1 (1997): 255–74.

Kingston, Maxine Hong. *China Men*. New York: Knopf, 1981.

Le, Thi Diem Thuy. *The Gangster We Are All Looking For*. New York: Knopf, 2003.

Lee, Chang-rae. *A Gesture Life*. New York: Penguin Putnam, 1999.

Lowe, Lisa. *Immigrant Acts: On Asian American Cultural Politics*. Durham: Duke University Press, 1996.

Miki, Roy. *Broken Entries: Race, Subjectivity, Writing*. Toronto: Mercury Press, 1998.

Miki, Roy, and Cassandra Kobayashi. *Justice in Our Time: The Japanese Canadian Redress Settlement*. Vancouver: Talonbooks and National Association of Japanese Canadians, 1991.

Miyake, Perry. *21st Century Manzanar*. Los Angeles: Really Great Books, 2002.

Ninh, Bao. *The Sorrow of War: A Novel of North Vietnam*. Trans. Frank Palmos. New York: Riverhead, 1995.

Nguyen, Viet Thanh. "*When Heaven and Earth Changed Places* and *Child of War, Woman of Peace*, by Le Ly Hayslip." *A Resource Guide to Asian American Literature*. Eds. Sauling Cynthia Wong and Stephen H. Sumida. New York: MLA, 2001. 66–77.

Okazaki, Stephen, dir. *Unfinished Business*, 1986.

Okihiro, Gary, and Joan Myers. *Whispered Silences: Japanese Americans and World War II*. Seattle: University of Washington Press, 2001.

Park, Therese. "To give a voice." *Legacies of the Comfort Women*. Eds. Stetz and Oh. 218–22.

Pham, Andrew X. *Catfish and Mandala: A Two-Wheeled Voyage Through the Landscape and Memory of Vietnam*. New York: Farrar, Straus and Giroux, 2000.

Ringnalda, Don. "Doing it wrong is getting it right: America's Vietnam War drama." *Fourteen Landing Zones: Approaches to Vietnam War Literature*. Ed. Philip K. Jason. Iowa City: University of Iowa Press, 1991. 67–87.

Sato, Gayle K. "Lawson Inada's poetics of relocation: weathering, nesting, leaving the Bough." *Amerasia Journal* 26.3 (2000–2001): 139–60.

Sato, Gayle K. "Momotaro's exile in John Okada's *No-No Boy*.' *Reading the Literatures of Asian America*. Eds. Shirley Geok-lin Lim and Amy Ling. Philadelphia: Temple University Press, 1992. 239–58.

Sato, Gayle K. "Nora Okja Keller's *Comfort Woman* and Chang-rae Lee's *A Gesture Life*: gendered narratives of the home front." *AALA Journal* 7 (2001): 22–33.

Shimabukuro, Robert Sadamu. *Born in Seattle: The Campaign for Japanese American Redress*. Seattle: University of Washington Press, 2001.

Simpson, Caroline Chung. *An Absent Presence: Japanese Americans in Postwar American Culture, 1945–1960*. Durham: Duke University Press, 2001.

Soh, Chunghee Sarah. "Prostitutes versus sex slaves: the politics of representing the 'comfort women.'" *Legacies of the Comfort Women*. Eds. Stetz and Oh. 69–87.

Stetz, Margaret, and Bonnie B. C. Oh, eds. *Legacies of the Comfort Women of World War II*. Armonk, NY: M.E. Sharpe, 2001.

Sturken, Marita. "Absent images of memory: remembering and reenacting the Japanese internment." *positions* 5.3 (1997): 687–707.

Sturken, Marita. *Tangled Memories: The Vietnam War, the AIDS Epidemic, and the Politics of Remembering*. Berkeley: University of California Press, 1997.

Tajiri, Rea, dir. *History and Memory: For Akiko and Takashige*. 1991.

Takezawa, Yasuko. *Breaking the Silence: Redress and Japanese American Ethnicity*. Ithaca: Cornell University Press, 1995.

Tal, Kali. "Speaking the language of pain: Vietnam War literature in the context of a literature of trauma." *Fourteen Landing Zones: Approaches to Vietnam War Literature*. Ed. Philip K. Jason. Iowa City: University of Iowa Press, 1991. 217–50.

Taylor, Sandra C. *Jewel of the Desert: Japanese American Internment at Topaz*. Berkeley: University of California Press, 1993.

Thong, Huynh Sanh. "Live by water, die for water." *Watermark: Vietnamese American Poetry & Prose*. Eds. Barbara Tran, Monique T. D. Truong, and Luu Truong Koi. New York: Asian American Writers' Workshop, 1998. vi–vii.

Truong, Monique. *The Book of Salt*. Boston: Houghton Mifflin, 2003.

Truong, Monique. "Into thin air." *Time* (18–25 August, 2003): 52–55.

Van der Kolk, Bessel A., and Onno van der Hart. "The intrusive past: the flexibility of memory and the engraving of trauma." *Trauma: Explorations in Memory*. Ed. Cathy Caruth. Baltimore: Johns Hopkins University Press, 1995. 158–82.

White, Geoffrey M. "Moving history: the Pearl Harbor film(s)." *positions* 5.3 (1997): 709–44.

Wong, Sau-ling Cynthia. *Reading Asian American Literature: From Necessity to Extravagance*. Princeton: Princeton University Press, 1993.

Woodward, Kathleen. "Grief-work in contemporary American cultural criticism." *Discourse* 15.2 (1992–93): 93–110.

Yamashita, Karen Tei. *Tropic of Orange*. Minneapolis: Coffee House Press, 1997.

Yang, Hyunah. "Revisiting the issue of Korean 'military comfort women': the question of truth and positionality." *positions* 5.1 (1997): 51–71.

CHAPTER 2

The Self in the Text versus the Self as Text: Asian American Autobiographical Strategies

Rocío G. Davis

Ethnic autobiography in the twentieth century has become an increasingly multilayered form of self-inscription, and Asian American life writers are expanding the possibilities of the genre to illustrate particular forms of belonging and knowledge. As these writers negotiate aesthetically what Paul Smith calls "positions of subjectivity" (xxxv), life writing has become experimental and revisionary.[1] To analyze Asian American life writing exercises effectively, we must move beyond an analytical model of merely reading the surface of texts for potential meanings and study the generic codes addressed by the authors to see what the texts achieve within literary contexts. In this chapter, I propose a reading that transcends the type of analysis that focuses primarily on ideas of political resistance and social change to consider the writers' generic and formal choices. We must bear in mind that writers sensitive to how differences in cultural contexts create specific responses manipulate established forms of representation to challenge conventional strategies of meaning. Consequently, readers who encounter these revisionary texts are obliged to reexamine their expectations and critical perspectives.

Asian American autobiographies generally highlight the protagonist's growing comprehension of the meaning or value that society places on questions and attitudes about ethnic differences, historical reconstruction, and the place of their communities in American societies. This approach recontextualizes earlier notions of both the self in autobiography and the life writing process, stressing the complex representation of the ethnic subject's self-awareness and self-inscription. Issues of representation in life writing – and its concerns with identity politics, the rewriting of history, and the attempt to claim the validity of personal and social experience – characterize the narrative strategies employed by Asian American writers. Their texts challenge the boundaries of traditional autobiography by blending diverse formal techniques with increasingly complex questions about subjectivity, self-representation, and the process of signification. Sidonie Smith suggests that autobiographical practices can be taken up as occasions to "critique dominant discourses of identity and truth-telling by rendering the 'I' unstable, shifting, provisional, troubled by and in its identifications" ("Memory" 40). The engagement with the act of narrative evolves into a strategy that blends selfhood and writing to stress evolving subjectivities, challenge contextual authority, or claim agency. In this chapter, I address some of the diverse narrative strategies that Asian American writers employ in their life writing texts as performative acts – where *saying* something is also *doing* something – that challenge traditional ideas of the self-in-auto-biography.[2] I begin my discussion by illustrating the shift in perspective on autobiography wrought by Maxine Hong Kingston's *The Woman Warrior*, and examine how other life writing texts revise established generic models to signal significant moments of subject awareness.

The title of this chapter describes the critical process enacted in life writing texts. When we attend to Kingston's model – the relational component of life writing presented through innovative formal strategies – we understand how previous paradigms may be modified to heighten meaning. Autobiography has been traditionally understood as the true account of a person's life, narrated by the most authoritative of all persons – the subject him/herself. Current writing and theory challenges this alleged authority, as well as the idea of the individual as the only subject of the text, and confers value to the *act* of writing as a constitutive part of narrative subjectivity. The self *of* the text frequently becomes the self *as* the text – the narrative strategies used reflect particular forms of perceiving and/or performing subjectivity. Selfhood in life writing is thus understood as a narrative performance and the text often exhibits the writer's process of self-awareness and struggle for self-representation through the narrative structure itself.

To understand the strategies that Asian American writers use, we need to be attentive to the ways formal and cultural modes interact, because many of these texts challenge inherited ideas of autobiographical structure and content. Contemporary life writing in North America reflects a multi-voiced cultural situation that invites the writer to examine the tensions between personal and communal discourse. Issues of ethnic representation are central to the autobiographical strategies employed by many of these writers and the manner in which each text performs the writer's process of self-awareness. As Traise Yamamoto writes of Japanese American women's narratives, "[w]hat is at stake here is not simply the question of whether the autobiographical form, as though it had a life of its own, empowers or dis-empowers its practitioners. At issue are crucial acts of discursive agency and the (re)appropriation of representational power, both of which are directly related to whether one reads these autobiographies as the intro-spective impulses of self-contemplation" (106–7). The act of reading, nonetheless, is directed by the process of actual writing, as much as by the themes in the texts. This reading of representative forms of life writing requires us to pay attention to these formal choices, and their implications regarding subjectivity, self-formation, and representation, as well as dia-logue with existing forms of autobiography.

VALIDATING ASIAN AMERICAN LIFE WRITING

The current canon of Asian American autobiographical production includes numerous works that present diverse formal strategies and the-matic concerns: early texts from the 1920s such as Etsu Sugimoto's *A Daughter of the Samurai*, narratives about Chinatown such as Jade Snow Wong's *Fifth Chinese Daughter*, narratives of the Japanese internment by Monica Sone, Jeanne Wakatsuki Houston, and Yoshiko Uchida, postmod-ern collagic texts like Kingston's *The Woman Warrior* and Garrett Hongo's *Volcano*, and more recent recuperations of historical connections and family histories like Connie Kang's *Home was the Land of Morning Calm* and Duong Van Mai Elliot's *The Sacred Willow*. Specifically, it was Kingston's subversive and controversial text that obliged writers, readers, and critics to rethink the possibilities of life writing in transcultural contexts.[3] Frank Chin's notorious critique of Kingston's text initiated a furious argument about the place of autobiography in Asian American writing. This debate hinges on a simplistic binary that Chin set up: the *real* – posited as works that have its uncontaminated sources in the Asian fairy tale and the Confucian heroic tradition – and the *fake* – works that supposedly emerge from Christian heritage and Western philosophy, history, and literature. In general terms, Chin's accusations centered on two issues: that Kingston, among others, invents Chinese history and misrepresents what he calls the "form and ethics of the classic heroic tradition" (4); and secondly, he challenges the use of the label "autobiography" because he claims it is a non-Chinese form.

Kingston's responses to Chin's accusations, most notably in her novel *Tripmaster Monkey: His Fake Book*, have made us rethink not only the issue of authenticity but the formal and aesthetic projects of Asian American life writers. Patricia Chu's thoughtful reflection of this debate shows how Kingston's novel disputes Chin's readings of heroic texts on two levels: she challenges his emphasis on the tradition's "hypermasculine, martial ethos," and notes his repugnance to what he deems current Asian American writing's feminization of men. Second, and more importantly for our purposes, Kingston "dramatizes an interactive reading strategy that emphasizes the texts' collaboration with various communities of readers" (171). Specifically, "Kingston's view of representation as a collaborative matter, and texts as the product of collusions (and collisions) between authors and readers, is illustrated within *Tripmaster Monkey* by her representation of Wittman's own art as a collective rather than individual achievement," highlighting the intertextual process involved in the fashioning of a play and, by extension, that of a novel or a life-writing text (Chu 173, 175). The relational approach to autobiography and textual construction becomes crucial to Kingston's revised paradigm of life writing. Moreover, Kingston adopts the postmodern perspective that invites a dialogue with readers, traditional texts, and interpretive communities, portraying literary composition "as a process enriched rather than threatened by dialogue, whether between a text and its predecessors, or between an author and her audience" (Chu 181).

Kingston's challenge to the notion of the individual as the prime subject of autobiography illustrates her understanding of the first person in autobiography as, according to Paul John Eakin, "truly plural in its origins and subsequent formation," as it addresses "the extent to which the self is defined by – and lives in terms of – its relations with others" (43). The links Kingston establishes between her evolving sense of self and a community of women prove stronger than any assertions of individuality. As King-Kok Cheung notes, "By giving voice to various female ancestors in this work of putative self-representation, she acknowledges the familial and cultural influences on her formation as an intertextual artist" (99–100). The basis of her itinerary of subjectivity and narrative performance lies in the intersection – even juxtaposition – of her life with those of the women in her family and community.

Awareness of multiplicity influences current autobiographical theory as well. Several recent critical studies on autobiography emphasize a new consciousness of manners of inscribing the self-in-relation, leading to original formal and aesthetic choices. Eakin, in *How Our Lives Become Stories*, defines the most common form of what he calls the "relational life" as those autobiographies "that feature the decisive impact on the autobiographer of either (1) an entire social environment (a particular kind of family, or a community and its social institutions – schools, churches, and so forth) or (2) other key individuals, usually family members, especially parents" (69). The writing subject therefore views and writes his or her story from the prism of intersecting lives. Susanna Egan uses the term "mirror talk" to describe this process, which begins

> as the encounter of two lives in which the biographer is also an
> autobiographer. Very commonly, the (auto)biographer is the child or
> partner of the biographical subject, a relationship in which
> (auto)biographical identity is significantly shaped by the processes of
> exploratory mirroring. [. . .] Such "reflections" within a text repeat
> processes common in lived experience, where one person is formed
> in proximity to another, often but not always by genetic inheritance
> as well as by proximity in life (7).

These perspectives require us to revise our notions about identity and self-representation on diverse levels, specifically the formal remembering and re-imagining of intersecting lives.[4]

Relational life writing challenges the fundamental paradigm of the independent self of traditional autobiography, as well as the concept of monologic representation. In a sense, this form of autobiographical inscription corresponds to a logical reality, as Michael Jackson explains: "Life stories emerge in the course of *inter*subjective life, and intersubjectivity is a site of conflicting wills and intentions. Accordingly, the life stories that individuals bring to a relationship are metamorphosed in the course of that relationship. They are thus, in a very real sense, authored not by autonomous subjects but by the dynamics of intersubjectivity" (23). Indeed, the renewed aesthetic experience of these autobiographical texts stems precisely from the tension created by this dialogue, which illustrates the reality of intersubjectivity. One of the constitutive thematic/textual markers of this life writing exercise involves an emphasis on the intersection of biography and autobiography, placing the narrating subject most often in the context of a community of women – family or ethnic group. This relational component, already present in Kingston's text, continues to mark the development of much subsequent Asian American life writing. This concern necessarily operates on a formal level as well, proposing a renewed vision that challenges the concept of the individuality of the narrator.

THE SHORT STORY CYCLE AS AUTOBIOGRAPHY

One specific form of this strategy involves the formal revisioning of established literary genres. For example, the short story cycle has been successfully used as an autobiographical model that emphasizes the constructedness of ethnic identity, the importance of the relational, and the power of textual formation. Groundbreaking Asian American autobiographies such as Kingston's *The Woman Warrior*, Michael Ondaatje's *Running in the Family*, Garrett Hongo's *Volcano,* and Sara Suleri's *Meatless Days* have signaled interesting possibilities for the form. These texts reveal subject identities that are multiple and discontinuous, denoting palimpsestic layers of reference and meaning through narratives that are themselves fragmented and disordered. Writers of short story cycles resist the reader's attempt to "fix" their identity by invalidating the basis on which identity is founded in traditional autobiography: chronology, personal history, and evolving perceptions of self.

The choice of the cycle form is highly significant for Kingston's and Ondaatje's memoirs.[5] Though the narratives reveal certain formal characteristics found in other autobiographies, the design and intention behind the textual innovations and the cultural implications of such fragmentation prove to be quite distinct. Cycles emphasize breaks, beginnings and rebeginnings, episodic structuring of lives and selves, inviting the reader to fill in the gaps and build meaning from the fragments retained in the memory and on the page. The story cycle presents the narrator's process of memory as non-lineal, associative, non-temporal, fragmented, and incomplete, making structure and content mutually reinforcing. The organization of the discrete narratives reflects the authors' attempts to control a series of fundamental memories, to understand their significance with regard to personal formation and self-representation, beyond the dictates of causality. Nonetheless, despite the fragmentary characteristic of these autobiographies, the texts exist as a coherent whole, united by a series of motifs and themes. *The Woman Warrior* and *Running in the Family* show a consciousness of the need for self-inscription and of the existence of text as the result of the intersection of stories told by and of others into the writer's personal narrative. Yet, as William Boelhower points out, "through a strategy of reconstruction, autobiographical interpretation defamiliarizes actual self and place by converting them into figurae, or tropes, which defer to an alternative cultural scenario" (134). These autobiographic cycles also carry cultural connotations that signify for the community, attesting to the complex interweaving of personal and cultural meaning. Indeed, the cyclical nature of the form, with its emphasis on recurring themes as well as its traditional resistance to closure, suggests a wider universe of significance for the writer and his or her stories. The diasporic nature of Kingston's and Ondaatje's personal and family chronicles, which foregrounds the need to return and rediscover a home – physically, imaginatively, representationally – is effectively enacted by the form.

Kingston's text dialogues with both the American tradition of the short story cycle and the immigrant tradition of the "talk story," creating a complex intercultural text.[6] Her memoir acknowledges its inheritance as it departs from its own traditions. Content is artistically shaped, as the storyteller's seemingly free association of ideas shifts attention from point to point in independent yet interdependent sections of the narrative. Kingston's life writing text evidences how traditional stories live on, but in revised forms that examine both cultural myths and the national contexts that shape the storytelling self.

The cycle's structure contributes to Kingston's dialogue with multiple traditions, which lead her to disregard traditional autobiographic portrayals of space and time, preferring instead the almost mythical temporal and spatial representation characteristic of the way memory works. The cycle form permits her to weave the separate accounts into a network of poetic connections. This technique locates Kingston's discourse clearly within a maternal cultural tradition. Importantly, the separate stories in Kingston's memoir center on the women who have significantly shaped her life and creative imagination. Though she continually asserts her individualism, she nonetheless foregrounds a community of women and her singular narrative voice originates in a relational/collective formation: she tells her own stories by and through those of others. She links these inherited stories with explanations and memories of her own, breaking up time, fusing memory and fantasy, embedding her life firmly in a female diasporic lineage, as she explores possible models for her own identity. These multiple protagonists may be considered versions of the self that Kingston entertains, or parts that make up her version/vision of her self. The interlinking stories allow her to explore the validity of these women's experiences in the context of her own developing self-consciousness and artistic impulse. The most outstanding model is clearly that of the woman warrior, influencing the author's life not merely through the revisioning of the ancient "Ballad of Mu Lan," in "White Tigers," but through her own mother's life chronicled in "Shaman." The stories of her aunts – the eponymous "No Name Woman" and Moon Orchid of "At the Western Palace" – also shape Kingston's perceptions of the possibilities and roles of women.

The metafictional component gives the stories an intimate air, reminding the reader of the close links between the story cycle and the oral narrative. Direct references to readers invite them into the story, notably in the last section. *The Woman Warrior* ends with a metaphorical resolution of the conflict between parent and child and, by extension, between cultures, with their collaboration in the story of Ts'ai Yen. "Here is a story my mother told me, . . . The beginning is hers, the end, mine" (184), says Kingston in "A Song for a Barbarian Reed Pipe." The story of Ts'ai Yen, a Chinese poetess captured by barbarians, issues from Brave Orchid's story of her own mother. Like Ts'ai Yen's children listening to her song in the desert, Kingston intertwines her voice with that of her mother, stressing the importance of maternal links and, more importantly for our purposes, noting the process of the inscription of the text we are reading. As such, in *The Woman Warrior*, Kingston offers a model of transcultural identity by presenting a generic model for writing about ethnic selfhood. Significantly, the final pages of the text celebrate the validity of a renewed life writing form as Kingston performs interethnic harmony through the integration of diverse art forms. As the woman warrior "learned to make my mind large, as the universe is large, so that there is room for paradoxes" (34), Kingston demonstrates through her manipulation of form that textual representation is often part of a new way of perceiving and writing about the self.

Ondaatje's *Running in the Family* also harnesses the potential of the story cycle to revision the history of a homeland and a family. Having left Ceylon for England and then Canada at the age of eleven after his parents' divorce, Ondaatje chronicles his return twenty-five years later, accompanied by his own family. The seemingly unstructured vignettes of varied lengths, interspersed with poetry, pictures of life in Ceylon and snapshots rescued from the family album, chronicle and recapture the world of his parents, Ceylon in the early decades of the twentieth century, which the author knew mainly from fragments of stories he had heard as a child. This structure symbolizes Ondaatje's process of recovery and inscription, of

reading clues into the most varied forms of pictorial and literary representation, to reconstruct a whole history from remaining fragments. The dis-
jointed, discontinuous structure articulates both the complexity of a
colonial inheritance and the intricacies of family connections. The interaction between the Tamils, Sinhalese, Burghers, Dutch, and colonial
English forged a Sri Lankan identity almost impossible to categorize,
much less objectify or define: the narrative's episodic nature textually illustrates this complexity. It was a society where intermarriage had caused
everyone to be vaguely related, where cultural differences were undefin-
able, and where "God alone knows" (41) each one's nationality. This intricate maze of social affiliations is what Ondaatje tries to disentangle by
gathering data on both Sri Lankan history and that of his family, as he
invites the reader to accompany him in the process of figuring out the
truth. When the facts fail to speak, he turns to myth to give explanations
and to fill in the gaps. The Ondaatje family history is thus laden with the
fictions and mythical elaborations of memory. The writer sees himself as
the chronicler of these linked histories: "During certain hours, at certain
years in our lives, we see ourselves as remnants from the earlier generations
that were destroyed. So our job becomes to keep peace with enemy camps,
eliminate the chaos at the end of Jacobean tragedies, and with 'the mercy
of distance' write the histories" (179). Ondaatje's shifts in perspective, the
independent narratives, the foregrounding of textuality, the anxiety to
belong and the need for distance, the awareness of history and the self-consciousness about historiography – all combine to create the effect of a
complex quest in which the notion of identity needs to be explored in all
its multiplicity (Kanaganayakam 35).

Ondaatje metafictionally enacts his process of discovery – the uncover-
ing and collecting of family and national history, as well as the awakening of
his consciousness to the implications of the realities he discovers and the
connections he perceives. This assignment he has given himself directs his
manner of recording: recurring images, foreshadowing and flashbacks,
themes taken up, discarded, and retaken, are the structural manifestations
of Ondaatje's involvement with his history. This overcrowding of data, the
inability to process them all at once and the exigency of time to recollect and
reflect is evident, for instance, in "Honeymoon." This chapter, set after
"April 11, 1932" (his parents' wedding day), seems to promise a logical
sequence of events. Unexpectedly, this vignette is crowded with newsclips,
flashes of miscellanea ranging from the death of Fred Astaire's sister to the
decrease of pythons in Africa to Charlie Chaplin's visit to Ceylon and the

fighting in Manchuria. Ondaatje implies thus that he would rather record stimuli than risk losing it, even at the cost of traditional autobiographical structure.

The purpose of Ondaatje's memoir is the discovery of his family. Family legend had immortalized Mervyn and Doris Ondaatje, a youthful, high-spirited couple, a Sri Lankan Scott and Zelda Fitzgerald. He reconstructs their world through the memories and the stories his relatives tell, using them to recover lost time. But the stories, however organized with "additions" and "judgements," do not satisfy him. For now, he realizes, only gossip remains, explaining "nothing of the closeness between two people: how they grew in the shade of each other's presence" (53–54). Nonetheless, Ondaatje's need to find – or create – stories to explain his family to himself goes beyond the discovery of his parents. There are continuous references to the act of writing and the power of words: the physicality of language, its concrete letters, is likewise a recurring motif in the text, as in the letters carved on gravestones or church floors that make "your own story a lyric" (66), and the beauty of the Sinhalese alphabet, "the self-portrait in language" (83). He refers to his father, moreover, as "one of those books we long to read whose pages remain uncut" (200), and pleads with the memory "Give me your arm. Give the word" (180).

Emphasis on the act of writing – of textual reconstruction – colors Ondaatje's and Kingston's accounts as they chronicle their existence within a wide familial and cultural context, representing themselves through the characters in their life stories. The stories prove to be significantly arranged to create a logical, aesthetically controlled structural pattern that supports the development of selfhood. Throughout the text, Ondaatje makes it clear that gathering and inscribing this history is his only way to seize his past and write himself into the text. This is a charge given to him by his family: "You must get this book right, my brother tells me, 'You can only write it once'" (201). Nonetheless, he must come to terms with the fact that, though family stories give life to the narration, his memoir will necessarily always remain "incomplete" as a history: "In the end your children move among the scattered acts and memories with no more clues" (201). As Ondaatje tries to recapture the stories that had long evaded him, he must resign himself to the fate of the writer and "confess that the book is not a history but a portrait or 'gesture'" and comfort himself with the thought that "in Sri Lanka a well-told lie is worth a thousand facts" (206).

THE SELF IN RELATION: INSCRIBING THE PROXIMATE OTHER

Apart from short story cycles, other forms of relational autobiography have become increasingly common in Asian American writing, such as Duong Elliot's *The Sacred Willow*, Adam Fifield's *A Blessing Over Ashes: The Remarkable Odyssey of My Unlikely Brother*, Sara Suleri Goodyear's *Boys Will Be Boys*, or Helie Lee's *Still Life with Rice*, where biography takes precedence over autobiography.[7] In these texts, the figure of the narrator, presented mainly through and in interaction with others, becomes a composite built up from the accounts of the other characters, highlighting the communal process of self-making and representation. Eakin considers the most common form of the relational life as "the self's story viewed through the lens of its relation with some key other person, sometimes a sibling, friend, or lover; but most often a parent — we might call such an individual the *proximate other* to signify the intimate tie to the relational autobiographer" (86). In some cases, the writer will present the biography of the other as constitutive of his or her own life writing exercise, to the extent of writing the "autobiography" of that other. When this happens, the narrator needs to establish the authority of his or her experience, for rhetorical reasons, based primarily on the existence and validity of the autobiographical pact. The role of the writer in relation to that of the subject is also noteworthy. For "the story of the self is not ancillary to the story of the other," and "because identity is conceived as relational in these cases, these narratives defy the boundaries we try to establish between genres" (Eakin 58).

Sara Suleri and Helie Lee write their personal stories through chronicles of the lives of their parents, grandmothers, and other relatives. The autobiographical self in the text appears obliquely, in relation to the other characters: the authors decenter themselves and substitute in their place other personalities, each bearing a profound psychological and emotional relationship to the narrator that helps unify the text. Suleri's *Meatless Days* emulates Kingston's strategy by positing a relational identity that involves the stories of the women and some of the men in her life. Specifically, *Meatless Days* is an elegy to her mother, a strategy she replicates in her next book. As she narrates the character and experiences of her highly singular family, she notes her father's (Z. A. Suleri, the journalist, known to his children as Pip) intention to write an autobiography entitled *Boys Will Be Boys*, and expresses her regret that he never wrote it (*Meatless Days* 184). Knowing Suleri's predilection for textual manipulation and the manner in which she links subjectivity to textuality,[8] we understand what this dream of his means to her and how seriously she takes his desire.

This regret and sorrow at her father's frustration because he believes: "I have written nothing [. . .] done nothing with my life" (*Meatless Days* 184), leads her to take up his truncated project. *Boys Will Be Boys*, subtitled *A Daughter's Elegy*, is a dialogue that Sara Suleri Goodyear establishes between herself and her father as she explores their shared past. Speaking in the first person, Goodyear positions her father as both the text's subject and its narratee, addressing, questioning, challenging, and acknowledging him continually: "When Pip died, I moaned. I thought some remnant of me had been discarded; I needed you to look at me and say, once again, with your unreplicated disgust, 'You children'" (39). This narrative strategy obliges the reader to constantly shift attention from Pip as subject and narratee, in order to understand the writer's complex relationship with her father and her memory of him. Though the text was written after her father's death, his presence as motivator, guiding force, and judge of the chronicle colors Goodyear's account, even as she acknowledges (or feels) his recognition of her gaze. As she quotes him: "On Judgement Day, I will say to God, 'Be merciful, for I have already been judged by my child'" (17). As such, the narrative is set firmly within Goodyear's memories of her father and her family, their negotiations, their peculiar use of language, their shifting loyalties. She portrays her father as a brilliant, irascible, blunt, yet tremendously endearing man who could treat his children cruelly and then come out in "great glee" to dance under the monsoon rains with them, making her realize, at the age of ten, that "Pip is just a child" (89) – signaling her growing understanding of this complex man.

Goodyear structures her fragmentary narrative in chapters titled with epigraphs, culled from translations of Pip's favorite Urdu poets, Yeats, a popular song, and the Pakistani national anthem. This highlights her father's passion for letters, and his lifelong commitment to writing, to Pakistan, and to Urdu. "I know how pained Pip would be – almost as pained as was I – when I went like a blunderbuss through the delicacies of Urdu, which surely remained his most favored language," she exclaims (56). By foregrounding this poetry, she illustrates her father's obsession with language and tries to atone for her inadequacy. These epigraphs also allow her to explore her memories of his preoccupations: building a new nation, the existence of friendship, the nature of Islam, and his attitude towards his children. As she chronicles her unstructured memories of life with her father, she simultaneously recounts his role in specific events, as she invokes his (sometimes physical, often imaginary) presence: "Listen, Pip. This is not a complaint. It is history. You were always so hither and thither, so much back and forth, that it is hard for me to be chronological" (38).

Though Goodyear never actually quotes her father, her account makes us aware of how his manner of speaking configured her own discourse: their discussions on the use of language, for example, of the ways he transformed the pronunciation of certain words to create a private family language ("no doubt," for example, becoming "no dort"; "'Anther' is Pip's rendition of 'another': it has entered our vocabulary, has it not Pip?" [43]), and how certain turns of phrase were among his favorites (like "far be it from me" [74]), and the hours of reading to him that Sara spent as she was growing up and later, when blindness set in. She also notes how his writing style transformed her own. As a young girl, she was frequently assigned the task of meticulously transcribing his articles into a legible hand, only to watch him "chisel" (his word for "revise") the piece, requiring her to rewrite page after page. "No wonder I have such an adamantly different style of writing," she notes, "when each word I put down on paper is both my first and my last. [. . .] It's Pip, the influence of Pip" (42).

Ultimately, the narrative is a valedictory for the father that loomed so large in her imagination. His children's collective frustration at his temper and unpredictability is balanced by their awareness of his fierce love for them. Describing a visit to her father's sickbed, Goodyear writes: "It is true, Pip: when one of us walked into your room, you would look up with such a radiance in your face, the one asked for nothing, nothing but the joy of presence. It was a very profound compliment that you conferred, which, however life enriching, was also curiously humbling. With humility we approached you, which is another way of expressing the joy we too were feeling, to be once again in the aura of your remarkable presence" (59). Their astonishment at how small their father's body actually was at the time of his death limns the manner of his presence in their life and imagination. As her brother-in-law Farooq explains: "I could not believe he was so small, [. . .] he always struck you as larger-than-life" (47). The conversation Goodyear establishes, therefore, challenges traditional forms of life writing: she authorizes herself to write her father's autobiography by blending the "elegy" with multiple acts of self-representation. By writing in this manner, she revises our perception of life writing, and of its possibilities for filling in gaps and fulfilling dreams.

Helie Lee operates a similar approach in *Still Life with Rice*, where she speaks in her grandmother's voice to claim a past she had previously refused to acknowledge. Lee's itinerary of self-formation and representation includes a process of intersubjective identification, where mutual recognition becomes necessary. As Jessica Benjamin explains, "[t]he idea of mutual recognition . . . implies that we actually have a need to recognize the other as a separate person who is like us yet distinct" (quoted in Egan 8). Lee undergoes the typical Asian American process of rejecting her mother and grandmother, punctuated by the "I am who I am. I'm not like you" (12) declaration of independence. As she narrates: "Once someone said to me I am my mother's daughter. I never believed it to be true and now I believe it even less. I've always hated being Oriental/Asian" (14). Lee's mother says: "Your father and me give up everything, our home, our life, to bring you kids to America, not to be American people, but so you can be Korean. Here, there is no Cold War, no hunger, no losses. . . . [w]hen others see your Oriental face, I want them to say, 'Ah, she Korean lady, they so proud people'" (13). This is precisely the identification that Lee rejects, until she impulsively leaves the US at twenty-five, to spend two years in Korea and China. Her serendipitous discovery of displaced Korean communities in China becomes an epiphanic moment: seeing them makes her want to recover their erased histories. And seeing her face in those *Hangooksahlam* – Korean persons – "I realize for the first time that I am my mother's daughter and my grandmother's granddaughter" (24).

There is a strong metafictional quality to Lee's narrative: she admits at the beginning, that "[l]ooking at myself through the prism of their lives, I've finally come to peace with who I am. The emptiness and chaos I once felt is now filled with the past I rejected and the future I will passionately embrace" (25). Having arrived at this conclusion, she proceeds to narrate her grandmother's story in the first person. A short third-person chapter that recounts her grandmother's birth separates the two parts of her text, which then centers wholly on the grandmother's story. This intelligent, independent, resourceful woman recounts the story of survival – the Japanese occupation of Korea, exile to China and a victorious return after the war – of the Koreans' indomitable pride and courageous fight for democracy, her husband's infidelities and her loyalty to him, the Christian faith that uplifts them, and the loss of her oldest son when the two Koreas were violently created. Appropriating her grandmother's voice, Lee explains to the implied reader numerous details of Korean life and customs – the rituals that surround birth, marriage, death, architecture, culinary customs, philosophy, and religion. The authoritative first-person insider voice implicates the reader as it attests to its own authenticity. Yet, because Lee admits to writing the text in order to connect with the grandmother she had refused to acknowledge, we understand that the principal implied reader is Lee herself. By performing her grandmother's voice, Lee gives herself the chance to listen to the stories she had previously ignored. Lee's appropriation of her grandmother's voice is complex and nuanced. She does not skim over the less positive episodes of the woman's life, like her experiences as an opium smuggler, recounting moments of selfishness and cruelty, balanced by the story of her genuine devotion to her family. Indeed, Lee does more than just appropriate her grandmother's voice, she enacts her life to provide herself with the basis of her experiential authenticity as an Asian American connected to a history and rerooted because of that history.

The moment of mutual recognition is the central point of the text. At the end, the grandmother narrates how her granddaughter, Helie, "has been gone two years, working in Korea and traveling through China. Just imagining her following my footsteps all over the Orient fills me with pride. Of all my grandchildren, she reminds me the most of myself. She has the same stubborn, spunky streak" (312). This affirming recognition validates Lee's role as granddaughter and authorizes her to write the text. Though we might read this affirmation as self-serving, we can also read it as necessary. Just as Lee learned how much she needed the connection to her foremothers, she feels compelled to establish the mutuality of that identification. The maternal story of *Still Life with Rice* concludes on this note of mirrored recognition.[9]

SELVES IN COLLABORATION: REIMAGINING THE "I" IN THE AUTOBIOGRAPHICAL TEXT

Another vital relational narrative strategy in auto/biographical inscription is collaborative writing (understood in this case as a text with two writers, rather than an as-told-to narrative), where the interaction between the writing voices becomes a contested site for meaning. Collaborative autobiographies challenge the fundamental idea of the unified self of traditional autobiography, as well as the concept of the monologic voice. Clark Blaise and Bharati Mukherjee's *Days and Nights in Calcutta* and May-lee Chai and Winberg Chai's *The Girl from Purple Mountain*, for example, demonstrate how the plural position of these writers reflects the shifting boundaries of memory, transcultural awareness, and representation. The multiple meanings generated by the narrative strategies these writers employ make further investigation into these revisionary texts imperative.

In this context, Sidonie Smith and Julia Watson posit remembering as a "collective activity" (19). The dialogues enacted in relational text foreground the collective nature of memory, which

> extends beyond the acknowledgement of social sites of memory, historical documents, and oral traditions. It extends to motives for remembering and the question of those on whose behalf one remembers. Precisely because acts of remembering are implicated in how people understand the past and make claims about their versions of the past, memory is an inescapably intersubjective act. (Smith and Watson 21–22)

In Asian American texts, where issues of politics and power are often the subtext of personal stories, the dialogue between two people often becomes a dialogue between two binary positions. The voices elicited in these texts are often posited as mirroring, highlighting the intersubjective and postulating the advantages of double-voicing in the process of life writing.

Most criticism on collaborative writing has centered on texts that involve the work of speakers/writers and editors, rather than on the dialogue of two persons who are ostensibly partners in the act of narration and where the text features independent sections by individual writers. The polyvocal form of dual-authored texts challenges the traditional definition of autobiography. Blaise and Mukherjee combine their journals to emphasize the intersection of ethnic, social, familial, and personal positions precisely because each of them, as individuals, occupies differing locations in the structure: questions of position, power, and agency are thus negotiated through the interaction of the two voices in dialogue. The two sections are mutually enhancing, contradictory and complementary at the same time, providing a sense of both performance and mutual spectatorship. As Egan argues, "[a]djustments between the two narrators also establish each one as the critical reader of the other. [. . .] Just as this journey calls into question the cultural securities of the Western white man, requiring him to listen in new ways to his Bengali wife, so too the qualities of narrative, shifting significantly from part one to part two, function responsively, pointing up both harmony and dissonance" (138).

The pivotal point of *Days and Nights in Calcutta* is the writers' dealing with the issue of immigration and ethnic affiliation, which influence their relationship and their writerly choices. The formal realization of this dialogue – the text itself – widens the modes of performing subjective meaning and multiplies the possibilities of Asian American writing. To have one's opinions, perspectives, and stories complemented or challenged by an (ostensibly) equally authoritative voice *within the text itself* stresses the dialogic element, making the relationship, rather than individuals, the center of the text. The manner in which Blaise's and Mukherjee's chronicles – written independently but placed side by side in the published text – gives the reader a renewed life reading experience and promotes the potentiality of narrative structuring in the context of life writing. By stressing the relational through performed dialogue, the text resists becoming a static artifact. Egan notes the importance of the "real presence" of the speakers, confirmed "by the responsiveness of each to the other and by the fact that their dialogue is comprehensible only in terms of the involvement of both" (9–10), and authorized by the autobiographical pact. *Days and Nights in Calcutta* is composed of simultaneous journals that Blaise and Mukherjee kept on a year's sabbatical in India, after a series of unfortunate accidents (Blaise breaks his wrist, their house burns down, and their car is wrecked) led them to decide to leave Canada with their two young sons. The journals are framed by a prologue by Blaise and epilogues, written for the book's publication in 1977 and reissue in 1995. The text is divided into two parts, the first written by Blaise and the second by Mukherjee; similar events, themes, questions, and changing perspectives are engaged by each writer. Their contrasting positions on cultural and ethnic affiliation, family obligations and ceremonies, the role of the writer, and questions of diasporic belonging oblige them to reexamine their relationship and the basis of their marriage. The juxtaposition of these two journals allows us to consider the experimental nature of autobiographical relationships. Mukherjee's account comes after that of her husband's, inevitably nuancing the perception of both narratives. Interestingly, the two sections do not directly refer to each other; there is no textual evidence that the two writers read each other's journals nor do they address each other's versions. Indeed, this structure shows how Blaise and Mukherjee locate the center of their autobiographical exercise precisely in the space between their individual positions and independent texts. The autobiographical occasion of this form of life writing occurs in the act and at the moment of dialogue, as it opens up a third space for relational selfhood. The literary interaction between two life writing texts provides the reader with an originative record that enacts this dialogue.[10]

Their diverse cultural histories and ethnic positions are the subtext of Blaise and Mukherjee's performances. In Canada, an officially multicultural nation, Mukherjee's Indianness was an issue she negotiated daily, particularly in her professional life. In India, this ethnic affiliation is also subject to question, particularly as it intersects with social position. But the position of each of the writers in their journals illustrates their changing ideas of self-hood, as individuals and in dialogue. This doubled journal stresses the separate individuals Blaise and Mukherjee are, and the surprising self-revelations that they each undergo in that year, linked to how diverse perspectives on ethnic affiliation torment their relationship. She now confronts the questions that Blaise often asked visiting Bengalis in Montreal: "'What have you given up? Is it worth it?' For the next year, I was to hear her answers, and it has shaken our marriage to its core" (104). As the couple examine their relationship through the prisms of ethnic and national affiliation and social class, their text becomes a reflection of their evolving perspectives. The chance to be in India, viewed almost as a rebirth after their home is consumed in flames, allows both subjects to engage a significant act of self-invention, a re-presentation in writing. Because of the lost home in Canada, and the journey to recover another lost homeland, these writers demonstrate a plurality of possibilities for self-formation. As both had renounced citizenships and made their place in another location, their multilocationality contributes to their processes of liminality. To perform these processes in a journal – the form that most clearly rejects finality – is significant in the context of life writing.

In a similar vein, May-lee Chai and Winberg Chai's father-daughter collaboration struggles to give voice to a lost character whose presence influenced their family. *The Girl from Purple Mountain* opens with family matriarch Ruth Mei-en Tsao Chai's instructions to bury her in "a spot where she would be encircled by strangers, where my father could not be buried, beside her" (1). This dictum unsettles the family and inspires her eldest son and biracial granddaughter to revisit her life – an odyssey of civil and foreign wars, revolution, betrayal, tragedy, and immigration. In her introductory note to the text, May-lee explains how, in the process of writing this story, she discovered that the story of her family did not involve "only what actually happened to them in China, but also how these events were later both remembered and repressed in America" (xi). Caught as a child between the tension of remembering and ignoring the past, May-lee collaborates with her father, in alternating chapters, to attempt to trace and understand the life of her remarkable grandmother, one of China's first college students.

The tension between forms of knowing is textually represented by the discrete chapters. The Chais' approach is complementary: May-lee provides historical background information that supplements Winberg's childhood memories. This strategy illustrates May-lee's own attempts to solve the confusion of her childhood. Because her first-hand knowledge of her grandmother was limited by their generational and cultural gap, she resorts to other forms of knowledge, in a sense, to contextualize her. As she explains, "it was this atmosphere of political intrigue, of paranoia, of assassinations and executions, that I needed to understand before I could begin to comprehend my grandparents' life" (189). Indeed, May-lee's chapters are historically and culturally grounded, based on scholarly insights rather than on the filial perspective Winberg provides. These complementary operations show a doubled relational strategy and a layered approach to biography. Nonetheless, despite the discerning juxtaposition of family stories, historical data, and cultural analysis, the axial point of this multilayered construct – the grandmother – remains elusive. What is enacted, however, is a renewed locating of both son and granddaughter in the larger story of twentieth-century Chinese history of revolutions and diaspora. As they tell Ruth's story, Winberg and May-lee stress their affiliation to that particular story and to the larger context of Chinese and American history, claiming a place for themselves in both spaces. But they also enact a liminal space – the gaps between their narratives attest to an irrecoverable loss – of a history, of unquestioning belonging, of family.

Crucially, the narrative enactment of these processes – for Blaise and Mukherjee and the Chais – requires the participation of both parties, a formal and aesthetic choice made consciously by the writers. For these writers, therefore, the construction of their story – individual, interacting, and intersecting lives – enacts a fundamental aspect of their distinct processes of selfhood. These collaborative life writing projects chart itineraries of subject dialogue and positionality that oblige us to reevaluate formal and aesthetic paradigms. The resulting text becomes dynamic chronicles that chart their writers' individual processes of adaptation and renegotiation of previously accepted models, prejudices, stances. Readers witness the formal dialogue that makes this change happen, and participate in the development of these relationships. *Days and Nights in Calcutta* and *The Girl from Purple Mountain* demonstrate how collaboration as a generic strategy effectively augments possibilities of inscribing the autobiographical project, attending to the relational quality of our lives and performing the dialogue that helps us comprehend it.

These diverse Asian American life writing texts – which privilege the relational as they challenge traditional generic forms – illustrate how the transcultural position of these writers offers new paths to self-representation.

Texts like these function as powerful tools for cultural criticism because of the discursive possibilities of the subversion of established forms of self-representation. The emphasis on the changing nature of subjectivity and its intersection with family and community, as well as the emphasis on textual manipulation offers ways to multiply meaning by challenging established forms. As writers negotiate life writing as relational, dialogical, or multiple, they accommodate not only issues of ethnicity, culture, or nation but, importantly, emphasize the formal approaches to the narrated subject in his or her act of inscription. These Asian American narrative strategies in life writing highlight performative acts that revise traditional concepts of the self-in-autobiography, leading us to rethink our ways of reading and writing lives.

NOTES

1. I use the term "life writing" because its inclusiveness accommodates the intersection – indeed the juxtaposition – of "biography" and "autobiography" and allows us to negotiate more precisely the multilayered processes at hand.
2. I use the term "performative" as Sidonie Smith does: autobiographical storytelling is "always a performative occasion" ("Performativity" 18).
3. I define "transcultural" as Janice Kulyk Keefer does, to refer to the manner in which the dominant culture "becomes part of a larger, looser structure within which literary texts which foreground the experience of 'minority' as opposed to 'dominant' groups both present themselves and are received as representative, even paradigmatic forms for an entire social formation, and not just for the ethnic or racial group with which the text's author is associated" (265).
4. See Michael M. J. Fischer's "Autobiographical Voices (1,2,3) and Mosaic Memory: Experimental Sondages in the (Post)Modern World" for more perspectives on the relational component to life writing.
5. This chapter centers on Kingston and Ondaatje. See my *Transcultural Reinventions: Asian American and Asian Canadian Short Story Cycles* for an analysis of how Asian Americans have appropriated and subverted this genre, and a discussion of Suleri's and Hongo's autobiographical cycles.
6. Though the short story cycle has its roots in traditional world literature, many critics, among them J. Gerald Kennedy and Rolf Lundén, have noted that the pragmatic affinity for short stories that shaped the literature of the United States decisively in the nineteenth century seems to persist in the form of a national inclination in the present century for organized short story collections: perhaps the very determination to build a unified republic out of diverse states, regions, and population groups, helps to account for this continuing passion for cycles (Kennedy viii). Lundén argues in favor of the short story cycle as a graphic expression of the coexisting conjunction of centripetal and centrifugal forces in American society and in the American character (108). In Wendy Ho's definition, "talk story" "includes women's experience and

imaginative stories [which] retell traditional stories and/or invent subversive stories" (28).

7. In certain cases, Asian American writers have reconstructed the life story of proximate others in books marketed as novels. Among these are Milton Murayama's *Five Years on a Rock* and Kien Nguyen's *The Tapestries*. Because the grandfather was left behind when Nguyen and his family abandoned Vietnam, the story recounted in his autobiography, *The Unwanted*, this text enacts a strategy of recovery – and attests to Nguyen's remembrance of his lost family. Frances and Ginger Park also inscribe a fictionalized version of their parents' story in *To Swim Across the World*.

8. See my "'A task of reclamation': Subjectivity, Self-Representation, and Textual Formulation in Sara Suleri's *Meatless Days*" for a detailed analysis of the juxtaposition of subjectivity and textual formation.

9. But Lee uses another story to extend her grandmother's narrative: the chronicle of her struggle to find the son who disappeared during the war at the age of fourteen. The life story thus ends with Lee's parents and her successful contact with her uncle, still trapped in North Korea, and with a grown family of his own. The story of the grandmother's only wish, to hold her son again, is deferred – Lee's final words are a celebration of her grandmother's devotion. The story of Lee's journey to North Korea to rescue her uncle and other family members is the subject of her next book, *In the Absence of Sun*.

10. Further, the 1995 prologue and epilogue by Blaise and Mukherjee, respectively, reframe the narrative. Mukherjee describes another journey – a relocation to the United States: "I shouldered my way into the country in which I felt minority discourse empowered me rather than enfeebled me. This time I was crossing a border because I wanted to cross it. This time I was repossessing a 'homeland' I had willed into existence, not inherited" (303).

WORKS CITED

Blaise, Clark, and Bharati Mukherjee. *Days and Nights in Calcutta*. 1977. St. Paul, MN: Hungry Mind Press, 1995.

Boelhower, William. "The Making of Ethnic Autobiography in the United States." *American Autobiography: Retrospect and Prospect*. Ed. Paul John Eakin. Madison: University of Wisconsin Press, 1991. 123–41.

Chai, May-lee, and Winberg Chai. *The Girl from Purple Mountain: Love, Honor, War, and One Family's Journey from China to America*. New York: Thomas Dunne Books, 2001.

Cheung, King-Kok. *Articulate Silences: Hisaye Yamamoto, Maxine Hong Kingston, Joy Kogawa*. Ithaca: Cornell University Press, 1993.

Chu, Patricia P. *Assimilating Asians: Gendered Strategies of Authorship in Asian America*. Durham: Duke University Press, 2000.

Davis, Rocío G. "'A task of reclamation': Subjectivity, Self-Representation, and Textual Formulation in Sara Suleri's *Meatless Days*." *Asian North American Identities Beyond the Hyphen*. Eds. Donald Goellnicht and Eleanor Ty. Bloomington: Indiana University Press, 2004.

Davis, Rocío G. *Transcultural Reinventions: Asian American and Asian Canadian Short-Story Cycles*. Toronto: TSAR, 2001.

Eakin, Paul John. *How Our Lives Become Stories: Making Selves*. Ithaca: Cornell University Press, 1999.

Egan, Susanna. *Mirror Talk: Genres of Crisis in Contemporary Autobiography*. Chapel Hill: University of North Carolina Press, 1999.

Elliot, Duong Van Mai. *The Sacred Willow: Four Generations in the Life of a Vietnamese Family*. New York: Oxford University Press, 1999.

Fifield, Adam. *A Blessing Over Ashes: The Remarkable Odyssey of My Unlikely Brother*. 2000. New York: HarperPerennial, 2001.

Fischer, Michael M. J. "Autobiographical Voices (1, 2, 3) and Mosaic Memory: Experimental Sondages in the (Post)Modern World." *Autobiography and Postmodernism*. Eds. Kathleen Ashley, Leigh Gilmore, and Gerald Peters. Amherst: University of Massachusetts Press, 1994. 79–129.

Goodyear, Sara Suleri. *Boys Will Be Boys: A Daughter's Elegy*. Chicago: University of Chicago Press, 2003.

Ho, Wendy. *In Her Mother's House: The Politics of Asian American Mother-Daughter Writing*. Walnut Creek, CA: AltaMira, 1999.

Hongo, Garrett. *Volcano: A Memoir of Hawai'i*. New York: Vintage Departures, 1995.

Houston, Jeanne Wakatsuki, and James Houston. *Farewell to Manzanar*. 1973. New York: Bantam, 1995.

Jackson, Michael. *Minima Ethnographica: Intersubjectivity and the Anthropological Project*. Chicago: University of Chicago Press, 1998.

Kanaganayakam, Chelva. "A Trick with a Glass: Michael Ondaatje's South Asian Connection." *Canadian Literature* 132 (Spring 1992): 33–41.

Kang, K. Connie. *Home was the Land of Morning Calm: The Saga of a Korean-American Family*. Reading, MA: Addison-Wesley Publishing Co., 1995.

Keefer, Janice Kulyk. "On Being a Canadian Writer Today." *Multiculturalism and the Canon of American Culture*. Ed. Hans Bak. Amsterdam: VU UP, 1993. 261–71.

Kennedy, J. Gerald. *Modern American Short Story Sequences: Composite Fictions and Fictive Communities*. New York: Cambridge University Press, 1995.

Kingston, Maxine Hong. *The Woman Warrior: Memoirs of a Girlhood Among Ghosts*. London: Picador, 1981.

Lee, Helie. *In the Absence of Sun: A Korean American Woman's Promise to Reunite Three Lost Generations of Her Family*. New York: Harmony Books, 2002.

Lee, Helie. *Still Life with Rice*. New York: Touchstone, 1996.

Lundén, Rolf. *The United Stories of America: Studies in the Short Story Composite*. Amsterdam: Rodopi, 1999.

Murayama, Milton. *Five Years on a Rock*. Honolulu: University of Hawaii Press, 1994.

Nguyen, Kien. *The Tapestries*. New York: Little, Brown, and Co., 2002.

Nguyen, Kien. *The Unwanted*. New York: Little, Brown, and Co., 2001.

Ondaatje, Michael. *Running in the Family*. New York: Penguin, 1982.

Park, Frances, and Ginger Park. *To Swim Across the World*. New York: Miramax, 2002.

Smith, Paul. *Discerning the Subject*. Minneapolis: University of Minneapolis Press, 1988.

Smith, Sidonie. "Memory, Narrative, and the Discourses of Identity in *Abeng* and *No Telephone to Heaven*." *Postcolonialism and Autobiography*. Eds. Alfred Hornung and Ernstpeter Ruhe. Amsterdam: Rodopi, 1998. 37–59.

Smith, Sidonie. "Performativity, Autobiographical Practice, Resistance." *A/b: Auto/Biography Studies* 10.1 (1995): 17–31.

Smith, Sidonie, and Julia Watson. *Reading Autobiography: A Guide for Interpreting Narratives*. Minneapolis: University of Minnesota Press, 2001.

Sone, Monica. *Nisei Daughter*. 1953. Seattle: University of Washington Press, 1991.

Sugimoto, Etsu. *A Daughter of the Samurai*. 1925. Rutland, VT: Charles E. Tuttle, Co., 1966.

Suleri, Sara. *Meatless Days*. Chicago: University of Chicago Press, 1987.

Uchida, Yoshiko. *The Invisible Thread*. New York: Simon and Schuster, 1991.

Wong, Jade Snow. *Fifth Chinese Daughter*. 1945. Seattle: University of Washington Press, 1989.

Yamamoto, Traise. *Masking Selves, Making Subjects: Japanese American Women, Identity, and the Body*. Berkeley: University of California Press, 1999.

CHAPTER 3

Asian Americans Imagining Burma: Chang-rae Lee's *A Gesture Life* and Wendy Law-Yone's *Irrawaddy Tango*

Cheng Lok Chua

Burma as a location of the fictive imagination has played a notably important role in two recent novels, Burmese American Wendy Law-Yone's *Irrawaddy Tango* (1993) and Korean American Chang-rae Lee's *A Gesture Life* (2000). Although Lee imagines a Burma of the past (during the Japanese Occupation of the 1940s) and Law-Yone projects a Burma of the future (as the fictional state of "Daya"), they both imagine it as a land of extremes, the extreme being a location beyond measure (to echo a concept of Homi Bhabha's). In Lee, Burma represents the geographical and cultural extreme of Japanese imperialism; in Law-Yone, the socio-political excess of state-sponsored military coercion. Burma is such an extreme that it is almost beyond the remembering for Lee's narrator-protagonist who nearly burns down his prized American home inadvertently when the memories of his Burmese days return to him. And the Burmese military dictatorship is so extreme that it is beyond the usual mimetic telling for Law-Yone who sets her novel in a nonexistent dystopia in order to censure its continuing existence. This experience of extremism acts as a catalyst for the revelation of a profound human truth in each work – in Lee's, the road through Burma leads to the truth about an individual human psyche (his protagonist's) while in Law-Yone's, the road back to Burma leads to the truth about a human society and polity (the protagonist's originary land).

In Lee's complexly crafted *A Gesture Life*, his Burma is compared and contrasted with three other cultural locations. Lee's narrator and protagonist is an aging Japanese American nicknamed "Doc" Hata who is making a retrospective evaluation of his life that has been materially successful but emotionally bankrupt and impotent. Hata's retrospective focuses on two pairs of symmetrically parallel but culturally contrasting locations, a North American pair in the present of the novel and a Southeast Asian pair of the past. The two present American locations are the upper-class town of Bedley Run and the contrasting working-class town of Ebbington. The two past Southeast Asian locations are Singapore during 1942 and Burma during 1944 when Hata had served as a medic in the Japanese Imperial Army during World War II. In addition, the essential qualities of each of these locations is emblematized by a house – Hata's high-end residence in Bedley Run, his runaway daughter's drug house in Ebbington, the Japanese officers' clubhouse in Singapore, and the comfort women's cubicles in Burma.

The culture of Bedley Run is that of an upper-class American community of orderliness and civility. Bedley Run's homes are well maintained, their grounds are manicured, and the businesses are prosperous. It is even "a picturesque town" (1). In Bedley Run, the narrator-protagonist "Doc" Hata (which is what everyone calls him though he makes it no secret that he is a pharmacist and not a doctor) has built up a thriving medical supplies store, and his residence is a prime piece of real estate: "My house isn't the grandest in town, but it's generally known that . . . [it] is one of the special properties" (16). He is a model of the Asian American success story and a pillar of his community. But behind the façade of his success lies the failure of Doc Hata's intimate emotional life – he fails to make a commitment to his lover, the attractive widow of a doctor living next door, and he fails to maintain a connection with his adopted Korean daughter who runs away from home to live in a drug house in nearby Ebbington. Ebbington's culture is that of a town in decay, and it forms a contrast to robust Bedley Run. Ebbington's businesses are failing, its streets ugly with trash, its neighborhoods deteriorating, and its inhabitants teetering on the brink of drugs and welfare: "Ebbington is . . . a working-class suburb of drab, unadorned homes and small motel-style apartment complexes. . . . There are what seems a disproportionately high number of auto garages and beauty salons and churches and bars, all half-failed and dilapidating in their own fashion" (65). One evening Hata seeks out his adopted runaway teenage daughter, Sunny, in Ebbington. He traces her to a drug house there only to see her engaging in consensual oral sex with a black man with a police record (112–16). Ebbington, then, in contrast to Bedley Run, is a culture of disorderliness and depravity.

These two North American locations have their counterparts in Southeast Asia. Singapore in 1942, as experienced by Lieutenant Hata, is an orderly and well controlled garrison of the Japanese Empire. Here Lieutenant Hata feels a sense of camaraderie and wellbeing, and he spends his leisure hours in the officers' club – "a grand house which was once a prominent British family's residence, . . . a yellow two-stor[e]y colonial structure with a double veranda and white columns" (105). In Singapore, the Japanese Empire of the Rising Sun seeks to inherit the culture of the British Empire on which the sun supposedly would never set.

Lee has said in an interview that his initial impulse in writing this novel was to depict the lot of the Korean "comfort women" who were pressed into servicing the Japanese Army (Garner 6). It is in Singapore that Lieutenant Hata notices the presence of these comfort women for the first time, but he has been propagandized into thinking of them as "volunteers" (163), even though one of them leaps to her death from a window (107). And he has no contact with them, confining his sexual patronage to an unexciting middle-aged Japanese prostitute whom he respectfully addresses as Madam Itsuda (111).

The culture of orderliness and wellbeing that Hata remembers experiencing in the Singapore of 1942 is radically changed to one of malaise and perversion when the location of his recollections shifts to the Burma of 1944. Geographically, Burma is at the extreme edge of the Japanese Empire, "the most far-flung sector of the occupied territory" (170). Culturally, it is also the rawest and most remote outpost of Japanese civility. In Burma, Hata's unit is isolated and encamped in the middle of the jungle, surrounded by a hostile Burmese population and waiting for the inevitable *coup de grâce* from the Allied forces amassing around them. The Japanese Colonel is an isolated eccentric who bares his body to mosquitoes daily "as a way of bleeding himself" (171). Lt Hata's superior officer Captain Ono is a skilled but ruthlessly sadistic surgeon who experiments horrifyingly with open-heart massage on a living Burmese subject (76). The men are sex starved, and one corporal is a sex-crazed collector of pornography (155–57). Into this degraded situation comes a troupe of five Korean comfort women, and Hata is charged with keeping them healthy for servicing the troops. Through his closer contact with them, he now realizes that they are not volunteers but abductees and sex slaves. Just as the drug house in Ebbington emblematizes the culture of decadence in Ebbington, so the comfort house epitomizes the culture of dehumanization in this Japanese encampment in Burma. Lee describes it with chilling precision and symbolism:

There were five compartments, . . . one for each of the girls; these were tiny windowless rooms, no more than the space of one and a half tatami mats, not even wide enough for a tall man to lie across without bending his knees. In the middle of each space was a wide plank . . . meant for lying down on, with one's feet as anchors on either side. At the other end, where the shoulders would be, the plank was widest, and then it narrowed again for the head, so that its shape was like the lid of a coffin. This is how they would receive the men. (179)

Unlike the other Japanese military personnel, Hata is really an ethnic Korean (Korea having been annexed into the Japanese Empire after the Russo-Japanese War of 1905–6), and he can speak to the Korean comfort women in secret and in their forbidden native language.[1] He is attracted to and falls in love with one of these women named Kkutaeh who reciprocates his feelings. Captain Ono, however, has reserved Kkutaeh for some mysterious personal experiment and isolates her in the camp infirmary under the supervision of Hata. Hata enters into a passionate sexual relationship with Kkutaeh, and one of their intense encounters is depicted through the house imagery that is so effectively recurrent in Lee's novel:

She did not hold me but she did not push me away. I never meant for this but I could no longer balk, or control myself, and then something inside her collapsed, snapped clean, giving way like some storm-sieged roof, and then I descended upon her, and I searched her, every lighted and darkened corner, and every room. (295)

Hata gets into a fight with Captain Ono over Kkutaeh, and when Ono threatens to shoot Hata, Kkutaeh kills the captain by severing his carotid artery with a scalpel (298). She then begs Hata to shoot her and end her miserable existence. In an enormous failure of nerve and an equally immense denial of reality (for Hata plans a life together with Kkutaeh after the War), he cannot bring himself to do it. Kkutaeh therefore forces the issue by empowering herself and attacking her arresting officer who turns her over to the tender mercies of a gang of twenty-five men. They take their pleasure of her and eventually dismember and hack up her body in a frenzy of extreme cruelty. Hata does not witness the extremes to which Kkutaeh is subjected, but he watches her executioners returning from their deed: "The men. . . . Some were half-dressed, shirtless, trouserless, half-hopping to pull on boots. They were generally quiet. The quiet after great celebration. They were flecked with blood, and muddy dirt. . . . One with his forearms as if dipped in crimson . . ." (304). To Hata is left the medic's task of picking up the pieces of human remains and to discover the fetus that Kkutaeh was carrying (305). (This memory returns to haunt him, of course, when he has to assist in his adopted Korean daughter's late-term abortion [282–83].)

Burma, then, is the traumatic Asian location that lies behind the appearance of Hata's apparently fulfilled dream of American success and assimilation. And it utterly poisons his model American lifestyle of privilege, country clubs, a desirable lover, and a high-achieving adopted Korean daughter. So insidious is its effect that, when he is burning some papers and memorabilia of his Burmese days, Hata sets fire to his prize home in a Freudian accident that almost destroys himself and the façade of successful respectability that he has so carefully cultivated in his pristine American location (34–35).

Whereas Korean American Chang-rae Lee imagines a Burma of the past that plays an essential role in his novel, the Burmese American Wendy Law-Yone projects a Burma of the future for her novel *Irrawaddy Tango*. In this novel Law-Yone imagines Burma as a dystopia that she ironically names Daya which its tourist guidebooks explain to mean "The Land of Compassion," but which, Law-Yone's narrator points out, may also mean "wound" (9). In her experimental narrative method, Law-Yone uses a hybridizing "bricolage"[2] to construct her protagonist and her dystopian state and thereby deconstruct contemporary Burmese politics.[3] The hybridizing elements are sometimes drawn from contrasting Asian and Western cultural locations (for example, obviously in the novel's title the name of the protagonist/narrator herself – a hybridizing of an Asian space and a Western tempo). Most fundamentally for the novel, however, the originary locations of the hybrid elements are either in the First World or in the Third World. The bricolage by which Law-Yone unified a mosaic out of these disparate elements is especially apparent in the construction and evolution of the protagonist-narrator Irrawaddy Tango, the construction of whose character is also a *bildungs* process that passes through three stages. First, there is an awakening to ego and self-interest, second, an awakening to alterity and the interest of others, and third, an awakening to self-empowerment for altruistic ends. The whole evolutionary process is a bricolage that hybridizes First-World and Third-World history and myth. Each evolving phase of Tango's identity can be seen as a hypertext behind which can be glimpsed a hypotext of female subjectivity located in First-World or Third-World culture.

Thus Tango's *bildung* begins with a Third-World phase, drawing upon the history and the myth of Eva Peron of Argentina. In this Cinderella-like phase, the humble small-town girl succeeds in the big city and becomes a mighty dictator's wife. Next, Law-Yone takes her protagonist through a First-World phase, drawing upon the history and myth of quintessential North American Patty Hearst (the granddaughter of "Citizen Kane," no less!). In this Maid Marian-Robin Hood phase, a wealthy woman socialite is kidnapped by guerrillas and then is persuaded to bond with, sleep with, fight for, and speak for her abductors. Third, Tango matures into a Third-World spider woman phase (as depicted in Native American orature as well as the work of Argentine bricoleur Manuel Puig[4]); in this phase a female empowers herself sexually, mates, and demolishes her mate. Through these phases of subjectivity, Tango's character moves and develops, like the Argentine dance itself, full of exhilarating dips and lifts of fortune, dizzying turns and reversals of plot, in movements charged with a sinister sense of power and unsated sensuality, all performed by a character cool to the point of superciliousness. In using this method of constructing and narrating her Asian American woman protagonist, Law-Yone seems to be working like a bricoleuse, entering easily into the semiotic locations of Third-World and First-World culture and appropriating for her creation the shards of female subjectivity to be found there.

The novel actually opens *in medias res*, near the spider-woman phase with its atmosphere of prison, torture, and sexuality. In it, Tango returns to her native Third-World location of Daya (Law-Yone's fictionalized Burma) as some sort of high-profile political prisoner after twenty-five years' domicile in the First World of the United States. The details of Daya/Burma are vividly and strategically evoked: the garish airport frescoes mythologizing the dystopian nation's history in which Tango reads a cruel and bloody national character, Tango's journey blindfolded through the sounds of a tropical night, the dreary particulars of her cell, the mind-boggling bureaucracy that requires Tango to sign a receipt for her body's being in captivity (17). Once the reader's interest is engaged by this initial situation, the first-person narrative flashes back to the antecedent formative stages of Tango's career.

The details of Tango's girlhood and adolescence resemble the Third-World history and myth of Evita Peron of Argentina. As V. S. Naipaul for one has made known (in his *Return of Eva Peron*), Maria Eva Duarte was born and grew up in the small pampa town of Toldos in Argentina. Her mother ran a boarding house; and when Evita was fifteen years old, she left her humble origins to sleep her way to a fairytale-like fame and fortune in Buenos Aires, her Big Apple (to use Andrew Lloyd Webber's phrase). Evita's is veritably a Latin American and naughtier enactment of the Cinderella story (which is, after all, Chinese in origin). Tango is likewise born and grows up in the small town of Irrawaddy whose Asian particularities Law-Yone delineates with vividness. The river boats with their cargoes of rice and elephants, the gibbon tethered to the Indian dry-goods store, the playmate with the soft spot in her head, the neighbor boy who produces his "pet worm" kept in his pants for Tango to fondle (62), all these become palpable presences in Law-Yone's pages of crisp descriptive writing. Against this backdrop is Tango's subjectivity formed. She emerges as an oddly Westernized and individualistic, even egocentric, subject while located in an Asian and Buddhist culture of self-denial and transcendence. Her father had first nicknamed her Mew because, as he explains, "You acted like a cat. No love for anyone but yourself" (21). This egocentricity is confirmed by Tango herself: "From time to time I felt a hardening inside, around the very spot warmed supposedly by love and goodwill . . ." (21). It is this egocentricity that allows Tango to mock her father's imperfect English and her mother's poor taste in music. After a particularly stormy confrontation with the teenage Tango, her mother decides to transcend the material world and retreat to a Buddhist nunnery. By contrast, Tango decides to embrace the material world and use her physical talents to rise from her humble origins.

For Tango's developing interests and talents have channeled themselves towards dancing the tango. Tango's dance instructor and partner is nicknamed Carlos, a local product of Portuguese descent and an erstwhile student in Argentina of the tango king, Carlos Gardel. Tango develops a passion for this Argentine dance which, unlike Burmese dance forms, allows her to be and to assert herself: "A dance that allowed me to stand up straight and tall, it didn't oblige me to crouch as if my back had just been broken. I wasn't pulled by invisible strings – I was guided and wooed by a partner who strode and leapt as one with me. A partner from whom I could swivel or twist away in seeming pique but could still trust to sweep me off my feet" (76). Tango and Carlos enter a national talent competition where they are standouts even though the prize goes to a politically correct indigenous dance. But Tango attracts the attention of a be-medaled Colonel, who marries her, just as Evita married Juan Peron when he was a Colonel. Not long afterwards, Tango's husband becomes General Supremo, and then military dictator of Daya with Tango as his first lady. With her marriage,

Tango becomes a socialite with the appurtenances and appearance of comfort, power, and prestige.

Tango soon discovers, however, that existence at the pinnacle of her material world leaves something to be desired. Her public life of languid days of poolside preening and glittering nights of diplomatic balls soon becomes boring. Her private life with Supremo is a dysfunctional existence of mental and physical abuse in which she must obey Supremo's every wish, even pet a crocodile at his command (109–10), and where she must fan the fading embers of his virility oddly enough by urinating on their bedroom floor (93). Supremo's near impotence again parallels the rumored impotence of Juan Peron, and Tango's duties of sexual arousal parallel Eva Peron's "reputed skill in fellatio" (as Naipaul puts it – 107). It is clear, then, that in this phase of character construction where Tango first awakens to self awareness and attains the goals set by her self-interest, her trajectory mirrors that of the legendary and historical figure of Third-World Argentina's Eva Peron.

There is a sudden tango-like reversal of plot direction when, at the apogee of Tango's socialite and material ascendancy, she is kidnapped by a band of hill-tribe guerrillas (117). Unlikely as it may seem, this kidnapping begins the second phase of Tango's subject formation – an awakening to alterity. And for this phase, Law-Yone appears to be mirroring the subjectivity of her protagonist with the First-World history and legend of the kidnapping of American socialite Patty Hearst in the 1970s.

In the case of Tango, she is captured by a band of dissident guerrillas and held for ransom and as a bargaining chip for the release of three imprisoned guerrilla leaders. The guerrillas call themselves the Jesu Liberation Army (the JLA). When the ransom is not paid and the prisoners not exchanged, Tango is held captive for more than a year, sharing the deprivation, fear, and fatigue of the fugitive guerrilla life and interacting with her captors. During this time, Boyan, the guerrilla leader, is attracted to Tango and becomes her sexual partner, a situation to which Tango reacts ambivalently. After Boyan is killed in a firefight with security forces, Tango begins to play a more substantial role in the guerrilla movement and becomes their spokesperson and media image. At this point, Tango evolves from her egoistic subjectivity towards one that is capable of sympathizing with others: "I began to understand . . . the nature of freedom. . . . When you are part of a purpose bigger than your single life, you feel free in a different way" (155–6). Subsequently, Tango is captured by the security forces, branded as a traitress by the state and her uncaring husband, charged with treason, jailed, and exquisitely tortured in a game of

Russian roulette played with a revolver inserted in her vagina (178–9). Eventually, Tango is freed from prison by an American humanitarian worker belonging to a group called INRI (Jesus Nazarenus Rex Judaeorum – Jesus of Nazareth, King of the Jews).[4]

The hypotext for this Asian sequence of events is the First-World kidnapping, trial, and pardon of Patricia Hearst during the 1970s. The story of Patty Hearst was a media frenzy in its time, almost equivalent in impact to the O. J. Simpson trial or the Monica Lewinsky scandal of the 1990s. It was widely reported (making the cover of *Newsweek* and *Time* magazines) and analyzed in more than half a dozen books written by journalists (for example, Shana Alexander's *Anyone's Daughter*), by academics (Christopher Castiglia's *Bound and Determined*), by Patty Hearst herself (*Every Secret Thing*), and by her lover (Steven Weed's *My Search for Patty Hearst*). Patty Hearst, like Irrawaddy Tango at the time of her abduction, was a woman of wealth and privileged social position. She was the granddaughter of William Randolph Hearst, the newspaper tycoon immortalized as *Citizen Kane* by Orson Welles's film. (Patty Hearst herself became the title subject of a film directed by Paul Schrader.) In September 1975, while a student at Berkeley, Patty Hearst was abducted and held for ransom by a group of guerrillas just as Tango would be. The guerrillas called themselves the Symbionese Liberation Army – the SLA (an acronym that is noticeably similar to that of Tango's captors, the JLA, the Jesu Liberation Army). The SLA held Patty for ransom and for exchange of two jailed members, a circumstance that would be mirrored in Tango's kidnapping. The SLA subjected Patty to months of classic thought reform through debilitation, dread, and dependency, and, as would Tango, she became romantically involved with one of her captors, Willie Wolfe (aka "Cujo"). Like Tango, Patty began to sympathize with her captors and joined them, taking the *nom de guerre* of "Tanya," after one of Che Guevara's companions. She participated in the robbery of the Hibernia Bank in San Francisco, with the bank cameras recording her brandishing a gun. In Sacramento, after the Crocker Bank was robbed, Patty was seen driving the getaway car. Eventually, after a SWAT team shootout in which two SLA leaders (including Willie Wolfe) were killed, and after several car bombings, Patty and an Asian American comrade Wendy Yoshimura were arrested. After a trial and much tribulation which whittled her weight down to eighty-seven pounds at trial's end (Hearst 372), Patty, as Tango was to be, is sentenced to twenty-five years in jail. Finally, just as Tango would be freed by a Christian liberator, Patty was pardoned – after serving six months – by President Carter, one of the most actively Christian of American presidents.

Considering the similar social positioning of Tango and Patty, the circumstances of their abduction, their conversion from being captives to becoming collaborators, from being victims to becoming participants, and their eventual arrest by the police, their conviction, and their release, one may reasonably conclude that the history and legend of the First-World American woman is the hypotext for Wendy Law-Yone's fictional character during this phase of the *bildung* of her subjectivity.

The third and final phase of Tango's evolving subjectivity concludes with her self-empowerment for the good of others. In this phase, Law-Yone uses a Third-World archetype as her hypotext for the climactic end of her novel. The mythic material originates in Native American orature and has been popularized in *The Kiss of the Spider Woman*, by that master bricoleur, the Argentine Manuel Puig.[5] In Puig, the spider woman is a symbol of female fecundity and fatality, of creativity and destructiveness: for the female spider mates with the male and then destroys it. Precisely this pattern of events, of mating and killing, structures the closing sequence of *Irrawaddy Tango*.

After her liberation from Daya, Tango becomes an Asian immigrant in America where the American Dream constantly eludes her. She is unhappy in her marriage to her American liberator, becomes embroiled in meaningless serial promiscuities, and drifts into a state of anomie. However, an opportunity to play an important role in the politics of her originary country presents itself. She is invited to return to Daya, where the Dayan astrologers have foreseen the coming end of their dictator's power, but they feel that his downfall may be forestalled by a reconciliation between him and "the first woman sanctioned to receive his life milk" (262). Tango agrees to cooperate and returns to Daya. (The moment of her return is the opening chapter of the novel.) Once back, Tango is kept as a VIP prisoner until the propitious hour for attempted reconciliation arrives. The ensuing episode, which concludes the novel, is a graphic piece of erotic writing[6] detailing Tango's heroic powers of sexual resuscitation as she brings her desiccated former husband to consummation. Then the novel ends with Tango's supreme act of self-empowerment and self-creation. As her mate lapses into a post-coital slumber, Tango uses duct tape to enclose him in their sheets, creating an insect-like "cocoon" (283). She then bludgeons him to death, and in so doing, frees a nation from its loathsome dictator. In the configuration of the events of this finale and of the antecedent kidnapping, it seems clear that Law-Yone was engaged in writing a witty, tongue-in-cheek work of bricolage which depends upon American hypotexts to construct her narrative of her protagonist's return to Asia.

In these three phases of her protagonist's evolving subjectivity – from egocentricity, to alterity, to altruistic self-empowerment – Law-Yone has employed a witty bricolage that hybridizes elements of First-World and Third-World history and mythology into a mordant condemnation of contemporary Burma and a thinly veiled call to action.

In sum, both of these Asian American novelists, Lee and Law-Yone, whose sensibilities and personal histories have derived from cultural locations both Asian and American, both Third World and First World, have imagined a Burma that plays a crucial role in their works. Chang-rae Lee has constructed the site of his imagined Burma of the past through the memories of the Korean comfort women whom he interviewed and studied in his native Korea. Law-Yone created her imagined "Daya" by using a bricolage of cultural artifacts drawn from the First World and the Third World as well as her own memories of her early life in Burma as the daughter of Edward Law-Yone, the editor of Burma's best-known English-language newspaper who became a political prisoner and then an exile first in Thailand and eventually in America (Yoo and Ho 283). Lee's purpose leans towards the psychological, and he examines the façade and interior of his protagonist's psyche through the apt symbolism of houses placed in contrasting Asian and American cultural locations. Law-Yone's purpose tends towards the socio-political, and she condemns and deconstructs an extreme tyranny by constructing out of Third World and First World cultural objects an intricate *bildungsroman* of an empowered female political assassin. In both works, Burma is used to represent an extreme in disorder and inhumanity, an area of extreme darkness in the uneasy heart of Southeast Asia. In these Asian American works, then, Burma represents a past of which the world should promise "Never again," and a future to which the present must say "Never ever."[7]

NOTES

1. In his memoir about his mother's death, "The Faintest Echo of Our Language," Lee has written feelingly about the antipathy of some Koreans towards Japanese – views that are, to be sure, not shared by all Koreans:

   My mother often showed open enmity for the Japanese, her face seeming to ash over when she spoke of her memories, that picture of the platoon of lean-faced soldiers burning [Korean-language] books and scrolls in the center of the village still aglow in my head . . . , and how they tried to erase what was Korean by criminalizing the home language and history by shipping slave labor, draftees, and young Korean women back to Japan and its other Pacific colonies. How they taught her to speak in Japanese. And as she would speak of her childhood, of the pretty, stern-lipped girl . . . who could only whisper to her sisters in the midnight safety of their house the Korean words folding inside her all day like mortal secrets, I felt the same burning, troubling lode of utter pride and utter shame still jabbing at the sweet belly of her life, that awful gem, about who she was and where her mother tongue and her land had gone. (31)

2. To use Claude Levi-Strauss's term describing a mosaic-like approach to creativity that he describes in his *Savage Mind*, 16–33.
3. Leslie Bow's *Betrayal and Other Acts of Subversion*, 137–53, provides a lucid account of the Burmese politics underlying Law-Yone's novel. See also her interview of Law-Yone in *MELUS*, Winter 2002.
4. The letters "INRI" are initials for the Latin title that Pontius Pilate had written over the head of Jesus Christ on the cross (John 19:19). The words were "Iesvs Nazarenvs Rex Ivdaeorvm." Latin uses "I" instead of the English "J," and "V" instead of "U" (i.e. Jesus Nazarenus Rex Judaeorum). The English translation is "Jesus of Nazareth, the King of the Jews."
5. For a discussion of Puig's bricolage, see Lavers's *Pop Culture into Art*.
6. Law-Yone's short story "Drought" is included in the anthology of erotica *Slow Hand*, edited by Michele Slung.
7. This article is dedicated to the memory of its author's father, Chua Yew Cheng, teacher and soldier, who died in a prisoner-of-war camp in Southeast Asia.

WORKS CITED

Alexander, Shana. *Anyone's Daughter*. New York: Viking, 1979.

Bhabha, Homi K. *The Location of Culture*. London: Routledge, 1994.

Bow, Leslie. *Betrayal and Other Acts of Subversion: Feminism, Sexual Politics, Asian American Women's Literature*. Princeton: Princeton University Press, 2001.

Bow, Leslie. "Beyond Rangoon: An Interview with Wendy Law-Yone." *MELUS* (Winter 2002): 183–200.

Castiglia, Christopher. *Bound and Determined: Captivity, Culture-Crossing and White Womanhood From Mary Rowlandson to Patty Hearst*. Chicago: University of Chicago Press, 1996.

Chiu, Monica. "Illness and Self-Representation in Asian American Literature by Women." Dissertation, Emory University, 1996.

Garner, Dwight. "Adopted Voice: Interview." *New York Times Book Review* 5 September 1999: 6, 20.

Hearst, Patricia Campbell with Alvin Moscow. *Every Secret Thing*. New York: Doubleday, 1982.

Jackson, Kevin, ed. *Schrader on Schrader*. London and Boston: Faber, 1990.

Lavers, Norman. *Pop Culture Into Art: The Novels of Manuel Puig*. Columbia: University of Missouri Press, 1988.

Law-Yone, Wendy. "Drought." *Slow Hand: Women Writing Erotica*. Ed. Michele Slung. New York: Harper, 1993. 27–40.

Law-Yone, Wendy. *Irrawaddy Tango*. New York: Knopf, 1993.

Law-Yone, Wendy. Telephone interview, 29 June 1999.

Lee, Chang-rae. "The Faintest Echo of Our Language." *Family: American Writers Remember Their Own*. Eds. Sharon Sloan Fiffer and Steve Fiffer. New York: Pantheon, 1996. 27–42.

Lee, Chang-rae. *A Gesture Life*. New York: Riverhead, 1999.

Levi-Strauss, Claude. *The Savage Mind*. Chicago: University of Chicago Press, 1996.

Naipaul, V. S. *The Return of Eva Peron with the Killings in Trinidad*. New York: Knopf, 1980.

Puig, Manuel. *The Kiss of the Spider Woman*. Trans. Thomas Colchie. New York: Random, 1979. (Trans. of *El Beso de la mujer arana* [1976].)

Schrader, Paul, dir. *Patty Hearst*, Atlantic/Zenith Films, 1988. (Based on Patty Hearst's book *Every Secret Thing*.)

Weed, Steven. *My Search for Patty Hearst*. New York: Crown, 1976.

Yoo, Nancy, and Tamara Ho. Interview with Wendy Law-Yone. *Words Matter: Conversations with Asian American Writers*. Ed. King-Kok Cheung. Honolulu: University of Hawaii Press, 2000. 283–302.

Perspectives on Gender Roles and Representation

Globalization, Masculinity, and the Changing Stakes of Hollywood Cinema for Asian American Studies

Karen Fang

In 2002, Roger Ebert became a leader in Asian American issues. The well-known film critic and television personality enthusiastically praised *Better Luck Tomorrow*, a film by an Asian American director, Justin Lin, and starring an entirely Asian American cast. At the important Sundance Film Festival, where the film had screened, Ebert had been at the center of controversy when a white audience member upbraided Lin for making a movie so "empty and amoral for Asian Americans." During the ensuing debate, the critic fiercely defended the director's artistic freedom; because of Ebert's fame, the debate sparked numerous press reports that would further publicize the film. At one point using his familiar portly figure to command attention by jumping up on his theater seat, Ebert countered, "Nobody would say to a bunch of white filmmakers, 'how could you do this to your people?'" In his opinion, Ebert argued – to much applause and cheers – "This film has the right to be about these people, and Asian American characters have the right to be whoever the hell they want to be."[1]

In this notion that "Asian American characters have the right to be whoever the hell they want to be," Ebert defends the rights of ethnic characters, under artistic license as well as the Constitution, to follow a path determined by their actions and motivations rather than by their racial makeup. Such a claim opposes the "burden of representation," the predicament that minority filmmakers often face when audiences expect them to depict stories that explicitly promote their public identity, as was implied by the Sundance audience member who demanded of Lin, "Don't you have a responsibility to paint a more positive and helpful portrait of your community?"[2] It is significant that it should be Ebert, a middle-aged white man whose nationally syndicated film reviews for the *Chicago Sun-Times* and various television networks have shown him to be an exemplar of mainstream, middle-brow movie-going taste, who should defend ethnic artists. For such a paragon of mainstream inclinations to become the film's unlikely champion must mean that much of America is capable of recognizing the same idea, and is indicative of a greater cultural sensitivity at large. For Asian Americans, Ebert's criticism of the burden of representation is particularly meaningful because of their historical status as the "model minority," a confining label that corrals Asian Americans into docile conformity under the guise of praising their industriousness and adaptability.

How did Ebert – and the mainstream American movie-going audience that he represents – come to this position? The economic and cultural transformations of globalization have been instrumental in this history. By the millenium, the global supremacy of the American movie industry was a uniquely interdependent phenomenon, wherein "Hollywood" catered to a global marketplace from which as much as half of its income resulted from foreign exports. Such an expansion in scope, however, transforms prior notions of the majority population that Hollywood targets, and hence necessarily also transforms what defines mainstream fare itself. For Asian Americans, the most systematically erased racial minority in Hollywood cinema, these changes would compel increasingly sensitive approaches towards ethnic Asian subjects, as Hollywood films after the late 1980s and early 1990s demonstrate. Ebert's insight into the cinematic rights of representation for Asian Americans only reflects this progressive trend.

Significantly, the critical and cultural progress that *Better Luck Tomorrow* emblematizes overturns the notion, once common in Asian American studies, that independent cinema is the sole province of positive representation. It also suggests, because of its origins in globalization, an expanded conception of Asian America similar to the reexamination of the discipline currently ongoing in diaspora, Asian, and Asian American studies.[3] Globalization confounds the very categories of "Asian" and "American," and thus seems to require a reevaluation of the Asian American label. Cinema is a particularly visible instance of these transformations, as is apparent in the stylistic interchange of Asian and Hollywood cinema – of which the violent action at the center of Lin's film, I will argue, is a key example. Masculinity is a more general cinematic subject in which violence figures, and because it has long been a key site of Asian racial stereotype, it often is inextricably bound up with the racial issues that globalization transforms.

These factors put pressure on the traditional disciplinary dichotomy in Asian American studies between Hollywood and independent cinema. After all, although Hollywood film is typically characterized by "universal" narratives designed to appeal to a broad audience, such an inclination towards the universal is also a defining attribute of globalization. Not surprisingly, then, post-global Hollywood representations of Asian Americans show mainstream cinema assimilating a sympathetic and non-racially-circumscribed minority perspective previously thought possible only in independent film. Indeed, this transformed sense of universality – universality as multiculturalism rather than a homogenous, de facto white majority – does not only transform the terms of Asian American identity: it also elevates Asian Americans into a prototype for today's transnational, culturally hybrid world after globalization.

This chapter explores the recent progress of Hollywood representations of Asian Americans by comparing Better Luck Tomorrow with The Joy Luck Club, an early attempt to advance Asian American cinematic representation which the later film, as suggested by the echoing of titles, revises. The Guru, a romantic comedy released around the same time as Better Luck Tomorrow, also figures in this history. A Hollywood film that Asian American studies overlooked, presumably because of its mainstream origins, The Guru is a paean to heterosexual virility that deserves recognition for its revisionary depiction of Asian American masculinity. Admittedly, my interest in masculinity and Asian American representation in relation to The Joy Luck Club may seem familiar, but my focus on these three films – and particularly the achievements of the two postmillenial movies – is the revolution in gender and genre that globalization has wrought upon the current status of Asian American identity in Hollywood film. One way, therefore, to think of this work is as a follow-up to both Eugene Franklin Wong's seminal On Visual Media Racism and Russell Leong's edited collection Moving the Image.[4] If Wong's historical study traced the limitations of Asian representations in American film up to 1977, and Leong and his contributors heralded the accomplishments of independent cinema from 1970–90 in contesting this history, my hope is to reveal how market-driven advances in mainstream media since 1993 reverse this history, instead exhibiting a gradual synthesis of Hollywood universalism and minority perspectives that currently places mainstream cinema as the leading edge of Asian American studies and activism.

THE BURDENS OF REPRESENTATION

Any exploration of minority representation in cinema must first acknowledge the various kinds of representation that the term implies. In film history, the term refers to both the nature and content of the dramatic story (often, stereotype and convention) as well as to the industrial history that brought the film into being and subsequently distributed it in theaters. This latter aspect involves casting, other affiliated creative talent, and the kinds of audiences reached by the film's status as either an independent or Hollywood feature. The "burden of representation," a third aspect of cinematic representation, developed to counter adverse or restricted representation in the two other conditions but, as the name implies, can be a burden itself because of the dramatic and artistic limitations it imposes. Film scholarship and minority activism thus are most effective when they move beyond these multiple burdens of representation to demand cinematic portrayals of minority characters in which their minority status is irrelevant, as occurred in Hollywood's historical representation of African Americans. Since African American moviegoers comprise about a third of the American movie-going audience, Hollywood efforts to appeal to this community have given rise to a whole sub-industry of current films virtually indistinct from mainstream Hollywood features except for the race of their African American leads.

By contrast, the apparently limited market potential of Asian Americans provides Hollywood little reason to change existing representational practices. Asian Americans compose between four and five percent of the US population and represent a proportionately miniscule fraction of the movie-going audience. The limited returns that this population represents therefore not only permit filmmakers to stereotype with impunity; it also motivates the infrequency of their appearances, preempting studios from considering Asian American topics or actors. In 1992, for example, a report from the Screen Actors Guild showed that only 1.3 per cent of all lead roles in films that year went to Asian/Pacific Islanders, considerably less than even the small fraction Asian Americans compose in the national population.[5] Nearly a decade later, in 2000, the year of blockbuster *Charlie's Angels*, co-starring Lucy Liu, this figure barely improved to 1.7 per cent – a leap for Asian Americans, but still a small step in real numbers.[6] The Hollywood history of Asian American screen appearances thus is arguably most typical in not being present at all. As the *New York Times* film critic, Elvis Mitchell, recently observed, despite being "the group most often orphaned into stereotypical behavior by teenage films," Asian Americans are so infrequent in Hollywood cinema that they were "even left out of the joke-compilation *Not Another Teen Movie*."[7]

The only significant alternative to this legacy of Hollywood invisibility has historically been independent cinema, as its centrality in Asian American studies attests. As Russell Leong, Marina Heung, Jun Xing, and Peter Feng have all demonstrated, independent cinema both offers powerful counter-images to the stereotypes in the dominant cinema and is a sanctuary for those Asian American actors and filmmakers that the mainstream industry over-looks.[8] But a comparison of the relative audiences reached by independent and Hollywood films demonstrates the value in maintaining mainstream cinema as an object of scholarship and activism. *Thousand Pieces of Gold* (1991), for example, is an independent film that frequently figures in Asian American scholarship. Although the film was critically well regarded, it earned less than a million dollars through the festival and arthouse screen-ings to which it was limited, and it received its final national airing as a television broadcast on PBS. *The Joy Luck Club*, by contrast, was a studio production with the full weight of the Disney Corporation behind it. As the most heavily promoted film featuring an Asian American cast in Hollywood history, the movie earned a remarkable thirty million dollars. But even if it achieved unprecedented crossover success, it still could be easily eclipsed by any genre or star-driven picture with greater mainstream appeal. *Rising Sun*, one of the top twenty box office hits of the same year, is an example. An action film set in Japan and portraying the secondary Japanese characters as sadistic, unscrupulous and inscrutable people deservedly thwarted by stars Sean Connery and Wesley Snipes, *Rising Sun* earned over sixty million dollars. With twice as many tickets sold for *Rising Sun* than *The Joy Luck Club*, we can be sure that that film's violently xenophobic depiction of Japanese greatly undermined any achievements of *The Joy Luck Club* – espe-cially among the non-Asian American audience that did not see that film.

The representational sites by which Hollywood stereotypes Asian Americans are precisely the same sites in which progressive representation can occur. These issues, which are all related, are (1) the gender dichotomy that singles out Asian American men for the brunt of Hollywood erasure; (2) the narrative conventions applied to Asian races that ensure these anti-masculine conditions are slow to change; and (3) the longstanding belief in the absolute otherness of Asian Americans that globalization would turn to advantage. I will deal with the third issue more fully in the second section of this chapter.

On the first issue, previous stereotype criticism has shown how stereotypes of Asian ethnicity frequently center upon gender. The Asian race is conventionally associated, in western perception, with thinner, shorter, and more hairless bodies than the normative white body, and with polite, modest behavior perceived to be typical of their rigidly ancient culture. Because of these connotations, heteronormative gender ideals accord Asian men and women entirely different cultural status, a fact that film reflects. Asian women, who are thought to be submissive and exotic creatures accustomed to suffering and to accommodating male pleasure, lend themselves easily to Hollywood, a film style reliant upon a profoundly heterosexual identification. They thus are an exception to the invisibility of Asian races in Hollywood, as they occupy a fairly common – even co-starring – presence in Hollywood cinema. Her various appearances, as Renee Tajima catalogues, range from "the Lotus Blossom Baby (aka China Doll, Geisha Girl, shy Polynesian beauty), [to] the Dragon Lady (Fu Manchu's various female relations, prostitutes, devious madames)," but all belong to a stock type, the "homogenous mass of Mama Sans."[9] Ironically, however, Asian men are conceived in western perception as effeminate and sexless beings, for precisely the same reasons that Asian women are thought to be hyper-feminine and over-sexed. Their stereotypes range from the demonic evil of Fu Manchu to the shuffling Ah Sings, whose deferential nature may confirm the servility of Charlie Chan or mask the unscrupulous oriental businessman's Fu Manchu-like greed. This is not to say that Asian men are always portrayed as asexual, because western anxieties about miscegenation – the underside of the orientalism that enthusiastically claims the exotic Asian woman – manifest in frequent depictions of lecherous Asian men whose sexual rejection is only ensured by their latent homosexuality or the impotent diminutiveness of his body. Obviously, this tradition does not posit Asian men as likely candidates for the active, heterosexual male protagonists privileged in Hollywood film. The historical invisibility of Asian Americans in Hollywood cinema thus is, more specifically, an invisibility of Asian men, whose rare appearances are always as secondary characters and only occur when such stereotypes are useful.

"Racial castration" is the term that David Eng, in one of the most astute explorations of cinema and Asian American masculinity, calls this symbolic emasculization performed by Hollywood.[10] For Eng, the term describes the visual depreciation exercised upon Asian Americans by stereotypes and erasure, but it can also apply to the way in which spectatorship further alienates Asian American men. Again, the African American model offers a useful comparison. The African American feminist critic, bell hooks, has pointed out how Hollywood can be a pleasurably transgressive experience for black men, despite its status as a mainstream medium. This occurs, as hooks notes, because the white male perspective that is the presumed audience of a Hollywood film enables a black male spectator to exult in the opportunity to identify with the autonomy of the Hollywood protagonist, a socially proscribed experience epitomized by the opportunity, in Hollywood spectatorship, to gaze upon white women. It is black women, hooks reveals, whom Hollywood neglects, by doubly excluding their race and gender in "a cinematic context that constructs our presence as absence."[11] It should be apparent, however, that for Asian Americans this gender split in spectatorship is reversed: Asian American women viewing Hollywood films understand their ethnicity as highly acceptable to American culture (albeit in highly stereotyped ways), whereas Asian American men are the absent presence in most Hollywood films. Already culturally and visually constructed as emasculated, impotent creatures, they are even precluded from the spectatorial transgression accorded the black male Hollywood moviegoer. This means that the male Asian American viewer of mainstream film experiences spectatorship as yet another symbol of his racial castration, in which the passive watching of a Hollywood film underscores the actual physical union that stereotypes within American culture assume Asian American men cannot achieve.

Genre segregation, the second defining problem in Asian American cinematic representation, connects with the gendered determination of visibility and stereotyping by using narrative form to reiterate masculinity's troubled status. "Genre segregation" is the likelihood that ethnically Asian roles appear only in storylines where such a racially specific character is useful, such as in an immigration history or as a model student in a teen drama or comedy. I derive the term from the patterns in casting that Eugene Franklin Wong identifies to describe how Hollywood systematically marginalizes ethnic Asians from industrial representation.[12] Genre segregation arguably is far more responsible for the limited opportunities for Asian American actors than the role constrictions that Wong identifies. After all, Hollywood production decisions are guided by market potential, and since genre is an aspect second only to stars in predicting a film's commercial success, it is a deciding factor in which projects get made. Because action, comedy, and romance are the leading box office genres in the US, and genre segregation limits Asians to ethnically relevant roles, few significant opportunities arise for Asian American actors. This is particularly the case for male actors, whose only hope for significant speaking parts may lie in the infrequent war film.

As one of the most likely opportunities for Asian American representation, the genre of history poses additional problems. Many Asian American narratives are immigrant histories and take the form of autobiography; the predominance of this theme exists because of the value of authenticity to counter past orientalist representations. Lisa Lowe and Werner Sollors, however, have both argued that the plots of generational conflict frequently at the center of such immigrant narratives inadvertently essentialize ethnic American culture.[13] According to Lowe, "the reduction of ethnic cultural politics to struggles between first and second generations" is undesirable because they imply the impossibility of hybridity by portraying immigration history "in terms of a loss of the 'original' culture in exchange for the new 'American' culture."[14] Similarly, the always combative Frank Chin has claimed that autobiography is a Christian tradition, and consequently condemns the use of that form as tantamount to ethnic renunciation.[15] Chin's admittedly controversial claims aside, autobiography and immigrant histories certainly limit artistic achievement. These genres underscore the "burden" in the burden of representation by upholding narrative conventions, and by thus engaging in genre segregation they fail to demonstrate artistic originality. One would think that Asian Americans, used to being thought of as an indistinguishable and unimaginative mass, and already feeling the strain of confinement in the model minority label, ought to be eager to shatter such sources of stereotype.

The Joy Luck Club illustrates the various problems in Hollywood representations of Asian Americans as previously outlined. The film, based on Amy Tan's bestselling novel of the same name, was produced by prestigious Oscar-winning director Oliver Stone, whose service in the Vietnam War sparked a lasting personal interest in Asia.[16] Both Stone and screenwriter Ronald Bass were determined to maintain the sensitivities they perceived in the original novel. Bass, for example, agreed to adapt the work on the condition that all of Tan's original stories be retained in the film, and Stone's commitment to authenticity and sensitivity was evident in his appointment of Wayne Wang, the director of the critically acclaimed independent film, *Chan is Missing* (1982), to direct. But if Wang's appointment to the project was indicative of an emerging willingness in Hollywood to disseminate sensitive and authentic images of Asian Americans, the film did not achieve its promise. Not only was it eclipsed by more commercial vehicles such as the Connery-Snipes actioner, but it failed to transcend the Hollywood conventions of gender privileging and genre segregation that have long conspired to limit Asian American cinematic representation. Both the immigrant genre and the invisibility of masculinity distinguish *The Joy Luck Club* movie, though as many contemporary reviews of the film pointed out, the mothers' stories in China were more interesting, which suggests how little Hollywood is capable of portraying a compellingly American vision of Asian identity.[17]

Significantly, then, gender and genre conspire in *The Joy Luck Club* to extend inclusion into American society only at the price of the women's willing erasure of their own ethnicity. In the three romantic relationships with which the film concludes, two women have white husbands and the Asian boyfriend of the third woman, unlike the other consorts, gets no close-up. In her study of this recurring scenario in Hollywood film, Gina Marchetti shows how these cinematic instances of Asian woman/white man romances naturalize western or white racial supremacy.[18] The implication is clear: because the women resist their racial heritage, as embodied in their rejected Asian suitors, the film suggests that hybrid identity ultimately is not possible. As Jessica Hagedorn notes of the film, the daughters "had lost all sense of self."[19] The film's resistance to the continuity of a wholly ethnically Asian family is apparent in one scene in which the camera lingers lovingly over the mixed-race child of one of the interracial couples, whose honey-colored hair and skin are offered as the optimistic embodiment of the (racially) brightened future of Asian Americans.

Both the promise and failure of *The Joy Luck Club* illuminate the value of positing mainstream or Hollywood cinema as the focus of Asian American activism. The previous notion of independent cinema as the privileged site of progressive Asian American representation exists because of independent cinema's strong associations of art with politics, as in the socially critical, guerilla filmmaking of *Chan is Missing* and *Who Killed Vincent Chin?* Asian American cinema studies reflect this commitment through its own predominately political critical approaches, which diverge from the more philosophical and psychoanalytic approaches common in film theory in general. But if Hollywood art inflicts injuries upon a population that are countered by the politically oppositional art of independent film, the very power of that dominant art demonstrates its value – and capacity – to be redirected for similarly progressive political purposes. Yoshio Kichi, a prominent Hollywood film editor (he was associate editor on *Raging Bull*) as well as a veteran Asian American activist, is a compelling proponent of this view. According to Kichi, talent that exclusively concentrates on alternative media, "loses out on the training and experiences needed to compete beyond the ethnic enclave," and ultimately may lose an opportunity to change the stereotypes and invisibility that prevail within Hollywood.[20] Starting in the late 1990s, globalization would provide the enabling conditions for such a change. It would do so because of the way in which it reframed the criteria – and particularly the stakes – of the perceived foreignness that previously shaped Asian American cinematic representation.

GLOBALIZATION AND THE RISE OF ASIAN COOL

The Hollywood portrayal of people of Asian ethnicity as foreign and non-American – the third defining aspect of Hollywood representations of Asian Americans – has always reflected the political and especially the economic relationship of the US to the Asian nation to which the characters supposedly belong. As Robert G. Lee and Eugene Franklin Wong have shown, Hollywood portraits of ethnic Asians run the gamut of romantic novelty, sinister labor threat, Communist agent and war victim, reflecting the various ways in which immigration laws and US military involvement have figured Asian people relative to default white America.[21] As a mode of racial representation that always implies their fundamental foreignness, this emphasis upon ethnic Asians in relation to another space – unlike the stereotyping leveled at African Americans – is particularly apparent in the ethnic specificity by which such characters are presented on film. It is a significant fact that despite the common western notion that members of the Asian race all look alike, Hollywood portraits of Asians have been so closely indexed to contemporary politics that their dramatizations often presuppose the ability to understand, for example, the relevance of Chinese vs. Japanese citizenship in a film from 1941–5. Similarly, more recently Hollywood has noted South Asian immigration to the US by scripting Indian and Pakistani taxicab drivers and convenience store clerks. These characters, which replaced African Americans as the new race for these stock working-class figures, are nearly always minor roles whose limited dialogue usually exists to make cheap comic shots at their language and culture.

In the 1980s and early 1990s, such a tendency to portray Asian ethnicity as nationality was spurred by the growing economic agency of ethnic Asians, both in the US and abroad. As the 1980s witnessed the rapid enrichment of Japan, Korea, Hong Kong, Singapore, and Taiwan, this event was paralleled, in film as in the national imagination, by the domestic rise of the

Asian American model minority – as was trumpeted on a cover issue of a campus edition of *Newsweek* magazine in 1984. In Hollywood, contemporary representations of Asians maintained such national othering by hiring Asian American actors for highly stereotyped roles as foreigners. The career of respected Japanese American actor Gedde Watanabe illustrates this tendency. In 1986, Watanabe had second billing in the Paramount comedy, *Gung Ho*. In the film, about the culture clash when a Japanese firm buys an American automobile factory, Watanabe and others were humorless and tyrannical technocrats, the straight men to the irrepressibly free-spirited American union laborers, who are supposed to be loveable despite their antagonism towards the company that bails out their dying industrial town. More embarrassingly, two years earlier in the John Hughes adolescent romance, *Sixteen Candles* (1984), Watanabe provided comic relief as "Long Duk Dong," a Chinese exchange student lodging with an American family. In addition to using race as the sign of the social outcast (in which the hunched posture and thick glasses of the Asian American super-student marks his place in high school's dreaded "out" crowd), the name of Watanabe's character was the character's main joke. Decades of stereotypes of Asian emasculation, which manifest in popular beliefs that "Asian men have small penises," were supposed to make the very idea of a "Long Duk Dong" hilariously funny. The film recaps the improbable humor of the character's sexuality in a scene in which the diminutive character slumps in bliss over the matronly bosom of a much taller white woman. The impact of this film is immeasurable. Ask any American teenager who came of age watching John Hughes movies; *everyone* remembers the name of Long Duk Dong.

Possible solutions to the problem of Hollywood depiction of Asian American masculinity have been discussed since Frank Chin's 1972 essay, "Confessions of the Chinatown Cowboy," in which he describes how "movies were teachers" that "[i]n no uncertain terms . . . taught Americans that we were . . . a race of sissies." For Chin, this "wrong movie" about Asian Americans needs to be corrected by the "right movie," a "good movie" that, for Chin at least, was not fulfilled by Hollywood but rather by "the Chinese movies I grew up with" – that is, Asian martial arts dramas which provided the same "ballsy individuality" as Hollywood westerns.[22] Significantly, however, Chin's solution to restoring masculinity to Asian Americans remains firmly grounded in mainstream film discourse, as his turn to genres of Chinese martial arts and his own self-reference (as a "Chinatown Cowboy") blend Asian ethnic heritage with Hollywood iconology. Similarly, in his essay for *The Big Aiiieeeee!*, the landmark anthology of Asian American literature, Chin rejects autobiography by specifically advocating a "fighting" consciousness modeled on martial arts or other indigenous traditions accessible in popular Asian cinema.[23] Therefore, significantly, this cinematic version of racial empowerment turns not to independent film but rather to an alternative that seeks the power of mainstream genres but with a racially familiar image.

To be sure, the chauvinistic rhetoric in Chin's cinematic ideal of "ballsy individuality" has problems. Most disturbing, as King-Kok Cheung has importantly pointed out, is the way in which Chin's alternative to the orientalist commodification he associates with Kingston and Tan runs the risk of being anti-woman, urging Asian Americans to empower race at the cost of gender.[24] This dichotomy exists, however, because of the strong association of gender with genre implicit in cinema, and it is under this generic concern that Chin's manifesto for aggressive masculinity is relevant. Asian Americans don't need another *Joy Luck*, but rather a Hollywood movie that features – for once – a powerful Asian American male. Such a hero would have to go beyond Bruce Lee, the most iconic Asian American film star to date, by insisting upon romantic qualities that Lee's films did not contain. In fact, although *Joy Luck* garnered most of the attention, arguably the more important movie of 1993 to consider Asian American issues was *Dragon: The Bruce Lee Story*, a biopic whose straightforward homage to the movie icon also included a number of critically progressive elements. These included emphasizing Lee's sexual appeal, beginning with his early years as a dance champion in Hong Kong, through this interracial marriage – and thereby also sympathetically depicting the injuries of prejudice and stereotype. The film is especially acute on the issues of cinematic representation itself, portraying the limited opportunities Lee found in Hollywood and also incorporating stereotype criticism in a remarkably sensitive scene in which he walks out of a screening of the beloved Hollywood movie, *Breakfast at Tiffany's*, because of that film's notorious caricature of a Japanese man.[25]

The reception of recent major Hollywood productions reveals a maturing sensitivity to matters of Asian American representation that *Dragon* inaugurated. In 1999, *The Phantom Menace*, the long-awaited follow-up to the *Star Wars* trilogy, appeared. Among the new characters created for this installment were Jar Jar Binks, a lanky, awkward, and rather dumb sidekick with dreadlocks and a large posterior, and who spoke a slurred Caribbean pidgin exactly like that of black slaves in old Hollywood movies, and the opportunistic Nemoidians, a hive-dwelling, hoarding tribe "known for their exceptional organizing abilities" as a visual dictionary marketed with the film explained.[26] In the film the Nemoidians speak in a lisp that blurs the /l/ and /r/ sounds in the same way that film actors employ a Chinese accent as an all-purpose Asian voice. As numerous film critics, fans, and journalists quickly recognized, both characters reprise cornerstone cinematic stereotypes. Jar Jar was described as a cross between Sambo, Stepin Fetchit, and Butterfly McQueen, and the Nemoidians were "stock Asian villains out of black-and-white B movies of the 1930s and 1940s, complete with . . . a space-age version of . . . Fu Manchu clothing." Indeed, the most recent referents for the unscrupulous, inscrutable Oriental businessman the Nemoidians evoked were the characters in *Gung Ho* and *Rising Sun*.[27] Two things are remarkable about this widespread critical distaste. First, the outcry over *The Phantom Menace* suggested growing cultural sensitivity in the mainstream population, in which Hollywood stereotypes of Asian Americans were no longer tolerated. This was true regardless of the appeal of the film, as there can hardly be a movie more ensured of enthusiasm than an episode in the Star Wars franchise. Second, the recognition of the stereotyping that simultaneously applied to the Nemoidians and Jar Jar Binks suggests a new capacity to see both the Asian American and the African American perspectives with the same multicultural empathy. Such an insight moves away from the longstanding tendency to perceive Asian ethnicity as foreign that persisted as late as six years earlier, in the year of *Rising Sun* and *The Joy Luck Club*.

What brought about such radical change? Arif Dirlik summarizes the role of globalization: "the emergence of Pacific Asian economies as key players in the global economy has had a transformative effect on the Asian American self-image, as well as on the perceptions of Asian Americans in the society at large."[28] In the early years of globalization the growing economic might of Asia was threatening, but as it accelerated both the increasing imbrication of multinational corporations and the implosion of the Asian economies in the later 1990s rendered these paranoid portraits of Asian business anachronistic. Hollywood's ascendency from a national industry to dominate most foreign markets is part of this change, in which the domestic outcry against *The Phantom Menace* foreshadows how globalization brought upon Hollywood a greater responsibility for fashioning non-offensive, easily exportable material. In other words, the "American" hegemony of global Hollywood actually created a global village whose multicultural landscape had the benefit of improving multicultural conditions back in the US. As Dirlik notes, "Asian America is no longer just a location in the United States, but is at the same time on a metaphorical rim" whose horizon expanded with the economic and cultural effects of globalization.[29] This redirection in Hollywood regarding Asian representation is consistent with contemporary shifts in the Asian American population, of which currently two-thirds were born in Asia, and who maintain strong trans-Pacific ties enabled by jet travel and telecommunications. Importantly, this history, a push-pull model of cultural change, influenced film production in Hollywood through the Asian nationals upon whom the industry now relies rather than the Asian Americans, who, as previously noted, constitute too small a market to effect change themselves.

Pearl Harbor, the big "event" movie of the summer of 2001, exemplifies the progressive dividends of these new commercial responsibilities. The subject matter of the film – that is, the Japanese air attack on American soil that took over two thousand American lives and provoked the internment of tens of thousands of American citizens of Japanese descent – is one of the most divisive moments of Asian American history, and certainly was the source of the most deleterious cinematic images of ethnic Asians. Given this history, activism to protest the film began with news of its development and consolidated until its release.[30] Significantly, though, those efforts were anticipated by Disney, the studio behind the film, which already had consulted with leaders of Japanese and Japanese American groups from the very beginning of development. The changes made in the script thus stemmed, importantly, not so much from Asian American activism as from internal recognition of the extranational conditions of globalization – that is, the lucrative Japanese market that can alone generate twenty-five to thirty per cent of the foreign box office on a Hollywood blockbuster. *Pearl Harbor* displays this newfound sensitivity by omitting the term, "dirty Jap," by portraying the Japanese public against provoking the US, and by generally shifting the emphasis away from the attack and towards the courage demonstrated by both forces.[31] In a crucial sequence in the film, for example, which depicts the Japanese preparations for the attack, a minute and a half of hagiographic slow-motion close-ups of handsome Asian men are accompanied by a barely accented voice-over, from a pilot to his father, that re-present the formerly vilified *kamikaze* as an elite warrior whose actions partake in a ritual of national honor and filial piety. These images and narration sharply counter the notion of a "ruthless" personality and "squat Mongoloid" features that once were thought to distinguish the Japanese, as described in a notorious *Life* magazine feature that appeared shortly after the Pearl Harbor bombing.[32]

However cynical and mercenary, then, the motivations underlying the millennial re-telling of Pearl Harbor nevertheless contribute to advances in the Hollywood representations of ethnic Asians. Indeed, the cultural change that *Pearl Harbor* suggests calls into question the relevancy of the "Asian American" category at all, as the narrative changes that recuperated the Pearl Harbor history for Asian Americans originated out of concerns for the film's reception among Asian nationals. A more accurate way to think of the current Asian American mediascape thus would be to acknowledge the newly positive influence that Asian nations have upon Asian Americans, in which the longstanding tendency of Hollywood to portray ethnic Asians as foreign now earns its sanguine reinvention as a business practice that improves representational conditions for Asian Americans precisely because of its obligation to lump all Asian ethnicities and nationalities into one mass. Such a global mediascape, moreover, also transforms Hollywood by assimilating foreign cinemas that previously were only present in America among Asian immigrants and first-generation Asian American viewers, like the Chinese martial arts movies that Frank Chin enjoys. In his influential study of diasporic cinema, Hamid Naficy calls this syncretic propensity "refusion," a blend of ethnic and mainstream elements that is "not a refusal of dominant traditions but an assimilation of that with more esoteric features."[33] Although independent cinema is usually the source of refusion, as Naficy notes, the momentum of globalization is sufficient to move alternative aspects into the mainstream. Significantly, when this occurs Asian Americans are constituted not so much as a minority group but rather as a prototype for globalization, whose postcolonial hybridity is evoked on film by a postmodern refusion of both Hollywood and non-Hollywood styles.

The Indian and Hong Kong film industries were key sources in this stylistic transformation of Hollywood. Both nations foster vibrant film industries whose product and audience offered Hollywood stylistic inspiration and an enthusiastic movie-going audience worth targeting. India, which leads the world in annual film production, is inextricable from the spectacularly excessive musical romances that are its favorite genre. The camp appeal of its musicals was the site of some coveted roles in 2001, when award-winning director Baz Luhrmann recycled American pop hits for his Bollywood homage, *Moulin Rouge!* The following year, the expanded scope of Asian America was further demonstrated when *Bend It Like Beckham*, a rousing comedy about a tomboy daughter of Sikh immigrants in England, became the highest-grossing film by a non-white director in British history.

Although the film, by Gurindher Chadha, is not American, Hollywood's stakes in pursuing the hybrid blend of east and west associated with Asian Americans were evident when American studios battled over the rights to Chadha's next film.

Hong Kong, which at its height had the world's highest rate of per capita film consumption, influenced Hollywood conventions of Asian Americans because of its generic focus on action films, the single most lucrative genre for Hollywood, in both domestic and global markets. Hong Kong movies are known for dynamic action that makes the languorous iconography of American action stars pale in comparison. Its specific attributes are kinetic speed, often heightened with aggressively fast editing techniques, but based primarily upon the acrobatics, stunts, gunplay, and other physical accomplishments that exhibit a specifically Asian martial arts heritage. The best known of the directors, John Woo, is known for the gun battles in which a favorite star, Chow Yun-fat, fights holding guns in both hands. As the latest incarnation of the "ballsy" Chinese movies that Frank Chin espoused, these films transformed the context in which the Asian male body was seen, particularly for the American studio executives and moviegoers who discovered them. In the later 1990s, Hong Kong-style action films emerged as a major studio trend. The blockbusters, *The Matrix* (1999) and *Charlie's Angels* (2000), both imported master Hong Kong action choreographers for their fight sequences, and as further evidence of the revolution in connotation that Asian cinema signified to Hollywood audiences, the fact of action choreography by a Hong Kong martial artist was often mentioned in movie trailers and theater taglines. Indeed, American enthusiasm for Hong Kong-style martial arts movies was so great that it even propelled the Chinese-language film, *Crouching Tiger, Hidden Dragon*, by Taiwanese American director Ang Lee, to blockbuster status, becoming the highest-grossing foreign-language film in US history. Interestingly, both *The Matrix* and *Charlie's Angels* seem to tangentially acknowledge these debts to Asian cinema, as the key role of Morpheus in *The Matrix* was initially offered to Chow Yun-fat, and *Charlie's Angels*, a remake of a classic American television series, exchanged one of the three white leads in the original show for the Asian American actress Lucy Liu.

In pop culture terms, globalization made the Asian American body cool. By "cool," I am deliberately differentiating these millennial trends from the "Asian chic" that were heralded in a 1993 *Time* magazine feature which celebrated the unprecedented visibility of Asians and Asian Americans in *Joy Luck, Dragon*, and Ang Lee's *The Wedding Banquet*, a Chinese-language comedy set in New York, which had the highest-percentage gross on cost of all American films that year.[34] Because "chic" implies a fashion, however, it implicitly trivializes its object's impact and intimates its exhaustion. As such, the epithet never indicated unqualified cultural inclusion. The term "cool," by contrast, connotes something prior, and therefore enduring, as well as an ineffability that resists trivialization and reduction to mere consumerism. Coolness is central to cinematic iconography and, as Hollywood movie idols show, it is also, originally, a distinctly American phenomenon. Coolness therefore is a far better index of assimilation than the orientalizing othering of chic, and it required a phenomenon on the scale of globalization to usher the conversion of chic into cool. It was coolness that underlay Bruce Lee's appeal in the US in the 1970s; it also describes part-Asian Keanu Reeves' memorable turn as the hero of *The Matrix*. As these male examples of cinematic cool suggest, the gendered connotations of coolness have been instrumental in rehabilitating Asian American masculinity. Because the operative adjective for the sexual appeal of female film stars is not cool but "hot," it must be a male star, rather than oriental pinup fantasy Lucy Liu, whose ability to project cool will be the most valuable component in the representational progress of Asian Americans.

The romantic comedy, *The Guru*, illustrates this transformed status of Asian American men in current Hollywood film. The 2002 film, from Universal Pictures – a studio whose name aptly echoes contemporary global trends – participates in the fashion for Bollywood-style cinema by featuring a South Asian male lead. As such, the film is historically significant as the first mainstream feature to depict an ethnic Asian male as a romantic interest for white women – to depict him, that is, as the lead in a comedy, unlike the ways in which Asian men had been rejected or punished in past Hollywood pictures. The achievements of this unprecedented casting are significant: in keeping with the general romantic invisibility of Asian men, South Asians had been erased from Hollywood romances as late as 1996, when the Oscar-winning film, *The English Patient*, drastically minimized the romance between a Sikh soldier and a white nurse that constitutes much of the novel upon which the movie is based.

The numerous revisions of Asian American cinematic representation that *The Guru* exerts begin with the start of the film. The film starts as a familiar immigrant narrative, with an opening sequence in Delhi, and soon shifts to New York, where the protagonist Ramu works in a restaurant and survives in a slum. Ramu's ambition, however, is to make it as an actor, and it is in this slight twist in genre – where immigrant story morphs into show-business fable – that *The Guru* begins its radical departure from previous Hollywood representations of Asian Americans. Cinematic visibility, *The Guru* smartly acknowledges, is the true test of inclusion into American culture. Romance intersects with this plot line as Ramu answers a casting call for an "ethnic male" and wins a film role opposite Sharonna (Heather Graham), the comely co-star with whom he'll soon fall in love. Because Sharonna is white, the romantic plotline metonymizes the issues of acceptance that *The Guru* portrays. The joke is that Ramu's role is in a porn shoot. Of course, such a plot device, where romance is overshadowed by graphic professional intimacy, is nothing new, but it is for the specific racial scenario that *The Guru* proposes. Previous Hollywood stereotypes about Asian masculinity would have rendered such a casting unthinkable (indeed, given the previous stereotypes about black men, "the ethnic male" the casting ad presumably called for probably intended an African American). That *The Guru* presupposes the desirability of an Asian man to the extent of dramatizing it on two levels only underscores its achievement. The movie posits Ramu as a romantic interest while the film-within-the-film insists upon his erotic appeal.

The Guru bolsters this progressive version of Asian American masculinity by both countering prohibitions against interracial romance as well as criticizing the reduction of Asian culture to orientalist consumption. The film achieves these ends by showing Ramu's sexual appeal to be widespread and acceptable, and by distinguishing this romantic enthusiasm from the fetishization of Asianness that the film gently satirizes in a subplot about Ramu's success as an Indian mystic. These developments begin at a party for dilettante spiritualist Lexi (Marisa Tomei), where Ramu charms everyone as a "sex guru" who dispenses mantras about emotional well-being by way of sexual fulfillment. While these scenes of Ramu's evident charm set up his appeal to Sharonna, they also satirize those Americans who buy into Asian chic, much as Vijay Prashad argues that Deepak Chopra profits from Western consumers.[35] To underscore the appeal of Asian American masculinity, Ramu and Lexi have sex the very first night that they meet, an audacious transgression of conventions of Asian emasculation which the film further naturalizes by having Lexi make the first overture. Similarly, the "morning after" scene shows a relaxed and glowing Lexi on the telephone already enthusing about Ramu's prowess, while her manicurist and acupuncturist are unsurprised when her lover emerges from the bedroom, in a classic film convention for post-coital relations, wrapped only in a towel.

It is important to emphasize that *The Guru*'s interracial romance does not replicate the problems of white male/Asian female relations previously described. This is because the default white perspective in Hollywood that privileges Asian women by erasing Asian men requires the idealized depiction of white female/Asian male miscegenation in order to advocate the idea of Asian masculinity to Asians as well as to the non-Asian mainstream. In this situation, white women viewing the film perceive the scenario as unproblematic, and Asian American women, who are accustomed to viewing Hollywood films from the same default white perspective, ironically are encouraged to curtail those white man/Asian woman romances precisely because they see their own race appreciated on these terms. To emphasize the appeal of ethnic difference, *The Guru* does not compromise upon its star's Asianness. Jimi Mistry, who plays Ramu, looks South Asian, rather than displaying the whitewashed features usually required of ethnic actors to break into mass entertainment (as in the brothers, Russell and Michael Wong, who are mixed). Mistry is very thin, lacking the chiseled hardbody usually required for a Hollywood leading man, and his smaller frame is further contrasted to that of the burly actor (Dash Mihok, *The Perfect Storm*, *The Thin Red Line*) who is cast as Sharonna's quintessentially American boyfriend. Yet Ramu's frail physique is never elided; indeed, the porn plot of the film usefully requires it to be frequently displayed. *The Guru* pursues this point even to granting Mistry a "butt shot," a recent screen requisite for many leading men. Similarly, it is Ramu's competitor whose masculinity is problematized by a homosexual denouement.

Porn functions in *The Guru* as a facetious metaphor for the eroticization of ethnic bodies that the film itself performs. If Ramu's porn gig is awarded because of the director's enthusiasm for his "interesting look – kind of [an] oriental, cabana boy thing," the real film, *The Guru*, makes numerous references to other Hollywood films to specifically present Ramu as the global heir of prior Hollywood icons. The casting of Heather Graham, for example, plays upon her previous role as a porn star in *Boogie Nights* (1997), in order to lightheartedly suggest Ramu's interchangeability with her previous co-star, former Calvin Klein model, Mark Wahlberg. Other intertextual references include John Travolta in *Grease*, Tom Cruise's career-launching, underwear-clad lip-sync scene from *Risky Business*, and the climactic, church-crashing finale of *The Graduate* – a particularly effective reference because of that film's history in making a megastar out of another physically diminutive actor. And, if I may be excused for the pun, the film's biggest achievement in revising Asian American male stereotypes occurs by way of its use of the porn setting to foreground Ramu's sexual organ, which is scrutinized during Ramu's audition. That Ramu gets the part would suggest that it isn't an issue. The scene thus overturns the "small dick" stereotype that has long plagued Asian men, making *The Guru* the retort, long overdue, to Long Duk Dong. If there is any film character that Ramu references, it is "Dirk Diggler," Mark Wahlberg's role in *Boogie Nights* – another character whose name was a phallic joke, but one renowned for the length, rather than the inadequacy, of his penis.

Of course, it would go too far to praise *The Guru* as the *Guess Who's Coming to Dinner?* for Asian Americans. The film, "from the makers of *Notting Hill* and *Bridget Jones' Diary*," as the print ads announced it, is a studio genre piece whose superficial engagements with Bollywood stylistics barely mask the predictable dialogue, tired scenario, and superficial characters that are hardly distinguishable from a conventional romantic comedy. That's the point: by progressively featuring an ethnic gender group usually visible only in independent film, the mainstream movie is already revolutionary. It is not surprising that reviews of the film in the general press were the first to recognize *The Guru*'s historical achievements. Because general interest reviewers were most aware of the mainstream film's variations on Hollywood and Bollywood formulas, their discussions recognized the film's risk in an opening without any recognizable stars and praised Mistry's performance amidst the genre's stock roles as the "least stereotyped" of the film's characters.[36]

MAINSTREAM CINEMA AND ASIAN AMERICAN ACTIVISM

It is useful at this point to review the changes towards a progressive depiction of Asian Americans in mainstream cinema that preceded *Better Luck Tomorrow*. Because Asian American studies, like most ethnic scholarship, began with political activism, the discipline privileges the political commitments of independent cinema over Hollywood's historical promulgation of Asian American stereotypes. But such an exclusive focus on independent cinema overlooks the new possibilities that globalization brought to the mainstream, as Sandra Liu has recently argued. Citing how industrial and economic changes of the 1980s and 1990s eroded the divisions between "good" independent cinema and "bad" mainstream film, Liu contends that the market-oriented nature of the US film industry suggests that "film activism cannot" – and should not – "be the sole responsibility of filmmakers."[37] This idea that Hollywood cinema can change based on audience and executive pressures from above and below is echoed by Rey Chow, whose thoughtful discussion of *The Joy Luck Club* underscores the importance of generic revolution. Reiterating how the "*political* imperative of vindicating the neglected fate/history of an entire culture and people" that characterizes the ethnic film only entrenches the ethnic, Chow's criticism of the burden of representation reveals how cultural inclusion will be achieved only when Asian Americans are portrayed as the site of universal human narratives rather than specifically ethnic issues.[38]

Significantly, Wayne Wang, the director of *Joy Luck*, outlined these issues in terms that exactly anticipate the rhetoric of Ebert's later defense of *Better Luck Tomorrow*. Complaining that studios considering him for a directing job "always would ask me what made me think I could direct a movie about [non-Asian American material, such as] teenagers in Minnesota," Wang recounts, "I'd say to them, 'Would you ask Ridley Scott or Tony Scott that same question?'" Like Ebert's comment, Wang's comment reveals the racial prejudice that presumes an ethnic filmmaker cannot produce films for the general audience. Moreover, by contrasting himself with directors Ridley Scott and Tony Scott – who are British – Wang's comment also reveals the misconceptions in that logic. The false emphasis on race over culture, Wang points out, ignores the fact that as a naturalized American citizen who arrived in the US in 1967, he is more "American" than the other directors, as he has "been here much longer than they have."[39] Again, the history of African American representation in Hollywood provides a useful model for the freedom from the burden of representation that confronts Asian Americans in Hollywood. The gradual diffusion of independent sensitivity in Hollywood that Asian Americans require occurred for African Americans in two phases: Hollywood developed the highly stereotyped genre of blaxploitation in an effort to capitalize on the African American audience; these images, however, were criticized, and ultimately were further corrected by a de-romanticizing strain of gritty ghetto realism as well as by the emergence of bourgeois genre pictures that put black actors in roles usually reserved for whites. For Asian Americans, globalization induced an expansion in Hollywood's ethnic Asian audience comparable to the historical significance of African American audiences within the domestic market – hence films after that time, like *The Guru*, are the Asian American equivalent of *Waiting to Exhale*, progressively depicting ethnic characters in traditional mainstream genres.

Similarly, *Better Luck Tomorrow* can be considered the Asian American *Boyz in the Hood* or *Menace II Society*, countering stereotype by specifically portraying them in the genre of violent crime. The particular intelligence of *Better Luck Tomorrow* in rewriting Asian American stereotypes was its use of the more recent associations with Asian bodies after the Hong Kong action pictures that helped undo earlier connotations – an inspired intervention that would reposition Hollywood as the progressive frontier of Asian American studies and activism.

From its inception, *Better Luck Tomorrow* was conceived to combat genre segregation and the other strictures limiting Asian American representation in Hollywood. Justin Lin, the director and co-screenwriter, is a Chinese American born in Taiwan but raised in the US. Only thirty years old when he completed *Better Luck Tomorrow*, Lin had been a teenager at the time of *Sixteen Candles* and a college student during the open casting calls for *The Joy Luck Club*, and hence came of age during the era of change in media representation of Asian Americans. Yet even during film school at UCLA, Lin felt confined by the genre ghetto and the burden of representation that applies to most minority filmmakers. "When I was a film student," he has recounted, "I could only make personal movies. When you're Asian American, everyone would say, how can you ever make a Hollywood film?"[40] Clearly, the implication in such comments was the familiar industrial conception that racial minority status necessarily precludes the capacity for universal storytelling that Hollywood requires. In rejection of this predicament, and in an effort to create work for fellow Asian American talents without repeating such tired themes, Lin began a fictionalized account of a high school murder that had taken place in Southern California in 1993, not far from where Lin grew up. This history, which the contemporary press dubbed the "Honor Roll Killing," had involved both white and Asian American honor students who had murdered their classmate, Stuart Tay. In their script Lin and co-author Ernesto Foronda emphasized the apparent paradox in the press rubric by depicting how the pressure-cooker environment of academically driven students can easily slide into fraud, drugs, and other criminal acts. In his casting, however, Lin chose only Asian American actors. The film thus resembled *The Joy Luck Club* in that it featured usually underemployed actors. Unlike the earlier film, though, *Better Luck Tomorrow* exhibits the changed cinematic status of Asian Americans after globalization. While the audition tape of Jason Tobin, one of the leads, consisted entirely of walk-ons as food delivery boys, one of the other leads, Sung Kang, had been one of the handsome faces recently depicted in *Pearl Harbor*.

Lin's revisions of Hollywood conventions regarding Asian American representation were multiple. First, by rewriting the circumstances of the actual history upon which the movie was based, so that the film's ensemble cast was entirely Asian American, Lin offered unprecedented opportunity for minority actors to assume a role that for historical accuracy, at least, should have been partially allocated towards white performers. Lin maintained this commitment even as he sought sponsors, choosing to continue shopping the script around rather than change some of the leads to Latin or African American characters, as some producers suggested. (Interestingly, it was former rap star, MC Hammer, who Lin reports is "very sympathetic to the issues of minority artists," who provided the funds to set the film into production. Such recognition of Lin's predicament by an African American artist testifies to the new recognition of Asian Americans as a companion American minority). Second, by offering an ensemble cast of men rather than women, *Better Luck Tomorrow* made visible the gender that bears the brunt of Hollywood erasure of Asians. This change in gender was motivated by genre, which wrought additional benefits. Thus, third, by yoking a crime story to its ethnic cast Lin dealt death blows to both the old Asian American stereotype of the immigrant model minority as well as the more recent association with violent action pictures. These Asian Americans, the film shows, are both honor students and a "Chinese mafia," as they are described at one point in the film. The sum of the film's various revisions of Asian American representation is a film with the same agenda of *The Joy Luck Club* but with an entirely different aesthetic strategy. As many of the contemporary reviewers of the film were quick to note, "'Better Luck' is the antithesis of 'Joy Luck.'"[41]

The title of *Better Luck Tomorrow* deftly summarizes Lin's simultaneous revisions of old and new Asian American stereotypes. The name echoes both *The Joy Luck Club* and *A Better Tomorrow* (1986), a John Woo film starring Chow Yun-fat that had been one of the most famous of the Hong Kong movies that impacted Hollywood in the 1990s. By merging both titles into his own Lin acknowledges the blending of both heritages while also insisting, by that corruption, upon its status as a new thing altogether. According to Lin, the title began as his film school thesis project, when the director felt acutely marginalized because of his ethnicity. That original project "was a spoof on a Hong Kong action film, but with the sensibility of *Joy Luck*," devised because those seemed the two possibilities that Hollywood allots Asian talent. His explanation of why the title appealed to him aptly positions his film as a corrective to both the older and more recent genres: "it [the title] had to say what we had to explore, as Asian Americans."[42]

The identity "between" the various Asian American stereotypes that Lin describes is, paradoxically, the idea that the visible ethnicity of these characters is not narratively significant at all. This is the single most significant of the film's several historical achievements. Importantly, nowhere in the film's dialogue does any character make reference to any ethnic or cultural pressure as motivation for their actions. The female love interest, for example, who is Asian and is academically driven, is the adopted child of a white family, thereby complicating any possible cultural stereotypes (to underscore this point, Lin has her brush aside doubts by insisting that her adopted parents "*are* my real family"). Similarly, secondary characters – such as the other members of the school academic quiz bowl team, on which the main characters serve – are of a variety of different races. This is not to say that race and stereotype don't come up: racial slurs surface, a character perceives his token status on the school athletic team, and a prostitute hired by the boys asks "what are you guys, a math club?" But race, as Roger Ebert later explained in his published review, works in the film "[l]ike African American films that take race for granted and get on with the characters and the story." This film is, as Ebert furthermore noted, about a "generation [that] no longer obsesses with the nation before the hyphen."[43]

This idea that *Better Luck Tomorrow* should be accepted as a story in which race is incidental to the plot is affirmed through the film's treatment of generational identity, that particular trope of Asian American immigrant narratives that has been so hampering for acculturation. In *Better Luck Tomorrow*, significantly, generational conflict is absent, lost in a vacuum that is a biting indictment of the need for social guidance in general. Almost no adults are shown in the film, and although at least one of the characters, Daric Loo (Roger Fan), is said to "live alone in a house while his parents send him money from Vancouver," like so many American children of affluent Asian parents who live abroad, the implication is that of youth gone amok because of the absence of adult guidance. As many critics noted, the film was not so much an ethnic film as the latest in a long line of Hollywood films about the dissipation of American youth, including *The Asphalt Jungle*, *The Graduate*, *Risky Business*, *Fast Times at Ridgemont High*, and *Dazed and Confused*.

The melding of independent and Hollywood media in *Better Luck Tomorrow* is another way to think of the film's revisions that is definitive of the film's historical status. Lin made the film on digital video, completing it on a $250,000 budget; it was only the director's second feature-length film. But slickly shot and heavily overlaid with a pop/rock soundtrack, *Better*

Luck Tomorrow was readily positioned for pickup by a Hollywood distributor. The sharp style and storytelling got the film into the important Sundance Film Festival, an annual exhibition of independent films which has increasingly become the province of Hollywood studios trolling for cheap sleeper hits. At Sundance in 2002, response to the film was so positive and so swift that Lin has said that he and his fellow producers were mobbed by willing buyers within thirty minutes of the opening credits. The distributor that Lin eventually selected to market the film epitomizes the mainstream: MTV Films, an offshoot of the powerful music video network and partner of Paramount, whose primary audience of eighteen to thirty-four-year-old males is the largest demographic for Hollywood as well. The enthusiasm of MTV Films for *Better Luck Tomorrow* demonstrates the acceptance the film enjoyed as an exemplar of mainstream, rather than specifically Asian American, subjects. As one MTV representative recounted their reasons for acquiring the film, "We thought our audience," which is "a very diverse group," "would be very interested in this film."[44]

Better Luck Tomorrow's revolutionary effect on the status of cinema in Asian American studies consolidated as the film became the center of debate over whether it was an independent or mainstream picture. This controversy, which resulted in massive activism, demonstrates the important position Hollywood now occupies in returning Asian American scholarship to the political activism with which the discipline began. As the movie's distributor, MTV Films slated *Better Luck Tomorrow* for platform release, meaning that it would open first in only a few select cities, and then proceed throughout the nation only in stages, with each new opening dependent upon its evaluated success in preceding markets. This process differs from the simultaneous nationwide opening that is the industry practice for Hollywood films, and is usually applied to independent, foreign, and art films – that is, those films deemed relevant to only limited audiences. In an effort to promote the film, Lin circulated by internet an "open letter to Asian Americans," urging them to see the movie, and the film's actors traveled the country publicizing the necessity of box office success. As more and more Asian Americans learned of the issue, these campaigns expanded into additional print, web, and live efforts that began without any association with the film itself. *Better Luck Tomorrow*, Asian Americans were told, was poised to be "their *She's Gotta Have It*," referring to the breakthrough film by Spike Lee that made possible new trends in movies for and by African Americans. Were *Better Luck Tomorrow* to fail, it would be perceived within Hollywood as definitive proof of the limits of Asian American representation, and thus would be a disaster for the Asian American community. These political efforts to promote the film did not go unheeded: in its opening weekend in Los Angeles and New York, the film turned a profit by grossing over a million dollars. Equally significantly, the racial makeup of the audience throughout its run was almost evenly divided between Asian and non-Asian viewers, a fact that reassured Paramount, which recorded the data in an obvious attempt to gauge the film's mainstream appeal, that a film featuring an all-Asian cast was capable of crossover appeal. *Better Luck Tomorrow* would go on to build its profit throughout its platform release, and by year-end the industry consensus was that the film was an undoubted success, with box office earnings representing sixteen times its cost and the potential to earn a great deal more by future DVD sales.

These grassroots efforts surrounding *Better Luck Tomorrow* to convert platform to national release reveal a political understanding of the important status of mainstream film in Asian American studies. By recognizing the political capital in commercial cinema, the activism surrounding *Better Luck Tomorrow* shows the Asian American community recognizing mainstream cinema as a primary objective of attaining cultural equality. Such a new understanding of Hollywood cinema in Asian American media was indebted to the new interdependency of the world economy, a process of globalization that advanced Asian American masculinity in *The Guru* and assimilated the Hong Kong action traditions. As the global village increasingly dictates Hollywood productions, Hollywood can only grow more supportive of Asian American representation. Indeed, as the radical revisions in *Better Luck Tomorrow* demonstrate, Asian Americans may just be the future of Hollywood cinema, as the optimistic *Joy Luck-* and John Woo-evoking title of the film implies. This is certainly the belief of Deepak Chopra and the critically acclaimed film director, Shekhar Kapur (*Elizabeth*), who recently formed a conglomerate to manage the Asian stars and creative talent that they predict will increasingly dominate the global entertainment markets previously monopolized by Hollywood. The significance of such a change will be remarkable, both in numbers and symbolic meaning. As globalization consolidates the whole world to the space of the simultaneous opening that Hollywood currently gives mainstream films in the US, says Kapur, "It is likely that by the end of this decade, a film like *Spider-Man 5* will open to a billion-dollar first weekend." Asia, which constitutes more than half the world's population, will then determine box office success – as Kapur forecasts, "Expect $700 million of that to be generated from Asia." More importantly, the centrality of Asia in global

Hollywood's revenue must precipitate changes in mainstream content. These will not register in gender and genre, but rather in the race of the new Hollywood hero of the post-global era. Thus Kapur heralds, "Expect, then, that when Spider-Man takes his mask off, he may be Chinese or Indian."[45]

NOTES

I am grateful for the comments of Hosam Aboul-Ela, Margot Backus, Maria Gonzalez, David Mazella, and Jane Park.

1. The exchange between Ebert, Lin, and the Sundance audience member appears in most press coverage of the film. E.g., Mac Daniel, "Deal Drugs. Commit Murder. Cram for Finals."
2. Jae-Ha Kim, "Critical Approval Means Lin's 'Luck' is Here to Stay."
3. Some of these approaches are collected in Kandice Chuh and Karen Shimikawa, *Orientations*.
4. Eugene Franklin Wong, *On Visual Media Racism*; Russell Leong, ed., *Moving the Image*.
5. Ed Moy, "Reality Shift?: America's Changing Perception of the Asian American Experience," 185.
6. Rebecca Louie, "Making Their Own 'Luck.'"
7. Elvis Mitchell, "Teenagers Determined to Damage Their Resumes."
8. Leong, *Moving the Image*, 1991; Marina Heung, "Representing Ourselves: Films and Videos by Asian American/Canadian Women"; Jun Xing, *Asian America Through the Lens*; and Peter Feng, *Identities in Motion*.
9. Renee Tajima, "Lotus Blossoms Don't Bleed: Images of Asian Women," 309.
10. David Eng, *Racial Castration*.
11. bell hooks, *Black Looks*, 118.
12. Wong's terms are "role segregation," "role freedom," and "role stratification." They name, respectively, the restriction of ethnic actors to ethnic roles only, the privilege enjoyed by white actors to cannibalize ethnic roles by appearing in costumed and cosmetized "race face," and the likelihood that the more prominent an ethnic role, the more likely that it will be cast with a white actor. Wong, *On Visual Media Racism*, 12–13.
13. Werner Sollors, *Beyond Ethnicity*.
14. Lisa Lowe, "Heterogeneity, Hybridity, Multiplicity: Marking Asian American Differences," 26.
15. Chin, "Come All Ye Asian American Writers of the Real and the Fake," in Jefferey Paul Chan et al eds., *The Big Aiiieeeee!*, 8–11.
16. In 1993, Stone also directed *Heaven & Earth* and served as executive producer on *From Hollywood to Hanoi*; both films deal with Vietnamese and Vietnamese American subjects.

17. Mike Clark, "'With Joy Luck,' 'Disney Grows Up.'"

18. Gina Marchetti, *Romance and the "Yellow Peril."*

19. Jessica Hagedorn, "Asian Women in Film: No Joy, No Luck," 76.

20. Yoshio Kichi, "Final Mix: Unscheduled," 164.

21. Lee, *Orientals: Asian Americans in Popular Culture*, and Wong, *On Visual Media Racism.*

22. Frank Chin, "Confessions of the Chinatown Cowboy," 66, 62, 66, 65, 66.

23. Chin, "Come All Ye Asian American Writers," 35.

24. King-Kok Cheung, "The Woman Warrior versus the Chinaman Pacific: Must a Chinese American Critic Choose between Feminism and Heroism?".

25. For an insightful discussion of this scene, see Meaghan Morris, "Learning from Bruce Lee: Pedagogy and Political Correctness in Martial Arts Cinema."

26. David West Reynolds, *The Visual Dictionary (Star Wars, Episode I: The Phantom Menace)*, 16.

27. Joe Morgenstern, "Our Inner Child Meets Young Darth"; Ron Givens, "Jar Wars: Fame and Blame"; John Leo, "Fu Manchu on Naboo".

28. Arif Dirlik, "Asians on the Rim: Transnational Capital and Local Community in the Making of Contemporary Asian America," 3.

29. Ibid. 13.

30. E.g., Gisele Durham, "Some Asian-Americans Eye 'Pearl Harbor' Opening with Unease," *Associated Press Dispatch*, 25 May 2001; Evelyn Nieves, "Some Upset by Twist on Pearl Harbor," *New York Times*, 28 May 2001.

31. E.g., Peter Hadfield, "Pearl Harbour Becomes a Love Story for Japanese," *London Telegraph*, 22 April 2001; Ilene R. Prusher, "On the Other Side, 'Pearl Harbor' is a Hard Sell," *Christian Science Monitor*, 13 July 2001.

32. "How to Tell Japs from the Chinese," 81.

33. Hamid Naficy, *An Accented Cinema*, 6.

34. Richard Corliss, "Pacific Overtures."

35. Vijay Prashad, *The Karma of Brown Folk.*

36. Robert K. Elder, "Bollywood Ending"; Stephen Holden, "Using Ditsy Maxims for Erotic Self-Help."

37. Sandra Liu, "Negotiating the Meaning of Access: Wayne Wang's Contingent Film Practice."

38. Rey Chow, "Women in the Holocene: Ethnicity, Fantasy, and the Film *The Joy Luck Club*," 204–21.

39. Corliss, "Pacific Overtures," 70.

40. Interview with Justin Lin, 8 September 2003.

41. Daniel Yi, "They're the Bad Seeds?"

42. Interview with Justin Lin, 8 September 2003.

43. Roger Ebert, "'Better Luck' an Insightful Look at Modern Youth."

44. Jason Song, "Building for 'Tomorrow.'"

45. Gail Schiller, *Hollywood Reporter*, 19 March 2004.

WORKS CITED

Cheung, King-Kok. "The Woman Warrior versus the Chinaman Pacific: Must a Chinese American Critic Choose Between Feminism and Heroism?" *Conflicts in Feminism*. Eds. Marianne Hirsch and Evelyn Fox Keller. New York: Routledge, 1990.

Chin, Frank. "Come All Ye Asian American Writers of the Real and the Fake." *The Big Aiiieeeee!*. Eds. Jeffery Paul Chan et al. New York: Penguin, 1990. 1–92.

Chin, Frank. "Confessions of the Chinatown Cowboy." *Bulletin of Concerned Asian Scholars* 4.3 (1972): 58–70.

Chow, Rey. "Women in the Holocene: Ethnicity, Fantasy, and the Film 'The Joy Luck Club.'" *Feminism and the Pedagogies of Everyday Life*. Ed. Carmen Luke. Albany: State University of New York Press, 1996. 204–21.

Chuh, Kandice and Karen Shimikawa, eds. *Orientations*. Durham: Duke University Press, 2001.

Clark, Mike. "'With Joy Luck,' 'Disney Grows Up.'" *USA Today*, 8 Sept. 1993.

Corliss, Richard. "Pacific Overtures." *Time*, 13 Sept. 1993.

Daniel, Mac. "Deal Drugs. Commit Murder. Cram for Finals." *Boston Globe*, 13 Apr. 2003.

Dirlik, Arif. "Asians on the Rim: Transnational Capital and Local Community in the Making of Contemporary Asian America." *Amerasia Journal* 22.3 (1996): 1–24.

Ebert, Roger. "'Better Luck' an Insightful Look at Modern Youth." *Chicago Sun-Times*, 11 Apr. 2003.

Elder, Robert K. "Bollywood Ending." *Chicago Tribune*, 31 Jan. 2003.

Eng, David. *Racial Castration*. Durham: Duke University Press, 2001.

Feng, Peter. *Identities in Motion*. Durham: Duke University Press, 2002.

Givens, Ron. "Jar Wars: Fame and Blame." *New York Daily News*, 3 June 1999.

Hagedorn, Jessica. "Asian Women in Film: No Joy, No Luck." *Ms.*, Jan./Feb. 1994: 74–79.

Heung, Marina. "Representing Ourselves: Films and Videos by Asian American/Canadian Women." *Feminism, Multiculturalism, and the Media: Global Diversities*. Ed. Angharad N. Valdivia. Thousand Oaks, CA: Sage Publications, 1995.

Holden, Stephen. "Using Ditsy Maxims for Erotic Self-Help." *New York Times*, 31 Jan. 2003.

hooks, bell. *Black Looks*. Boston: South End, 1992.

"How to Tell Japs from the Chinese." *Life* 11.25 (22 Dec. 1941): 81–82.

Kichi, Yoshio. "Final Mix: Unscheduled." *Moving the Image*. Ed. Russell Leong. Los Angeles: UCLA Asian American Studies Center, 1991.

Kim, Jae-Ha. "Critical Approval Means Lin's 'Luck' is Here to Stay." *Chicago Sun-Times*, 10 Apr. 2003.

Lee, Robert G. *Orientals: Asian Americans in Popular Culture*. Philadelphia: Temple University Press, 1999.

Leo, John. "Fu Manchu on Naboo." *US News & World Report*, 12 July 1999.

Leong, Russell, ed. *Moving the Image*. Los Angeles: UCLA Asian American Studies Center, 1991.

Liu, Sandra. "Negotiating the Meaning of Access: Wayne Wang's Contingent Film

Practice." *Countervisions*. Eds. Darrell Y. Hamamoto and Sandra Liu. Philadelphia: Temple University Press, 2000.

Louie, Rebecca. "Making Their Own 'Luck.'" *New York Daily News*, 8 Apr. 2003.

Lowe, Lisa. "Heterogeneity, Hybridity, Multiplicity: Marking Asian American Differences." *Diaspora* 1 (1991): 24–44.

Marchetti, Gina. *Romance and the "Yellow Peril."* Berkeley: University of California Press, 1993.

Mitchell, Elvis. "Teenagers Determined to Damage Their Resumes." *New York Times*, 11 April 2003.

Morgenstern, Joe. "Our Inner Child Meets Young Darth." *Wall Street Journal*, 19 May 1999.

Morris, Meaghan. "Learning from Bruce Lee: Pedagogy and Political Correctness in Martial Arts Cinema." *Keyframes*. Eds. Matthew Tinkcom and Amy Villarejo. London: Routledge, 2001. 171–86.

Moy, Ed. "Reality Shift?: America's Changing Perception of the Asian American Experience." *The New Face of Asian Pacific America*. Ed. Eric Lai and Dennis Arguelles. San Francisco: Asian Week and UCLA Asian American Studies Center, 2003.

Naficy, Hamid. *An Accented Cinema*. Princeton: Princeton University Press, 2001.

Prashad, Vijay. *The Karma of Brown Folk*. Minneapolis: University of Minnesota Press, 2000.

Reynolds, David West. *The Visual Dictionary (Star Wars, Episode 1: the Phantom Menace)*. New York: DK Publishing, 1999.

Sollors, Werner. *Beyond Ethnicity*. New York: Oxford University Press, 1986.

Song, Jason. "Building for 'Tomorrow.'" *Baltimore Sun*, 19 April 2003.

Tajima, Renee. "Lotus Blossoms Don't Bleed: Images of Asian Women." *Making Waves: An Anthology of Writings By and About Asian American Women*. Ed. Asian Women United of California. Boston: Beacon Press, 2001.

Wong, Eugene Franklin. *On Visual Media Racism*. New York: Arno Press, 1978.

Xing, Jun. *Asian America Through the Lens*. Walnut Creek, CA: AltaMira Press, 1998.

Yi, Daniel. "They're the Bad Seeds?" *Los Angeles Times*, 6 Apr. 2003.

CHAPTER 5

Gender Negotiations and the Asian American Literary Imagination

Wenxin Li

One of the most intriguing phenomena in Asian American literature has undoubtedly been the gender gap – a fission roughly along gender lines in Asian American thinking and articulation about ethnic identity. Since the early 1970s when Asian America began in earnest to define itself, two distinct impulses, which Elaine Kim defines as feminist and nationalist ("Such" 75), have been competing for expression and recognition. Otherwise known as the Asian American "gender war," this debate erupted upon the publication of Maxine Hong Kingston's fictionalized memoir *The Woman Warrior* in 1976.[1] While mainstream reviews were overwhelmingly positive, many Asian American writers and critics, in part reacting to its ready acceptance by white society, criticized the book for misrepresenting Chinese culture and tradition. The ensuing debate between the nationalist and feminist camps has dominated much of Asian American critical discourse ever since, resulting in heated exchanges on a number of issues concerning the roles of gender, race, and culture in the formation of an Asian American identity, with gender being the defining element.

While I value this debate for invigorating Asian American critical discourse and sharpening our critical perception, I also marvel at its tenacity and regret its personal nature because the prolonged warring atmosphere has divided the Asian American community. Insightful analyses of the gender strife by many Asian American scholars – including Elaine Kim, King-Kok Cheung, Sau-ling Wong, Jinqi Ling, and David Leiwei Li – have significantly contributed to our understanding of the key issues involved. By engaging their critiques, I hope to move beyond the Asian American gender divide toward the formulation of a more coherent Asian American identity. The purpose of this chapter is not to decide which side of the debate is right and which is wrong; rather, I am interested in reviewing both positions not from the perspective of gender opposition, but from the perspective of gender negotiation and reconciliation to maximize our common ground and minimize our differences. The polemic rhetoric of both sides has obscured the fact that we actually have more in common and that our differences are not as irreconcilable as we may think. It is high time we moved beyond the dogmatism of binary opposition and the narrowness of polemic politics to reconceptualize our vision and renegotiate a new twenty-first century Asian American subjectivity.

Without a doubt, a fundamental cause of the split in Asian American critical discourse is the racist exclusionary laws in the history of the US, which created a huge gender imbalance in the early Chinese immigrant population. This material basis determined to a large extent how Asian America was to perceive and express itself during much of its history. According to historian Ronald Takaki, the Chinese male to female gender ratio in the nineteenth century was a whopping twenty to one, and it had gradually improved to four to one in the early 1920s (235). Then the 1924 Immigration Act specifically barred the entry of Chinese female immigrants, and, combined with the anti-miscegenation laws already in existence, essentially rendered Chinese America into desolate "bachelor societies" on the brink of extinction. Until the 1940s, when Congress began repealing the 1882 Chinese Exclusion Act, most of the writings by Asian Americans had been written by male authors primarily reflecting the male experience. Prominent examples include Lin Yutang's *My Country and My People* (1935), Younghill Kang's *East Goes West* (1937), and Carlos Bulosan's *America Is in the Heart* (1946). The phenomenon of male-centered Asian American discourse remained true for the next three decades, though with the notable exceptions of Jade Snow Wong's *Fifth Chinese Daughter* (1945) and Monica Sone's *Nisei Daughter* (1953), until the publication of Kingston's *The Woman Warrior* in 1976.[2]

However, this historical perspective should not prevent us from realizing that there were more immediate causes as well for the gender divide in Asian American literary discourse. Broadly speaking, both the nationalist and feminist impulses were the products of the Civil Rights movement, but they were more closely aligned with the Black Aesthetic movement and Western feminism respectively. Benefiting from the generally more favorable opinions of Asians in the post-war era, Asian American nationalism no longer had to confront the stereotype of Fu Manchu as unfathomable

Chinese evil. The new stereotype was the so-called "model minority" – the Charlie Chan type of meek and asexual subjects. On the other hand, Asian American feminists were focused on defining a female identity through the portrayal of their hitherto largely unacknowledged experience. It is against this backdrop that I conduct my analysis of the Asian American gender controversy.[3]

I. SEPARATE SPHERES AND GENDER BLINDNESS

Years before the publication of *The Woman Warrior*, Frank Chin and his associates at the Combined Asian American Resources Project (CARP) had been engaged in a war against the dominant culture's "racist love," a term coined by Chin and Jeffery Paul Chan in a 1972 essay so titled. Reacting against the rhetoric of "the model minority" perpetuated by white society, Chin and Chan sought to rectify the stereotype of Asian Americans as docile and uncomplaining subjects, which in their definition was equated with emasculation. As was pointed out earlier, the historical grounding for this way of thinking is the legislative racism of the nineteenth century that deprived Asian American laborers of their women and forced them to work in occupations traditionally regarded as feminine, such as gardening and cooking. To ethnic nationalists like Chin, the most effective way to win true respect from the white patriarchal society was through the assertion of manhood, the characteristics of which they defined as "aggressiveness, creativity, individuality, just being taken seriously" ("Racist" 68).[4]

Due to this historical reason, *Aiiieeeee!* (1974), one of the first Asian American attempts at self-definition, was preoccupied with restoring Asian American manhood and showed a marked lack of gender awareness.[5] While many generally credit it with putting Asian American literature on the map, some regret that the anthology did not highlight Asian American feminist concerns. Four out of the fourteen authors in the anthology are women, but their presence and point of view are hardly discernable from the preface (vii–viii). The problem here is of course not the male perspective per se, but the lack of recognition that it is so. Phrases such as "Asian America" and "our whole voice" indicate that the all-male editors presumed to speak for the entire Asian American community even though the tenor of their preface was decidedly male oriented.

Conversely, Asian American feminists also had their share of gender blindness in articulating a female identity. Take this often-quoted passage from *The Woman Warrior*, a seminal work largely responsible for the dominant culture's acceptance of Asian American literature as a worthy subject of academic and intellectual study: "Chinese-Americans, when you try to understand what things in you are Chinese, how do you separate what is peculiar to childhood, to poverty, insanities, one family, your mother who marked your growing with stories, from what is Chinese? What is Chinese tradition and what is the movies?" (5–6). Kingston's narrator captures her confusion of growing up in Stockton, California's Chinatown in the immediate postwar years, and her experience resonates with those of many Asian Americans in their search for a cultural identity. What the narrator asks about – how one's cultural tradition and social class, in conjunction with the specifics of family upbringing, determine racial identity – constitutes key elements in the vexing process of ethnic identity formation. However, what the narrator does not ask – how one's gender partakes of and intersects with other factors such as race and culture in the process – proves to be more elusive, as evidenced by the momentary lapse of gender consciousness from her racial imaginary. Of course, this observation does not mean to suggest that *The Woman Warrior* lacks gender awareness; Kingston's literary debut is, by all accounts, the most influential Asian American feminist manifesto, or as Amy Ling puts it, "the supreme Chinese American feminist text" ("Maxine" 155). To return to the narrator's questions, we might say that the "Chineseness" one finds within oneself is likely to be gender-inflected and depends largely on whose stories one has heard and what kind of movies one has seen.[6]

What becomes clear now is a tendency, or a certain blindness if you will, in Asian American thinking and articulation that unwittingly passes on one's own gender-specific convictions as if they applied to the racial experience of the whole community. In other words, in our effort to articulate ethnic identity, we tend to take for granted our gender-specific perceptions without giving adequate consideration to other gender formulations in the process. This inherent gender blindness gave rise to two distinct impulses in Asian American thinking, which in the revolutionary atmosphere of the time went on a head-on collision course. As is true with any movement in its formative stages, Asian American cultural resurgence of this period carried more passion and fire than strategic vision and shrewd planning. Therefore, it is little wonder that the prevailing insensitivity to gender disparity and the lacking of understanding of its ramifications evolved into full-blown confrontations between the nationalists and the feminists.

The Question of Fictionalism

While most agree that the key arguments in this debate have revolved around the problematics of cultural representation in ethnic creative expression, critics have not paid adequate attention to the manipulative influences of the mainstream publishing industry in the whole affair. In a sense, the Asian American gender war is a casualty of the white publishing industry's relentless pursuit of profits and its historical neglect and suppression of Asian American artistic expression. The fuse of the war of words was the issue of genre, which Sau-ling Wong calls "the question of fictionalism," that is, "to what extent 'fictional' features are admissible in a work that purports to be an autobiography" ("Autobiography" 30). While the importance of "fictionalism" for the interpretation of *The Woman Warrior* is obvious, the issue of literary genre is only the first step toward understanding the larger issue of ethnic cultural representation, which by necessity has to negotiate constantly with both the dominant culture and the ancestral tradition.

Shortly before *The Woman Warrior* was published, Frank Chin had the opportunity to review a copy of the bound galleys. Chin clearly appreciated its literary style but was strongly opposed to its classification as nonfiction. "[T]he yellow autobiography is a white racist form . . . an insult to our writing and characterizes us as freaks, anthropological phenomena kept and pampered in a white zoo and not people whose world is complete and complex," he told Kingston in a rarely publicized letter. "[G]o for fiction with this book if you can and dump the autobiography. As fiction, I can like your stuff without necessarily liking or agreeing with the narrator or any of the characters and credit you with subtleties and knowing lapses I can't give to an autobiographer" ("Letter"). Regardless of Chin's definition of Asian American autobiography as a racist genre, his warning about the white publishing industry's historical manipulation and suppression of Asian American artistic expression should be taken seriously. It is crucial to remember that Kingston wrote *The Woman Warrior* as fiction. Kingston told an interviewer in 1977, "I thought of it as a novel when I mailed it out to the publishers. I felt it had to be defined in that form because of the fictional techniques I used in the story" (Kubota 2). According to Skenazy and Martin, Kingston continued to refer to *The Woman Warrior* (and *China Men* as well for that matter) as fiction until 1986 when she redefined her first two books as "the biographies of imaginative people" (xvii).[7] However, for the sake of higher sales Kingston's editor Charles Elliot wanted to classify *The*

Woman Warrior as nonfiction: "[F]irst novels are hard to sell," he said. "I knew it would stand a stronger chance of selling well as nonfiction autobiography. It could have been called anything else" (Chun).[8] Understandably, as a no-name author at the time, Kingston was unwilling to take on a major publisher like Knopf over the classification of her first book, but she clearly underestimated the colossal consequences this classification would cause for the future of Asian American literature for decades to come.

The significance of *The Woman Warrior*'s classification lies not in Asian American nationalists' perceived dogmatic insistence on the genre distinction between fiction and autobiography, which is pitifully inconsequential for the publishing industry's bottom line and downright meaningless to postmodernist formulations of blurred boundaries and collapsed borders; rather, it lies in its foregrounding of the unique problem of ethnic cultural representation, which subjects ethnic writers to what Deborah Woo calls "the burden of dual authenticity" (173), that is, cultural truthfulness and artistic legitimacy. This double burden generally does not apply to the production of the dominant culture. Within the interpretive community of the dominant culture, when the author and the audience share a common tradition of historical and cultural values, the tension between cultural authenticity and aesthetic freedom is decidedly less severe. For even when the audience recognizes a gap between what is being described by the author and what is understood to be true according to the audience's education and experience, poetic license is more readily granted to the author because whatever discrepancies are perceived can be modified and corrected in the security of the common cultural traditions and sociopolitical particularities that inform both the author and the audience.[9]

Suffice it to say that when indeed a rupture occurs within such an interpretive community, as when second-wave feminists brought about the gender revolution in the US in the 1960s and 1970s, the breakaway from the Eurocentric and phallocentric canon was relatively unproblematic. Radically reinterpreting the traditional canon while at the same time recovering a lost literary tradition of its own (at roughly the same time the Asian American gender war erupted), the feminist movement made an exhilarating and clean break from the tradition and firmly established gender as a defining element in articulating women's experiences. While the conservative core of the dominant literary establishment resisted and discounted the new women's literature on the ground of aesthetic value or lack thereof, the majority of women as well as men quickly caught on and embraced it. Elaine Showalter's *A Literature of Their Own* (1976), Nina Baym's *Woman's Fiction*

(1978), and Sandra Gilbert and Susan Gubar's *The Madwoman in the Attic* (1979) effectively put to rest any lingering doubt about the legitimacy of women's literature in the canon. In contrast, Asian American feminists' articulation of their cultural identity encountered unprecedented attacks from within the Asian American community. Nearly three decades after the gender war erupted, Asian America is only beginning to navigate out of the critical impasse of gender opposition.

Against this backdrop, it seemed particularly ironic that when the white literary establishment blatantly dismissed the literary value of *The Woman Warrior* by classifying it as nonfiction, albeit under the benign guise of commercial interests, Kingston deferred to the decision and declined Chin's invitation to reconsider its genre classification. This is strikingly inconsistent with Kingston's professed goal of artistic pursuit and aesthetic fulfillment as seen in her reply to Chin's letter:

> The genre *I* am avoiding is the political/polemical harangue, which I
> dislike because a) it keeps the writer on the surface of perception; b)
> it puts the Asian-Am. Writer on the same trip as the racist; we
> provide the other half of the dialogue, the yin to his yang, as it were,
> c) the blacks already wrote that way in the '50's; all we'd do is change
> black faces to yellow, no furthering of art. ("Letter")

Kingston did not appear to address directly the problem of ethnic cultural representation and aesthetic freedom which Chin's letter raised; instead, her reply was somewhat condescending, saying in effect that "yours is politics and mine is art, forever the twain shall stay apart." Sadly for the Asian American literary community, the door to future dialogues and negotiations between the two prominent representatives of the opposing camps was closed. Chin may well have been jealous of Kingston's commercial success, but his high sensitivity to white establishment's manipulation and censorship of ethnic creative expression did not start with *The Woman Warrior*. In the introduction to *Aiiieeeee!*, he recorded a similar exchange with Jade Snow Wong concerning the heavy-handed editing of her *Fifth Chinese Daughter* by her white editor, Elizabeth Lawrence. When Chin asked if she thought the significant deletions were justified, Wong replied, "Some of the things are missing that I would have wanted in, then, you know, it's like selling to Gumps or sending to a museum. Everybody has a purpose in mind, in what they're carrying out. So, you know, you kind of have to work with them" (*Aiiieeeee!* xxx). Chin emphatically rejected Wong's "good business" sense, and for the same reason Asian American nationalists accused Kingston of "selling out."

William Wei frames his discussion of the Asian American controversy around the tension between the socio-ideological and aesthetic modes in literature. According to Wei, Asian American nationalists by and large subscribe to the sociopolitical view of literature, which emphasizes literature's political dimension while Asian American feminists tend to take the aesthetic view of literature, which privileges artistic freedom (67). While Chin's stance is ideologically driven, Kingston believes in "the timelessness and universality of individual vision" ("Cultural" 65). "Why must I 'represent' anyone besides myself?" Kingston asks. "Why should I be denied an individual artistic vision?" (64). However, Wei's theory has its limitations because, despite their different emphasis, both sides would agree that literature without aesthetics is no longer literature but history or sociology and that the idea that literature transcends all ideology and belongs in the pure realm of timelessness and universality is an incredibly naïve fantasy. Although Chin's work is informed by a strong sense of ethnic pride and political conviction, it also exemplifies clear artistic vision and achievement. Similarly, while Kingston's work is noted for its stylistic sophistication, *The Woman Warrior* is clearly inspired by feminism, which is no less ideological. The real challenge, as Sau-ling Wong puts it, is striving for "a balance between self-actualization and social responsibility" ("Necessity" 5).

The Perils of Ethnic Cultural Representation

Due to the delicate nature of ethnic cultural representation, we should never underestimate the importance of the issue of genre for Asian American literature. While mainstream readers could compensate for perceived lack or inaccuracy of cultural representation in literature with their own life experiences or other works of literature, minority literature does not have this luxury of post-production adjustment due to its extremely limited exposure in the mainstream media. Whatever an ethnic writer portrays usually registers in the mainstream imagination as the "typical" because there is little or no system of reference to consult and compare. This is particularly true when an ethnic text is branded nonfiction, a genre bound by definition (at least in common usage) to actual experience.[10] The Orientalist reception of *The Woman Warrior* by the mainstream press justifies this concern. According to Kingston herself, about two thirds of the reviewers measured "the book and me against the stereotype of the exotic, inscrutable, mysterious oriental. . . . The critics who said how the book was good because it was, or was not, like the oriental fantasy in their heads might as well have said how weak it was, since it in fact did not break through that fantasy" ("Cultural" 55). The San Francisco Association of Chinese Teachers bluntly warned: "Especially for students unfamiliar with the Chinese background, it [*The Woman Warrior*] could give an overly negative impression of the Chinese American experience" (qtd. in Kingston, "Cultural" 62).

Given this context, many of the charges leveled at Kingston appear understandable. Katheryn Fong faults Kingston for her "distortions of the histories of China and Chinese America" and her "over-exaggera[tion]" of the Chinese misogynistic attitudes (67–68). Benjamin Tong argues that Kingston sold out Chinese culture and tradition "with white acceptance in mind" (6). Chin calls Kingston a "yellow agent of stereotype" who "falsifies Chinese history [and] vilifies Chinese manhood" (qtd. in Kim, "Such" 76), adamantly disagreeing with her handling of Mulan, a sixth-century legendary woman warrior who enlisted in the army in her aging father's place. In her revisionist recast, Kingston transplants the story of Yue Fei (1103–1142), a heroic male general whose mother tattooed a message in his back to inspire patriotism, onto Mulan, allegedly "to dramatize cruelty to women" (Chin, "Come" 3). To convey his exasperation to those unaware of Mulan's cultural significance in the Chinese tradition, Chin wrote a parody of *The Woman Warrior* which evokes Joan of Arc and hypothesizes a French reaction if the latter's story were altered.[11]

On the other hand, Jeffery Paul Chan and Benjamin Tong take issue with Kingston over her translation of the word *kuei* into "ghost" as proof that her overriding interest was white acceptance at the expense of Chinese America.[12] David Leiwei Li's historicization of *kuei*'s translation helps toward an understanding of the full implications of the term. According to Li, since the onset of Western invasion of China in the mid-nineteenth century, the word *kuei* has been routinely translated as "devil" when referring to foreigners (54). In replacing the word "devil" (which usually conjures up a sense of Satanic evil or wickedness) with "ghost" (which generally evokes an amorphous non-threatening specter), Kingston seems to minimize the negative connotations of *kuei* in order to "relieve the white man's historical burden" (55).

A similar example of linguistic maneuvering in *The Woman Warrior* is discussed by Jinqi Ling concerning Kingston's translation of the archaic pronoun *nu* (the female I) into "slave" (*Narrating* 116). While *nu* could mean "slave," Kingston's usage deflects the meaning of *nu* as a female self-referencing pronoun (which means "my humble self" [Ling 116]) as a social marker of status, in much the same way feudal lords used *nu* to address themselves before the emperor. Ling contends that while Kingston's linguistic maneuvering effectively called attention to Chinese American women's plight, it also obscured the fact that the oppression of Chinese American women could not be functionally separated from that of Chinese American men. Ling argues, "it is mainly against such an orientalized or dehistoricized dimension of Kingston's feminist critiques of Chinese American patriarchy that Chin and others direct their strong criticisms – criticisms that, unfortunately, are often made within unexamined patriarchal and even sexist frames of reference" (116).[13]

Tit For Tat: Up Close and Personal

Regrettably, this kind of cool-headed analysis was conspicuously missing during the heated exchanges throughout the 1980s when the debate was largely overshadowed by the strong personalities involved. The debate's highly personal nature not only deflected attention away from the underlying issues but also alienated those who did not feel that their interests and allegiance belonged exclusively with either camp. It is common to hear the debate referred to as the "Kingston-Chin controversy" (Wong, "Chinese" 51), the "debate between Kingston and Frank Chin" (Chu, *Tripmaster* 118), "the War of Words between Chin and Kingston," or even "the Kingston-Chin 'feud'" (Yin 234, 240).[14] The sometimes bizarre labeling, such as "yellow agents of yellow extinction" (Chin, "This" 110), "border town whore talk" (Talbot 8), or conversely "anti-female" (Kim, *Asian* 199), and "[misogynistic] assholes," was highly incendiary.[15] These terms are not only inaccurate but also counterproductive to a constructive dialogue between the two camps. The mistrust and animosity had cost many opportunities to negotiate the issue of cultural identification in ways that could genuinely benefit both sides. It is important to go beyond the rabble-rousing and fanfare typically accompanying strong personalities in rivalry and focus on the fundamental issue of ethnic cultural representation.

The debate about *The Woman Warrior* had so poisoned the relationship between the two camps that the foundation for constructive gender dialogues and negotiations was seriously undermined. When *China Men* was published in 1980, Asian American nationalists were reluctant to acknowledge its profound significance. After her story of growing up as an Asian American female in *The Woman Warrior*, Kingston set out to address the gender imbalance by focusing on Chinese men in her second book. A powerful record of the great perseverance of Chinese men who struggled against great odds – unusually harsh physical conditions and legalized racial discrimination, *China Men* is a book that Asian American nationalists should find consistent with their own goal of exposing the racial injustices toward Chinese men. Given Kingston's enormous popularity and prestige among mainstream readers, *China Men* has probably achieved substantially in terms of educating the general public on legalized racism against the Chinese, especially males. In all fairness, the codes of traditional Chinese heroism would call for Asian American nationalists to seize upon this occasion and recognize Kingston's positive contribution to the fight against racism. Unfortunately, the momentum of bitterness and the tenacity of pride again carried the day and no cross-gender dialogue and negotiation came to fruition. Perhaps the Asian American nationalists felt that *China Men* failed to rise to their standards of heroism and integrity. For example, the narrator's silent father seems to open his mouth only to utter profanities against women; the grandfather's preference for girls over boys comes close to redeeming him from the prevalent patriarchal values, but such a reading is quickly subverted by his insanity, a fact that seems to imply that Chinese paternal affection for the female can only exist as a form of perversion rather than the norm. Nevertheless, one cannot deny that Kingston wrote courageously about the men in her family. We should at least grant her the authority of experience, if not poetic license, which may not apply here anyway because *China Men* has been accepted as nonfiction much less problematically.

The unrelenting attacks from Asian American nationalists are perhaps also directed at a perceived unwillingness on the part of Kingston to acknowledge even apparent errors in cultural reproduction. A case in point is her mistranslation of "frog" as "heavenly chicken" in *The Woman Warrior* (65), which is an understandable error by nonnative speakers who confuse two Chinese homophones with different tones. *Tianji*, a common Chinese expression for frog, can sound like "field chicken" or "heavenly chicken" to someone who does not know the corresponding written characters. But for those who do, "field chicken" is the only correct translation of *tianji*. Apparently reacting to criticisms of her mistakes, Kingston in *China Men* shows awareness of the difference:

"A field chicken." It was not a chicken at all but a toad with alert round eyes that looked out from under the white cabbage leaves. . . .

"A field chicken," said Say Goong. He cupped his hands, walked
quietly with wide steps and caught it. . . . "A field chicken?" I
repeated. "Field chicken," he said. "Sky chicken. Sky toad.
Heavenly toad. Field toad." It was a pun and the words the same
except for the low tone of *field* and the high tone of *heaven* or *sky*.
He put the toad in my hands. . . . (165–66)

In this very creative recount, however, Kingston makes two more errors
while attempting to correct one. First, a "field chicken" is a frog, not a toad;
second, the characters for "field" and "heaven" are not the same. To
Benjamin Tong and other critics, Kingston's narrative must have seemed a
rather fanciful reconstruction because her Say Goong, being a native
Cantonese, was unlikely to either call a toad a field chicken or offer a child
such an unpleasant, even poisonous animal as a pet. Kingston's substitution
of "frog" with "toad" seems to mock her critics while acknowledging her
error, but her linguistic maneuvering comes across as a bit strenuous and
therefore counterproductive.

Kingston's counterattack continues in *Tripmaster Monkey*, a novel that,
despite its dazzling wit and rich literary allusions, is widely read as her not-
so-private revenge against her critics, particularly Frank Chin.[16] Amy Ling
expresses her disappointment in a review: "We, poor mortals, don't read
Kingston in order to watch her outchinning Chin. We read her to hear the
voice of Maxine Hong Kingston, and we wish there were more of that voice
in this book" ("Kiss" 9). Not only does Kingston "outchin" Chin in appropriating the classic heroic figure of Monkey King, she also takes a direct jab at
Chin's idea of "real" and "fake" Chinese culture by subtitling her novel "his
fake book" (the basic score from which musicians may improvise).[17] The most
devastating mocking of Chin may be Kingston's description of a failed love
scene between Wittman and his wife Taña after a brief foreplay of fencing:

He sat on the footboard, his sword between his knees. In the shining
steel handguard, his penis reflected huge. Behind it, his pinhead
peeped out a long ways off. How odd, his head, the container of his
mind, which contains the universe, is a complicated button topping
this gigantic purple penis, which ends in a slit, like a vagina (220–21).

Here Kingston not only pokes fun at Chin's exaggerated masculinity
through the optic illusion of a huge penis, she also neutralizes the imposing
dominance of the phallus by drawing attention to its small vagina-like

opening. Chin's response? A ninety-two-page essay entitled "Come All Ye Asian American Writers of the Real and the Fake" in *The Big Aiiieeeee!*, in which he makes his case for an Asian American masculinity based on the heroic traditions of ancient China and Japan. While his attacks on Kingston remain harsh as ever, he also broadens his targets to include Amy Tan and David Henry Hwang.

Toward a Theoretical Remapping of the Gender War

The 1990s saw a remarkable maturation in Asian American critical thinking. Many critics have crossed over the gender divide and analyzed both sides of the debate persuasively from a critically "neutral" vantage point. In 1990, three important critiques – Elaine Kim's "Such Opposite Creatures," Deborah Woo's "Maxine Hong Kingston: The Ethnic Writer and the Burden of Dual Authenticity," and King-Kok Cheung's "The Woman Warrior Versus the Chinaman Pacific" – appeared, marking a breakthrough in the gender debate. Kim's essay clearly favors a synthesis of men and women's voices, as seen in her praise of Kingston's *Tripmaster Monkey* for "[putting] the men and women together in a story that suggests a new kind of America" (87). An insightful study of the ethnic writer's conflicting burden of aesthetic fulfillment and social responsibility, Woo's essay rises above gender polemics. On the one hand, she affirms Kingston's creative practice in "moving away from a simplistic, static, and self-contained view of culture," which Asian American nationalists are presumably guilty of sustaining (188); on the other hand, Woo points to the necessity for Kingston to "concretely document an authentic cultural experience," which I interpret as one that cannot be too far removed from the shared traditions of the community (189). Cheung is the most explicit in calling for gender negotiations between Chinese American women and men. "Must a Chinese American Critic Choose between Feminism and Heroism?" she asks, apparently dissatisfied with the either/or dichotomy (234). Prompted by insights of recent gender studies, she looks to break away from the entanglement of gender opposition, declaring that "the time has come to look at women and men together" (245–46). She further suggests that while "Asian American men need to be wary of certain pitfalls in using what Foucault calls 'reverse discourse,' in demanding legitimacy in the same vocabulary, using the same categories by which [they were] disqualified," their female counterparts should try to "find a way to negotiate the tangle of sexual and racial politics in all its intricacies, not just out of a desire for 'revenge' but also out of a sense of 'loyalty'" (246).

Cheung's insight is particularly important for the Asian American gender debate at a time when feminist studies is being rapidly transformed by gender studies toward a reconceptualization of gender opposition. As Judith Kegan Gardiner observes, "[B]oth genders can and should cooperate intellectually and politically . . . Women contribute to masculinity studies, men to feminist theory as well as to masculinity studies, heterosexuals to queer theory, and gay-identified scholars to the study of heterosexuality even though the standpoints of differently situated scholars will not be identical" (12). In "Of Men and Men," Cheung develops a more theoretical critique of Asian American masculinity. Building on Judith Butler's concept of gender performativity, she reads Asian American nationalists' obsession with hegemonic masculinity as a result of being denied by the dominant culture to "*perform* 'masculine' roles" (173). She identifies *shusheng*, a kind of witty, gentle, and sexy poet-scholar in classic Chinese romance and opera, as an alternative masculine model, and adopts Nel Noddings's concept of "ethic of care" for another.

It is also in this spirit of gender negotiation and reconciliation that Jinqi Ling frames his discussion of the Asian American gender war. In "Identity Crisis and Gender Politics," Ling attempts to "reappropriate masculinity in ways that both resist a phallocentric economy and go beyond forms of feminism unable to evaluate the meaning of patriarchy outside the framework of male/female oppositions" in order to formulate "collective strategies for more comprehensive social change" (312). In highlighting the often obscured entanglement of Chinese American women's racial oppression with Chinese American men's, Ling aims at locating common ground for both. His plea to the whole community comes in the form of a provocative question, "Can an Asian American feminist discourse transform and strengthen rather than weaken an evolving Asian American cultural identity that embraces both men's and women's concerns?" (322–23). His own answer is embedded in a dissection of the "gender ambiguity or gender transgression" motif in Wendy Law-Yone's *The Coffin Tree* and Jessica Hagedorn's *Dogeaters* from "the mediational ground between male and female identities" (326).

The critical intervention by the hitherto silent queer scholars in Asian American critical discourse in the mid-1990s demonstrated in startling clarity the inseparable link between race and gender in ethnic identity formation, powerfully undercutting the simplistic and restrictive practice of gender antagonism. For example, in his perceptive study of David Henry Hwang's *M. Butterfly*, David Eng focuses on Song Liling's "castration" by white "racist love," a Western male chauvinism that summarily subjugates the racial Other into a feminine/sexual subject. Such a critique of white sexism not only puts Asian American queers on the same critical plane as Asian American feminists but also aligns them with Asian American nationalists. The latter point is highly ironic because Asian American nationalists, while condemning their symbolic emasculation at the hands of white patriarchy, have steadfastly disparaged homosexuality. In "Art, Spirituality, and the Ethic of Care: Alternative Masculinities in Chinese American Literature," King-Kok Cheung acknowledges a debt to Asian American queer studies by citing from Richard Fung's "Looking for My Penis" in an epigraph, and from David Eng and Alice Hom's "Introduction" to *Q & A: Queer in Asian America* in an opening quote. Building on the alternative masculine models of "poet-scholar" and "ethic of care" first developed in "Of Men and Men," Cheung articulates a model of Asian American gay masculinity through an analysis of Russell Leong's short story "Phoenix Eyes." The gay protagonist Terence's challenge to Western and Asian American hegemonic masculinity finds the most powerful expression in an armless artist who paints with his toes: this "emasculated" young man, Cheung points out, "redefines masculinity as inner resources rather than physical endowments" (280).

II. GENDER REVERSAL IN JOHN OKADA'S *NO-NO BOY*

Within this frame work of gender negotiation, I now turn to John Okada's novel *No-No Boy*, whose unique history of critical reception makes it viable for analysis in light of the gender debate in Asian American literature. First published in 1957, *No-No Boy* is the first Asian American novel on the Japanese American internment during World War II, but primarily due to its politically sensitive nature, it remained in obscurity for nearly two decades until the Combined Asian American Resources Project reissued it in paperback in 1976.[18] Asian American nationalists enthusiastically embraced the novel for protesting white racism. For example, in his introduction Lawson Inada calls the novel "a great and lasting work of art" (vi). In the "Afterword," Frank Chin writes, "The book was so good it freed me to be trivial" (254). On the other hand, Asian American feminists have been more critical, focusing on Okada's alleged sexism. In *Asian American Literature*, Elaine Kim recognizes *No-No Boy* as a central work on the internment experience by devoting a considerable amount of attention to it

(147–56), but she regards Okada's Japanese women characters as "stick figures" and "unidimensional" (197), although she does differentiate Okada from the *Aiiieeeee!* group by characterizing his stance as "not anti-female" (197). Other feminist scholars are less forgiving. For example, Gayle Fujita Sato takes issue with Okada for portraying Mrs Yamada negatively, calling her characterization "a parody of the Japanese mother's strength" (247) and her death scene "conspicuously ungenerous" (252). Likewise, Patricia Chu calls Okada's portrayal of Mrs Yamada "a political failure" for being unnecessarily "nationalistic, anti-American, irrational, and unfeeling as well as unwomanly *and* unmanly" (*Assimilating* 58).

Asian American feminists' charges against *No-No Boy*'s alleged anti-female bias appear to hit right on target, since overall critical attention has focused primarily on the novel's racial and cultural aspects, as if gender critique, a key approach to the works of Kingston and Hwang, were irrelevant or would just confirm the truthfulness of the charges. Perhaps mindful of this "defect," critics have remained conspicuously silent on the prominent construction of gender reversal in *No-No Boy*.[19] In the following analysis, I seek to free the novel from a critical discourse that, confined to dogmatic gender opposition, relegates it to "a crisis of masculinity in a home where a hapless son and an effeminate father are dominated by an 'unnaturally' strong mother" (Amoko 43). By studying the gender reversal between Mr and Mrs Yamada, we can better appreciate Okada's protest against the dominant culture's oppression of both Asian American men and women. The act of gender reversal not only helps to transcend gender opposition but also sheds light on the closely intertwined relationship between race and gender in the Asian American experience.

Part of the difficulty in such a reading is that gender reversal in *No-No Boy* is constructed as a defensive measure against racial oppression that does not explicitly challenge existing gender norms or sexual stereotypes, whereas dominant modes of gender reversal in both Western and Asian American traditions do.[20] For Okada, gender reversal is not an act of subversion or revenge, but a consequence of racial oppression. In this sense, Mr and Mrs Yamada are forced into their opposite gender roles by the dominant culture, a fact that, while foregrounding the Issei's victimization, does not implicate the traditional notion of family structure. However, Mr Yamada's emasculation in the traditional sense is complicated by what we now recognize as alternative masculinities such as the "ethic of care" suggested by King-Kok Cheung. In the absence of the traditional mother figure, Mr Yamada assumes the caretaking role effectively and courageously.

Likewise, Mr Yamada's decision not to resolve family conflict through confrontation should not be seen only as an indication of his emasculated state. He does not directly confront Mrs Yamada not because he is intimidated by her as is usually assumed, but because he cares enough not to drive her deeper into insanity. Upon her death, Mr Yamada mails food to her starving relatives in Japan. His quiet, yet firm resolve may not conform to the norm of hegemonic masculinity, but even Asian American nationalists must have recognized the powerful resilience of Mr Yamada as positive masculinity, for they have nothing but praise for Okada. By contrast, the current lack of critical attention to Mr Yamada as well as the blatant dismissal of him as effeminate and undesirable may be an indicator of how deeply ingrained hegemonic masculinist thinking is.

Conversely, Mrs Yamada's portrayal should not be summarily branded as anti-female simply because her appearance and behavior depart from our usual expectations of a "typical" Japanese mother. First of all, Okada created this character to embody the dehumanizing effect of racial oppression, particularly the internment of Japanese Americans. Asian American feminists' lack of empathy for this victim of monstrous racism and for the author who created her betrays the effects of the tenacious logic of gender opposition. Most would agree that Charlotte Brontë's mad Bertha is much more demeaning, but since she is clearly a victim of patriarchy (I would argue of racism too), it is hard to envision similar harsh criticisms of Brontë for the creation of Bertha Rochester. Asian American women have certainly reacted in more extreme ways than Mrs Yamada under similar circumstances, and one needs only to think about Pau Lin in Sui Sin Far's "The Wisdom of the New" (1912) to understand how violent and intense such protest against the dominant culture could be.[21] If we can understand Pau Lin as a victim of the oppressive forces of culture and patriarchy, why can't we see Mrs Yamada as a victim of racism and patriarchy that drove her to fanaticism and insanity?[22] The tragedy of Mrs Yamada lies not in her fierce determination to fill the power vacuum created by Mr Yamada's emasculation, but in her misguided gender politics. As Stephen Sumida points out, "First denied recognition of her and her fellow issei's decades of living and working in America, then seeing the American citizenship of her children, the family's future, denied as well, Ma [Mrs Yamada] is herself a complex allegory of reaction against and yet imitation of her oppressors" (224). In other words, Mrs Yamada's downfall is that in fighting racial oppression, she adopts her oppressor's logic of hegemonic masculinity, mistakenly believing that the only form of resistance is through domination and control. The divergent readings of the gender construction in *No-No Boy* thus underscore once again the inherent gender blindness in Asian American critical discourses.

CONCLUSION

Through a review of some of the key issues in the Asian American critical debate, I hope to have demonstrated that only through a cross-gender critical sensibility can we move toward resolving some of the lingering problems of ethnic identification and cultural representation. The tenacity and bitterness of this controversy suggests that we may never be able to mediate and settle the disputes to the complete understanding and total satisfaction of all the parties concerned. However, as Asian America moves on from its formative stages of cultural identification, we must try our best to disinherit our historical burden of segregated gender consciousness. The exhilarating development in gender studies in recent years has provided a new paradigm for us to articulate a more integrated ethnic identity that breaks down the barrier of gender antagonism. The implications of these theoretical formulations for Asian American literature are obvious: if scholars from different political, sexual, and racial groups can cross boundaries to promote social justice collectively, then Asian American men and women should also strive to go beyond the confines of gender opposition as the defining model of articulating an Asian American subjectivity.

NOTES

A version of this chapter was delivered at the Fifteenth Annual Conference of the American Literature Association in San Francisco, California, on 29 May 2004. I wish to thank Derek Royal and Wenying Xu for their comments.

1. While one side has consistently been referred to as Asian American feminists, the other side has been known by various terms: "Asian American cultural nationalists" (Lisa Lowe 34), Chinatown cowboys, masculinists, militants, angry young men, and so on.
2. For a detailed discussion of early Asian American writers, see Chapter 2 of Kim's *Asian American Literature*, "Early Asian Immigrant Writers."
3. The trajectory of Asian American literary discourse might not have followed its overly gender-determined path had we not been deprived of the legacy of Sui Sin

Far, whose remarkable vision at the turn of the twentieth century gave eloquent expression to both Asian American nationalist and feminist concerns. See my "Sui Sin Far and the Chinese American Canon."

4. Clearly influenced by African American writers such as LeRoi Jones and Ishmael Reed, Chin adopted such martial mottos as "Writing is fighting" and "Life is war" ("This" 129). Similar gender wars in African American literature and Mexican American literature suggest that ethnic gender strife is not a uniquely Asian American problem and warrants more critical attention from various ethnic scholars.

5. Other early articulations include Stanley and Derald Sue's "Chinese-American Personality and Mental Health," Kai-yu Hsu and Helen Palubinskas's *Asian American Authors*, and David Hsin-Fu Wand's *Asian American Heritage*.

6. Chin certainly recognized the importance of the issue when he asked a friend, "What are you singing your kids to sleep with? What tales do you tell them?" ("This" 109).

7. For more detailed discussions of Kingston's shifting genre emphasis, see Skenazy and Martin, xvi–xvii.

8. Lisa Lowe takes an unambiguous stand against the dominant culture's tendency to classify Asian American creative expression as nonfiction in order to downplay its artistic value: she not only calls *The Woman Warrior* a novel (63), but refers to Bulosan's *America Is in the Heart* and Monica Sone's *Nisei Daughter* as novels (45, 48).

9. Given his unparalleled status in the Western canon, Shakespeare would be an excellent example to prove this point. His less than elegant portrayal of Joan of Arc in *Henry VI, Part 1* is perhaps particularly relevant to the current discussion. It is unlikely that readers will confuse her fictional recreation with the historical person.

10. For recent academic definitions of autobiography, see James Olney's "Autobiography and the Cultural Moment" (3), and Paul John Eakin's *Fictions in Autobiography* (5).

11. See "The Most Popular Book in China."

12. Chan, "Mysterious," 41; Tong, "Critic," 6.

13. For a discussion of Kingston's nonlinguistic misrepresentations of Chinese culture, see Toming Jun Liu's "The Problematics of Kingston's 'Cultural Translation.'"

14. Some critics have suggested that professional jealousy and rivalry are responsible for the highly personal nature of the debate. For example, Sau-ling Wong points to the rivalry between Chin and Hwang in "Chinese," 52; Sheng-mei Ma sees Chin as feeling "threatened" by the success of female writers (33); Xiao-huang Yin notes Chin's jealousy of Kingston and his sense of betrayal by her (239).

15. The term "assholes" was originally used in Kingston's *The Woman Warrior* on misogynistic paternal figures of the family (189), but has since entered critical discourse (Fong 69; Woo 177).

16. Kingston's depiction of Wittman Ah Sing, the novel's protagonist, is eerily reminiscent of the speech and mannerism of Chin. According to Amy Ling, Wittman Ah Sing was modeled on Frank Chin, although Kingston was quick to add a few others (*Between* 149). Ling also reports that Shawn Wong telephoned Chin to say, "She must have been a fly on the wall when you were talking!" ("Maxine" 155).

17. For a detailed reading of the novel in the context of the Chin-Kingston debate, see Patricia Chu, "*Tripmaster Monkey*, Chin, and the Chinese Heroic Tradition."

18. For a history of the critical reception and the socio-political background of the novel, see Jinqi Ling's "*No-No Boy*, by John Okada."

19. Mr Yamada's "femininity" is established early in the novel. For example, when greeting Ichiro upon his return from prison, Mr Yamada "uttered the name preciously as might an old woman" (6). In this post-internment household, Mr Yamada assumes the role traditionally reserved for the mother – watching the store while Mrs Yamada tends to more important business (7), cooking and washing dishes (10, 40, 105, 109, 111), and general "mothering" such as putting Ichiro to bed (35) and giving him spending money (44). He is also described as soft-spoken (6, 11), mild-mannered (12), emotional (37), considerate (41), and passive (43), all known as feminine traits. On the other hand, Mrs Yamada assumes the role traditionally reserved for the father. For example, she walks to the bakery for extra supplies of bread (7), does the accounting for the business (103, 104), and re-socializes Ichiro into the community (20). She is also depicted as "the rock" (13), "hard" (20), and exhibiting "strength" (43). In Ichiro's phrasing, "[Pa] should have been a woman. He should have been Ma and Ma should have been Pa" (112).

20. For discussions of gender reversal in the Western tradition, see, for example, Sandra M. Gilbert's "Costumes of the Mind," Sabrina Petra Ramet's *Gender Reversals and Gender Cultures*, and Lisa Rado's *The Modern Androgyne Imagination*. For the construction of gender reversal in Asian American literature, see Sui Sin Far's short story, "The Smuggling of Tie Co," Kingston's *The Woman Warrior* (Mulan) and *China Men* (Tang Ao), and Hwang's *M. Butterfly*.

21. To save her son from being Americanized, Pau Lin poisoned him. Sui Sin Far, 42–61.

22. I do not have the space here to elaborate on Mrs Yamada's madness, but it is clear that Okada portrayed Mrs Yamada with compassion and intended to implicate racism rather than Japanese motherhood.

WORKS CITED

Amoko, Apollo O. "Resilient ImagiNations: *No-No Boy*, *Obasan* and the Limits of Minority Discourse." *Mosaic* 33 (2000): 35–55.

Baym, Nina. *Woman's Fiction: A Guide to Novels by and about Women in America*. Ithaca: Cornell University Press, 1978.

Chan, Jeffery Paul. "The Mysterious West." *New York Review of Books* 28 April 1977, 41.

Cheung, King-Kok. "Art, Spirituality, and the Ethic of Care: Alternative Masculinities in Chinese American Literature." *Masculinity Studies and Feminist Theory: New Directions*. Ed. Judith Kegan Gardiner. New York: Columbia University Press, 2002, 261–89.

Cheung, King-Kok. "Of Men and Women: Reconstructing Chinese American Masculinity." *Other Sisterhoods: Literary Theory and U. S. Women of Color*. Ed. Sandra K. Stanley. Urbana: University of Illinois Press, 1998. 173–99.

Cheung, King-Kok. "The Woman Warrior Versus the Chinaman Pacific: Must a Chinese

American Critic Choose Between Feminism and Heroism?" *Conflicts in Feminism*. Eds. Marianne Hirsch and Evelyn Fox Keller. New York: Routledge, 1990. 234–51.

Cheung, King-Kok, ed. *An Interethnic Companion to Asian American Literature*. New York: Cambridge University Press, 1997.

Chin, Frank. Afterword. *No-No Boy*. John Okada. 1957. Seattle: University of Washington Press, 1979. 253–60.

Chin, Frank. *Chinaman Pacific & Frisco R. R. Co*. Minneapolis: Coffee House, 1988.

Chin, Frank. "Come All Ye Asian American Writers of the Real and the Fake." *The Big Aiiieeeee!: An Anthology of Chinese American and Japanese American Literature*. Eds. Jeffery Paul Chan et al. New York: Meridian-Penguin, 1991. 1–92.

Chin, Frank. "This Is Not an Autobiography." *Genre* 18 (Summer 1985): 109–30.

Chin, Frank. "Letter to Maxine Hong Kingston." 13 July 1976. Qtd. in David Li, 51.

Chin, Frank. "The Most Popular Book in China." *Quilt* 4 (1984): 6–12.

Chin, Frank, and Jeffery Paul Chan. "Racist Love." *Seeing through Shuck*. Ed. Richard Kostelanetz. New York: Ballantine, 1972. 65–79.

Chin, Frank et al., eds. *Aiiieeeee! An Anthology of Asian American Writers*. Washington, DC: Howard University Press, 1974.

Chu, Patricia P. *Assimilating Asians: Gendered Strategies of Authorship in Asian America*. Durham: Duke University Press, 2000.

Chu, Patricia P. "*Tripmaster Monkey*, Frank Chin, and the Chinese Heroic Tradition." *Arizona Quarterly* 53.3 (1997): 117–39.

Chun, Gloria H. "Metaphysician of Orientalism: Maxine Hong Kingston." The Sixth National Conference of the Association for Asian American Studies. New York, 3 June 1989. Qtd. in David Li, 51.

Eakin, Paul John. *Fictions in Autobiography: Studies in the Art of Self-Invention*. Princeton: Princeton University Press, 1985.

Eng, David L. *Racial Castration: Managing Masculinity in Asian America*. Durham: Duke University Press, 2001.

Fong, Katheryn M. "An Open Letter." *Bulletin of Concerned Asian Scholars* 9.4 (1977): 67–69.

Fung, Richard. "Looking for My Penis: The Eroticized Asian in Gay Video Porn." *How Do I Look: Queer Film and Video*. Ed. Bad Object-Choices. Seattle: Bay, 1991. 145–68.

Gardiner, Judith Kegan. Introduction. *Masculinity Studies and Feminist Theory: New Directions*. Ed. Gardiner. New York: Columbia University Press, 2002. 1–29.

Gilbert, Sandra M. "Costumes of the Mind: Transvestism as Metaphor in Modern Literature." *Critical Inquiry* 7 (1980): 391–417.

Gilbert, Sandra M., and Susan Gubar, eds. *The Madwoman in the Attic: The Woman Writer and the Nineteenth-Century Literary Imagination*. New Haven: Yale University Press, 1979.

Hsu, Kai-yu, and Helen Palubinskas, eds. *Asian American Authors*. Boston: Houghton Mifflin, 1972.

Hwang, David Henry. *M. Butterfly*. New York: Plume, 1989.

Inada, Lawson Fusao. Introduction. *No-No Boy*. iii–vi.

Kang, Younghill. *East Goes West*. New York: Scribner's, 1937.

Kim, Elaine H. *Asian American Literature: An Introduction to the Writings and Their Social Context*. Philadelphia: Temple University Press, 1982.

Kim, Elaine H. "'Such Opposite Creatures': Men and Women in Asian American Literature." *Michigan Quarterly Review* 29.1 (Winter 1990): 68–93.

Kingston, Maxine Hong. *China Men*. 1980. New York: Vintage-Random, 1989.

Kingston, Maxine Hong. "Cultural Mis-readings by American Reviewers." *Asian and Western Writers in Dialogue: New Cultural Identities*. Ed. Guy Amirthanayagam. London: Macmillan, 1982. 55–65.

Kingston, Maxine Hong. "Letter to Frank Chin." 8 August 1976; qtd. in David Li, 45.

Kingston, Maxine Hong. *Tripmaster Monkey: His Fake Book*. 1989. New York: Vintage-Random, 1990.

Kingston, Maxine Hong. *The Woman Warrior: Memoirs of a Girlhood Among Ghosts*. 1976. New York: Vintage-Random, 1989.

Kubota, Gary. "Maxine Hong Kingston: Something Comes from Outside Onto the Paper." *Hawaii Observer* 28 July 1977, 27–28. In Skenazy and Martin, 1–4.

Li, David Leiwei. *Imagining the Nation: Asian American Literature and Cultural Consent*. Stanford: Stanford University Press, 1998.

Li, Wenxin. "Sui Sin Far and the Chinese American Canon: Toward a Post-Gender Wars Discourse." *MELUS* 29.3–4 (2004).

Ling, Amy. *Between Worlds: Women Writers of Chinese Ancestry*. New York: Pergamon, 1990.

Ling, Amy. "A Kiss and a Tweak." *New Asian Times* June 1989: 9.

Ling, Amy. "Maxine Hong Kingston and the Dialogic Dilemma of Asian American Writers." *Bucknell Review* 39.1 (1995): 151–66.

Ling, Jinqi. *Narrating Nationalisms: Ideology and Form in Asian American Literature*. New York: Oxford University Press, 1998.

Ling, Jinqi. "Identity Crisis and Gender Politics: Reappropriating Asian American Masculinity." *An Interethnic Companion to Asian American Literature*. Ed. King-Kok Cheung. New York: Cambridge University Press, 1997. 312–37.

Ling, Jinqi. "*No-No Boy*, by John Okada." *A Resource Guide to Asian American Literature*. Eds. Sau-ling Cynthia Wong and Stephen H. Sumida. New York: MLA, 2001. 140–50.

Liu, Toming Jun. "The Problematics of Kingston's 'Cultural Translation.'" *Journal of American Studies of Turkey* 4 (1996): 15–26.

Lowe, Lisa. *Immigrant Acts: On Asian American Cultural Politics*. Durham: Duke University Press, 1996.

Ma, Sheng-mei. *Immigrant Subjectivities in Asian American and Asian Diaspora Literatures*. Albany: State University of New York Press, 1998.

Okada, John. *No-No Boy*. 1957. Seattle: University of Washington Press, 1979.

Olney, James. "Autobiography and the Cultural Moment." *Autobiography: Essays Theoretical and Cultural*. Ed. James Olney. Princeton: Princeton University Press, 1980. 3–27.

Rado, Lisa. *The Modern Androgyne Imagination: A Failed Sublime*. Charlottesville: University Press of Virginia, 2000.

Ramet, Sabrina Petra, ed. *Gender Reversals and Gender Cultures: Anthropological and Historical Perspectives*. London: Routledge, 1996.

Sato, Gayle K. Fujita. "Momotaro's Exile: John Okada's *No-No Boy*." *Reading the Literatures of Asian America*. Eds. Shirley Geok-lin Lim and Amy Ling. Philadelphia: Temple University Press, 1992. 239–58.

Shakespeare, William. *The First Part of Henry the Sixth*. *The Riverside Shakespeare*. Ed. G. Blakemore Evans. Boston: Houghton Mifflin, 1974. 596–629.

Showalter, Elaine. *A Literature of Their Own: British Women Novelists from Brontë to Lessing*. Princeton: Princeton University Press, 1976.

Skenazy, Paul, and Tera Martin, eds. *Conversations with Maxine Hong Kingston*. Jackson: University Press of Mississippi, 1998.

Sone, Monica. *Nisei Daughter*. 1953. Seattle: University of Washington Press, 1979.

Sue, Stanley, and Derald Sue. "Chinese-American Personality and Mental Health." *Amerasia Journal* 1.2 (1971): 36–49.

Sui Sin Far. *Mrs. Spring Fragrance and Other Writings*. Eds. Amy Ling and Annette White-Parks. Urbana: University of Illinois Press, 1995.

Sui Sin Far. "The Smuggling of Tie Co." *Mrs. Spring Fragrance*, 104–9.

Sui Sin Far. "The Wisdom of the New." *Mrs. Spring Fragrance*, 42–61.

Sumida, Stephen H. "Japanese American Moral Dilemmas in John Okada's *No-No Boy* and Milton Murayama's *All I Asking for Is My Body*." *Frontiers of Asian American Studies: Writing, Research, and Commentary*. Eds. Gail M. Nomura et al. Pullman: Washington State University Press, 1989. 224–26.

Takaki, Ronald. *Strangers from a Different Shore: A History of Asian Americans*. Boston: Little, 1998.

Talbot, Stephen. "Talking Story: Maxine Hong Kingston Rewrites the American Dream." *San Francisco Examiner* 24 June 1990: 8.

Tong, Benjamin. "Critic of Admirer Sees Dumb Racist." *San Francisco Journal* 11 May 1977: 6.

Wand, David Hsin-Fu, ed. *Asian American Heritage*. New York: Simon & Schuster, 1974.

Wei, William. *The Asian American Movement*. Philadelphia: Temple University Press, 1993.

Wong, Jade Snow. *Fifth Chinese Daughter*. 1945. Seattle: University of Washington Press, 1989.

Wong, Sau-ling C. "Autobiography as Guided Chinatown Tour? Maxine Hong Kingston's *The Woman Warrior* and the Chinese American Autobiography Controversy." *Multicultural American Autobiography: American Lives*. Ed. James Robert Payne. Knoxville: University of Tennessee Press, 1992. 248–79.

Wong, Sau-ling. "Chinese American Literature." *An Interethnic Companion to Asian American Literature*. Ed. King-Kok Cheung. New York: Cambridge University Press, 1997. 39–61.

Wong, Sau-ling. "Necessity and Extravagance in Maxine Hong Kingston's *The Woman Warrior*: Art and the Ethnic Experience." *MELUS* 15.1 (1988): 3–26.

Woo, Deborah. "Maxine Hong Kingston: The Ethnic Writer and the Burden of Dual Authenticity." *Amerasia Journal* 16.1 (1990): 173–200.

Yin, Xiao-huang. *Chinese American Literature since the 1850s*. Urbana: University of Illinois Press, 2000.

CHAPTER 6

Long a Mystery and Forever a Memory: God vs. Goddess in the Ethnic Novel

Guiyou Huang

Amy Tan's first two novels, *The Joy Luck Club* and *The Kitchen God's Wife*, both deploy feminist/women's concerns against a cross-cultural combination of religious, historical, and family backgrounds. A cursory comparison of what is in the two books with actual events that happened in Tan's family would reveal some parallels.[1] While *Joy Luck* has been widely noted, *Kitchen God*, the central concern of my inquiry here, has not been a critical focus of studies. However, this is a feminist text that, in Lisa Lowe's words, "multiplies the sites of cultural conflict, positing a number of struggles – familial and extrafamilial – as well as resolutions, without privileging the singularity or centrality of one" (35). The novel zooms in on women's issues by exploring their relationships to males – often husbands, and male divinities – while depicting an assiduous quest for a female divinity that represents the female subjectivity. The images of God and goddess command a controlling presence in the book and will be analyzed through examining Tan's use of divine metaphors to critique Chinese patriarchy.

In this chapter, God is understood as the one Supreme Being that created and rules the universe, as well as in the Christian scientific sense of Him as the Supreme Being understood as Life, Love, Mind, Soul, Spirit, and Principle. This is the God that Pearl's Chinese American father Jimmie Louie praised and worshipped as a minister. The lower-case god is defined in two ways, first as a male deity presiding over some portion of worldly affairs, in the case of Tan's novel, Kitchen God, who is charged by the Jade Emperor to specifically watch over human behaviors; second, as a deified person, and in this particular case, Confucius, the Chinese educator and philosopher who is beyond any doubt the most deified figure in Chinese history. Finally, goddess refers to a female god or deity, and in the case of *Kitchen God* she is the divinity that the narrator invents to displace and replace Kitchen God and that represents the successful conclusion of her search for a goddess with whom she can identify.[2]

This chapter takes as pre-texts Hawthorne's *The Scarlet Letter* and *The Blithedale Romance*. In chapter four of the latter novel the narrator Miles Coverdale describes Priscilla's worshipful look at her half-sister Zenobia when Priscilla first arrives at Blithedale under Hollingsworth's guidance. Coverdale observes, "she evidently saw nothing else in the room save that bright, fair, rosy, beautiful woman [Zenobia]. It was the strangest look I ever witnessed; long a mystery to me, and forever a memory" (57). The adaptation from Hawthorne is meaningful because, like *The Scarlet Letter* and *The Blithedale Romance*, *Kitchen God* is a novel about mysteries and secrets that emotionally separate the mother and her daughter, and a novel in which memory provides the base material about the mother's past life in China that persistently and hauntingly affects her life in America. Furthermore, Tan herself and her two principal characters evoke Hawthorne and his major characters in *The Scarlet Letter* – Tan's father died early, as did Hawthorne's, just like Arthur Dimmesdale, Pearl's father, who was survived by Hester and Pearl. Another noteworthy – perhaps not accidental – similarity between Hawthorne and Tan is the shared name – Pearl – of the respective daughter in *The Scarlet Letter* and *Kitchen God*. Even more interestingly, both Pearls's fathers are ministers – servants and messengers of God – a fact that implies redemptive qualities that are meant to fulfill the role of rescuers.

Unlike *Joy Luck* where half the narratives focus on China and Chinese-born mothers and half on America and American-born daughters, *Kitchen God* deals almost exclusively with the traumatic past of one Chinese mother. The mother does not merely intend to educate her daughter about her Chinese past; she wants to establish stronger bonds with her daughter and create a deeper understanding by letting Pearl into her secret past, a past that she has hitherto neither been able nor willing to confront herself because it is so entangled with shame and fear that she is afraid Pearl would not only fail to understand, but would think of her as a terrible mother, the last thing that she wants to be perceived as by Pearl. Winnie's exhaustive narrative is thus a carefully calculated effort to enable Pearl to know the more private and historical side of her as a mother, and her long narration of a chain of related events is tantamount to a necessary psychological preparation for the long-awaited disclosure of an important, well-kept secret.

As the novel may not be familiar to all readers, a brief summary of its stories is in order. Before she emigrated from China to America, Winnie (then called Weiwei) had an abusive marriage with Wen Fu, by whom she had three children, none of whom survived because of war-related circumstances and human factors. Wen Fu was a rapist, an adulterer, a wife-batterer, and an arrogant minor officer in the Chinese air force in World War II, then trained by US air force officers led by the later famous general Claire Chennault. During the Sino-Japanese war years, Winnie maintained a strained friendship with Hulan (later Americanized as Helen), the wife of a higher officer, Jiaguo. Helen and her Auntie Du were witnesses of Wen Fu's domestic violence and sexual abuses as well as of Winnie's submissive, bitter suffering. Therefore they were privy to Winnie's secrets and painful past. While a few secrets are deployed throughout the narrative, the worst is that which Winnie tried to hide from her daughter Pearl that her real father was Wen Fu who raped Winnie right after their divorce and before she journeyed to America to join her new husband, Jimmy Louie, a former member of the US air force stationed in Kunming and now back in the US working as a minister. Pearl was born and raised in America and is experiencing great emotional difficulty accepting the death of her American father. Pearl, however, has a secret of her own: she has developed multiple sclerosis. She does not want her mother to know but has told Aunt Helen, who therefore holds the keys to both Winnie's and Pearl's secrets. For better or worse, Helen's knowledge of the secrets allows her to manipulate her relationship with Winnie. On the other hand, due to her age and a desire to disclose the secrets by herself rather than through Helen, Winnie decides to reveal her secret to Pearl, who finally also tells her mother about her own disease. Mother and daughter together confront their respective pasts and, thanks to this sharing, come to grips with the present, in which Jimmy Louie just died.

The novel's title, *The Kitchen God's Wife*, finds its origin in a story Winnie tells her grandchildren in chapter two, "Grand Auntie Du's Funeral," which provides an initial thematic insight into the world of its characters. The Kitchen God used to be a lucky farmer, Zhang, who married a hardworking, kind-hearted woman, Guo, but who later turned into a philanderer and squanderer. Zhang even brought home a woman who chased his wife out of her own house. When he had squandered all his money and been deserted by the woman, Zhang turned a beggar. Later, however, the man chanced upon his wife again and, pricked by a guilty conscience, jumped into the kitchen fireplace and was burned into ashes despite her efforts to rescue him. When his ashes flew into heaven, the Jade

Emperor made him Kitchen God for having the courage to admit his wrong-doing and charged him to watch over everyone's behavior. This grandmother story, told early on in the novel, structurally frames all the subsequent stories, thematically holds the book together, and forecasts the horrible stories of Wen Fu, who, as the novel no doubt implies, himself is a bad kitchen god. Put differently, farmer Zhang's mistreatment of his wife epitomizes Wen Fu's misogynistic conduct toward Winnie. Compared with Wen Fu, Zhang even appears to be the moral superior, for he at least feels shame in the end and expresses remorse about his sexual misconduct. Winnie, on the other hand, is none other than a Kitchen God's wife, abused and oppressed by a husband who wielded unlimited power over her, other women, and certain helpless people. The bad fate of being a Kitchen's God's wife is reversed only after Winnie lands in America and marries her Chinese American husband, who believes in the God of Christianity, not a pagan god like Kitchen God. The images of god and goddess henceforth become dominant symbols of significance in the book.

The story of the Kitchen God is occasioned by the death of Auntie Du, who in her will left presents to people she had loved. One present, an altar that has the picture of a man inside, is left to Pearl. "The man is rather large and is seated in regal splendor, holding a quill in one hand, a tablet in the other. He has two long whiskers, shaped like smooth, tapered whips" (87). This regal figure – equipped with emblems of power and prestige: a quill and a tablet – is Kitchen God, who had been Auntie Du's good-luck god. However, he is not Winnie's idol. After hearing Winnie's story of Kitchen God, Pearl's husband Phil remarks on the god's Santa Claus resemblance, which provokes Winnie's outburst of contempt and anger: "He is not Santa Claus. More like a spy – FBI agent, CIA, Mafia, worse than IRS, that kind of person!" (91). Such comparative and derogative judgments of Kitchen God clearly reflect Winnie's views of him as an abusive, intrusive, and destructive agency, and are based on her personal experiences of the cruelty and violence emblematized in the image of the male figure in the altar. Winnie obviously has Wen Fu, her first husband, in mind when she unleashes her anger at both crime organizations like the Mafia and government agencies like the IRS, suggesting that Wen Fu is worse than any or all of them. In de-Santa Clausing him and calling him a person, not a god, Winnie strips the figure of all his endowed godly qualities, thus reducing him to the level of a despicable human being.

The character of Wen Fu seems like one born with innate depravity. Like farmer Zhang he was not justly punished by higher authorities represented by the Jade Emperor who instead despotically made him a god rather than condemning him for justice's sake. In his male-dominated society, Wen Fu benefited from the protection of the existing patriarchal system, where no one had ever passed a judgment on his moral character and conducts until Jimmy Louie made his appearance at a party. The casual encounter of a Chinese man and a Chinese American man sets the stage on which moral values and personal characters are compared and contrasted, the outcome of which in the long run helps Winnie to make the choice of one over another as her lifelong partner.[3] At this social gathering Jimmy Louie was surrounded by Chinese women and men asking him to give them suitable English names. Thus Weiwei became Winnie, a name that implies win or victory. Wen Fu wanted something special (as he believed himself to be) for his English name, and so he was named Judas, only to find out later that he was insulted by Jimmy who was, ironically, to replace him as Winnie's husband years later. On the other hand, this naming act reveals Jimmy's foresight into the evil side of Wen Fu characterized by betrayal, embodied in the name Judas.

Kitchen God intertwines family history and national history lived in a Confucian society torn by war and stricken by poverty. While the narrator relentlessly exposes the evil character of Wen Fu and praises only two men, Helen's first husband Jiaguo and Winnie's second husband Jimmy, the novel, like *Joy Luck*, focuses almost exclusively on women – their lives, hopes, hardships, and turns of fortune alongside societal and political tidings, with Wen Fu as their antagonist. Wen Fu was literally a god in his household, positioned as unchallengeable and exercising control over Winnie's person and over their financial matters. Winnie's dowry money, for example, given to her by her father and now intended for use for "taonan,"[4] was seized by Wen Fu who squandered it on perverse pleasures, such as purchasing an old car and crashing it while driving around with a woman. Wen Fu's sexual and physical abuse traumatized Winnie and directly contributed to her silence about her painful past. Winnie's experience of "taonan" is depicted vis-à-vis Japanese atrocities perpetrated during the war; thus Wen Fu's violence and Japanese war crimes are presented such that they become parallel targets of Winnie's critique. While the Japanese are portrayed as invaders of Chinese territory and murderers of tens of thousands of innocent civilians, the Americans are presented as trustworthy allies of the Chinese and are therefore marked for praise, of whom Jimmy makes just one example. Similarly, while Winnie's Chinese husband is depicted as a monster, her American husband is characterized as a rescuing angel who embodies peace, justice, and love. While China was war-torn and famine-plagued, crowded with "taonan" people – citizens turned into refugees on their own land, America, by contrast, was the land of hope and prosperity where war was conspicuously absent; hence a desired destination of diasporic relocation for war victims like Winnie and Helen.

The eulogistic representations of America and critical portrayals of China led some Asian American critics to question the Orientalist overtones in the works of Tan, fueling the debate among Asian Americans between nationalism and feminism. While Kingston bears the brunt of these criticisms, Tan has not been spared. In an essay provocatively titled "This Is Not an Autobiography," Frank Chin voices his anger at several Chinese American writers who, he believes, orientalize China, Chinese, and Chinese Americans: "All characterize Chinese history and culture in terms of Christian stereotype and tell of the same Cinderella story of rescue from the perverse, unnatural, and cruel Chinese into the one true universe" (110). "The true universe" is presumably America. And although Chin was yet to include Tan in this group in several other essays he published years later, this criticism already anticipated her who, in *Kitchen God*, presents nothing less than a Chinese "Cinderella story of rescue": Winnie was not only named (and was therefore given a new identity) but was literally rescued by Jimmy Louie from the evil claws of "the perverse, the unnatural, and cruel Chinese" Wen Fu.

Kingston and Tan seem to have followed different cultural and literary traditions from Chin and his *Aiiieeeee!* colleagues, who enthusiastically study, appropriate, and disseminate what Chin calls "the heroic tradition" rooted in classic Chinese and Japanese literature, in opposition to the so-called tradition of the Christian autobiography that usually adopts the confessional first-person singular in narration. On the other hand, Sau-ling Cynthia Wong finds an anti-Orientalist strain in both *Kitchen God* and *Joy Luck*. As she argues, Tan, while consciously and/or unconsciously orientalizing the mother and China, offers "occasional anti-Orientalist statements made by the characters" (181). These anti-Orientalist statements constitute a device to attract readers:

> Specifically, for the feminist audience, the Chinese American mother/daughter dyad in *The Joy Luck Club* and *The Kitchen God's Wife* allegorizes a Third World/First World encounter that allows mainstream American feminism to construct itself in a flattering, because depoliticized, manner – an outcome unlikely to be delivered

by mother-daughter stories penned by writers from Euro-American traditions. (181)

In *Kitchen God* Winnie's entire narrative builds up to a story of liberation of one particular woman – herself. And as her American name foretells, she would emerge from her ordeals triumphant as a victor. Her former husband even dies before her, which literally sets her free and makes her a real survivor. In the story of Kitchen God, Zhang's wife tries to rescue her fallen husband from being burnt (suggestive of a hellish punishment), but in her own life situation Winnie wished many times that Wen Fu was dead so that she would achieve freedom from his abusive control. But Wen Fu entertained no thought of letting her go because, like Leonce Pontellier in Kate Chopin's *The Awakening*, he never doubted for a moment that he had proprietary rights over his wife *because* he was a man, or *the* man. This ownership, not partnership, dominates their relationship. The patrilinear system, informed and supported by the Confucian doctrine that stipulates that the husband is the head of the wife, endows the man with power over the woman. Even the Buddhist God, the Jade Emperor, is partial towards men because of his indifference to women's predicament of victimization. So the root of the problem, for both farmer Zhang's wife and Winnie, is not Kitchen God, who, according to Winnie's definition, "was not too important. Not like Buddha, not like Kwan Yin, goddess of mercy – not that high level, not even the same level as the Money God. Maybe he was like a store manager, important, but still many, many bosses above him" (87). Unimportant as he may be, Kitchen God was charged to watch over all families' behavior and report his observations to the Jade Emperor who would then deal out rewards and punishments accordingly. So from his inception as Kitchen God, he was appointed to a political office and was revered by people like Auntie Du. Winnie, on the other hand, realizing Wen Fu's similarities to Kitchen God, lost all respect for the god; this loss in turn creates a spiritual void that needs filling.

Like Edna Pontellier, Winnie did not have a mother to raise her and after her marriage, she was taught by her mother-in-law "how to be a good wife" and "how to be dutiful to a terrible person" (291). The absence of the mother in literature, from Shakespeare's *King Lear* to Henrik Ibsen's *A Doll's House*, from Chopin's *The Awakening* to Morrison's *Bluest Eye* and now Tan's *Kitchen God*, seems to be a persistent subplot. The mother's absence is in and of itself a poignant commentary on women's plight in general where they are often victimized in forms ranging from marginalization to madness to disappearance or death. Interestingly enough, in all the above-mentioned works, the fathers survive the mothers. King Lear is left with three daughters and struggles to rule his kingdom and maintain his fatherly and kingly authority. In *A Doll's House*, Nora Helmer's father died later than his wife and Torvald Helmer makes no bones about laying the blame of what he perceives to be his wife's irresponsibility on her dead mother, not the father. In *The Awakening*, Edna's father unwittingly coerced his wife into an early grave without even knowing it, and ironically, he coached his son-in-law Leonce to be strict with his wife, suggesting the use of force on his own daughter if necessary. In his father-in-law's opinion, Leonce lacked the manhood to exercise male authority, and that manhood is sustained by an ability and willingness to resort to force. As Viet Thanh Nguyen's critique of Gus Lee's *China Boy* indicates, a young man's successful completion of a struggle to establish manhood "culminates in the assumption of patriarchy itself, meaning the establishment of one's own authority recognized by the state" (246). Ironically, Leonce never seemed to be able to establish such a coercive manhood and assumed a weak patriarchal role despite his desire to control his wife under his roof.

Like Ibsen's play and Chopin's novel, *Kitchen God* looks into intergenerational relationships to examine the effects of such connections. Winnie's situation, for example, is linked to her mother, who committed an unforgivable act and became a family disgrace that only death seems able to dissolve. Born into a rich family and influenced by Western, modern thought, Winnie's mother did not bind her feet, a fact that in itself violated the gender code of her era. Judging by the time of the narrated events, Winnie's mother was born in the late nineteenth century and went to a missionary school in 1897 in Shanghai. That she attended school suggests that she grew up in an enlightened family and must have been one of the few highly privileged women of the time. According to Tani Barlow in "Theorizing Woman," "A rash of masculinist interest in the universal sign of woman had surfaced as early as the 1830s"; by the 1860s interest in the male/female relations in Western countries also developed; and by the late 1890s – the decade when Winnie's mother attended a missionary school – there appeared "antifoot-binding and profemale academy arguments" (138), which necessarily provided stimulus for women who sought new modes of life and desired new roles to play other than within the parameters of the kitchen and the bedroom. The last decade of the nineteenth century marked the beginning of feminist awakening for women like Winnie's mother, though the number of awakened women was rather limited.

In the beginning years of the twentieth century, however, it would still be rare for a woman not to bind her feet. Women like Winnie's mother were generally called "new women"; or in Winnie's own words, a "modern girl" (167); or in the language of the revolutionaries – communists and nationalists alike – a liberated woman. Barlow's review of the Chinese feminist movement explains how Chinese women in general have been treated and classified according to their age and changing roles from the late Qing dynasty to the post-Mao era. The different terms designating women in Chinese are quite revealing about their social, political, and marital status. For example, *funü* is the most common term for women, though as Barlow points out, it is a term greatly politicized by the government as a statist concept. *Fu* literally means wife; *nü*, daughter or girl; and *mu*, mother; *nüren*, as opposed to *nanren*, is a more sexually connotative term meaning woman or female. Winnie performed all of these roles in the life of a female: from a *nü* (daughter) to a *fu* (wife) and then to a *mu* (mother) – a full cycle of a traditional woman's evolving roles, all of which confirm her sexual identity as a *nüren* (female), as opposed to *nanren*, a male. So did Winnie's mother, the liberated woman who refused to bind her feet, which places her squarely in the category of rebellious/liberated women with pro-Western and anti-Confucian strains of thinking.

This labeling of her entails two different interpretations of women's role in early twentieth-century China: the traditional woman and the new woman.[5] The new woman, by entering the public domain, distinguished herself from women *en masse* who were confined to their feminine roles in the private domain (usually the home) and who continued to perform functions stipulated for them by males, while walking falteringly on tiny bound feet, a deformed symbol and signifier of traditional womanhood. The new woman started to dress in Western-style clothing that obviously was already a provocative dressing code in the eyes of traditionalists. Apart from refusing to bind her feet, the new woman went to school, while a school education had been almost exclusively a male privilege in pre-twentieth-century China. Many of these modern women turned out to be family rebels or joined the revolutionary ranks, as Little Yu's mother and Peanut did in *Kitchen God*. In their rebellion they emulated historical Chinese heroines as role models, a feminist theme of women's liberation that has been explored extensively in China's proletarian literature since the 1930s. Hua Mulan, a millennia-old folkloric character who has been utilized by feminists and communists alike and who is the prototype for Kingston's *The Woman Warrior*, is again a case in point. The highly influential Chinese ballet drama first staged in the 1950s, *The Red Army of Women*, narrates the heroic story of women joining the Red Army in the 1920–30s when oppression of women was unbearably rampant.[6]

Women joining the Red Army is a reified instance of rebellion partly inspired by Hua Mulan's heroics, but it represents a consciousness of self-determination in regard to their rights as women. To simply leave home or join the revolutionary ranks is the first step taken toward independence and liberation: Nora Helmer and Edna Pontellier both depart from their husbands' home and control, in late nineteenth-century Norway and America respectively. Winnie's mother, apparently a liberated, new woman, turned a rebel against her family and sought "free love" outside her arranged marriage. She appreciated her own looks – she narcissistically looked in a mirror every night – as a way of projecting or maintaining confidence and reaffirming her self-identity. This narcissistic act seems to emphasize her self-worth as a person and a woman. And yet the value of her womanhood was severely compromised by being forced to become the second wife of a rich merchant; she was even called "Double Second" because the merchant's original second wife had committed suicide and he married Winnie's mother to replace her. This demeaning vocative, much like the red letter A on Hester Prynne's chest, serves as a stigma that at best partially evokes the past of its bearer and is intended to shape the public's perception of the stigmatized, which in turn contributes to the consolidation of patriarchal control of the woman, who was doubly discriminated against because of her dual, and now dubious, identity.

This dual identity, like double chains on a prisoner, deprives Winnie's mother of her freedom and compels her to seek happiness and personal gratification from a man whom she had loved before her marriage to the merchant. Her mother's mysterious disappearance occasioned Winnie's relocation to Tsungming Island, where, Old Aunt told her, her mother had been buried. However, while there was a burial, the family did not hold funeral services for her, which suggests that the family withheld respect and recognition for her most likely due to her moral and sexual transgressions that, in their perception, disgraced the family, exactly like the fate of No Name Woman in Kingston's *The Woman Warrior*. Old Aunt thus by necessity became a surrogate mother to Winnie and inculcated into the young girl her own pristine understanding of a female's role in the home and in society at large, insisting that women should not be educated in schools, but rather by older women as to how to behave properly, and in a womanly way.

In pre-twentieth-century Chinese history, there were two fundamentally different types of education – education of males (and only the elite few) in the school sense, geared toward a public career outside the home, and "education" of females for use within the domestic sphere. As Tani Barlow's critique of the eighteenth-century Chinese scholar Chen Hongmou indicates, "Chen Hongmou sought to educate women in order to produce more xiannü or virtuous 'women' and thereby enhance the jia [home], that is all. Learning to act virtuously is coterminous with acting 'like a woman' in Chen Hongmou's view" (136). This so-called education of women is more properly an indoctrination of male chauvinistic, male-defined conduct code for women, a kind of training in deportment that has nothing to do with the acquisition of literacy but everything to do with practical knowledge, personal conducts, and social etiquette. The fact that almost all women in Chen's time had bound feet undergirds the theory Chen championed: working inside and around the house, a woman is not supposed or allowed to travel far beyond the boundaries of the home, which often constitutes the immovable center of her world; and anything she does will be measured and evaluated against her level of performance at home as daughter, as wife, and finally, as mother.

Old Aunt's philosophy and principles of life were informed and dictated by nothing save the Confucian doctrine that women are virtuous when they are devoid of literacy and talents,[7] which problematically contradicts Confucius's own insistence that "In instruction there is no separation into categories" (you jiao wu lei) (137).[8] Confucius's emphasis on self-perfection through education has been applauded universally, especially in East Asian countries, and more generally in other parts of the world. But only a minority of Chinese historically have been willing to fault the ancient thinker on his extremely prejudiced views on women. Confucius's well-known motto – instructing without separating categories – regardless of its high-sounding rhetoric, clearly does not include women, so "no separation" truly only applied to males. On one occasion, the world-famous educator, talking about compensation for his teaching, says, "I have never denied instruction to anyone who, of his own accord, has given me so much as a bundle of dried meat as a present" (86). Either because no woman had offered dried meat to him in exchange for his instruction, or Confucius refused to grant women this boon, he was not recorded to have had any female students in his influential teaching career. His anti-woman, if not misogynistic, strain of thinking and practice has bequeathed a 2,500-year-long legacy to China and the world, a glaring fact demonstrable in late twentieth-century Asian American writing in the US – a country that may well be the least influenced by Confucianism due to its historico-geographical distance from China and, more importantly, to a democratic system that has overall effectively resisted any despotic system characterized by Confucian advocacy of patriarchal rule.

This legacy lives on in the thinking of Old Aunt, who blames Winnie's mother's deviation on Western-style education. As she lectures Winnie about her mother:

> "Her education was the cause," Old Aunt would say. "They put Western thoughts into a Chinese mind, causing everything to ferment. It is the same way eating foreign food – upset stomach, upset mind. The foreign teachers want to overturn all order in the world. Confucius is bad, Jesus is good! Girls can be teachers, girls do not have to marry. For what purpose do they teach this? Upside-down thinking! – that's what got her into trouble." (171)

Thus Confucian teaching helped erect a formidable wall of resistance against invasion of new thought, foreign or not. Old Aunt accepts Confucian teaching without questioning its gendered biases and uncritically holds Western-style education accountable for Winnie's mother's moral downfall and demise. In a way she is right because education empowered Winnie's mother and enabled her to rid herself of ignorance and realize her unhappy predicament, and this realization steered her life in a direction that uneducated, ignorant/illiterate women would probably not take.

Winnie, conversely, traces the root of her mother's problems to Confucius, not her western-style education: "Her daughter could take care of her into her old age. That's what Confucius would have said. I don't know why everyone always thought Confucius was so good, so wise. He made everyone look down on someone else, *women were the worst!*" (173; emphasis added). This anti-Confucian articulation, through the mouth of a Chinese American woman in her seventies, indirectly affirms the value of Western education and the urgency of women's liberation. It has seldom been disputed that Confucius's emphasis on social and familial hierarchy lends an expedient philosophical rationale to advocates of social order and governmental/patriarchal authority, where government and patriarchy are complicitous and reinforce each other. When citizens/subjects of a state are properly stationed in their prescribed positions determined by the amount of power they have, hierarchy becomes inevitable, which in turn lends theory and facilitates practice for the ease of family and state governance.

In his at once famous and notorious answer to Duke Ching of Ch'i's question about government, Confucius says: "Let the ruler be a ruler, the subject a subject, the father a father, the son a son" (114). Blatant is the omission of women in this biased political discourse regarding state and family governance; conspicuous, too, is the absence of women in his vision for an ideal state;[9] and unequivocal is his advocacy of hierarchy for the expediency of running family and state affairs. In this hierarchy men and senior members perch on the top rungs of the social ladder while women and children occupy the lowest rungs. In this tightly structured social fixture, any attempt to violate the hierarchical order is perceived as transgressive and is therefore punishable. Winnie's mother was supposed to stay obediently in her feminine, wifely, and motherly roles, despite pressures from all sides caused by four wives vying for the attention of one husband whom she did not love. But when she chose the dangerous path of rebellion – a transgressive affront that defied the hierarchical order that represented and favored male authority – familial and social ostracization became inevitable.

The story performed in the ballet drama *The Red Army of Women* took place around the time Winnie grew up in the 1930s, when women started to question the subordinate position they were in. The cause of women's marginalization and subordination was not merely the high-handed rule of men over them, but also the end result of women's own acquiescence, as Old Aunt's criticism of Winnie's mother quoted earlier suggests. The way Winnie was brought up – "I did not know I was supposed to be angry. This was China. A woman had no right to be angry" (285) – is illuminating. Despite the oversimplification of the issue implicit in this statement, Winnie shows her daughter Pearl how a woman, especially a young wife, has to be silent in order to fit the bill of an obedient, good wife, and to fulfill the expectations of housekeeping and child-bearing responsibilities while remaining useful to parents-in-law and sexually available to the husband. The powerlessness of women is evident in the fact that there is no legal way wives can stop men from taking in other women as concubines or mistresses.

Kitchen God portrays men's privileges to emphasize the hardships of women, complicated by war, and worse yet, by the oppressive institution of patriarchy. For example, on their perilous journey to Kunming, fatigue and malnutrition affected Winnie's pregnancy and resulted in a stillbirth. But significantly, Winnie made it a point to look at her dead child and gave her a meaningful name: "Mochou, Sorrowfree, because she had never known even one sorrow" (428). The naming is significant because it is a self-consoling act on the part of Winnie in that Mochou, now dead, would not have to grow up suffering and abused as did Winnie herself; it is also important because it initiates a creative process of a search for a goddess, and counteracts the pulling down of Kitchen God, who represents males and invokes the suffering of women. The name also serves as the title of the last chapter of the novel, where Winnie resumes her narrative after Pearl's interruption to describe Bao-Bao's wedding in chapter twenty-five, which, like the first two chapters, is narrated by Pearl. These special chapters all perform symbolic and structural functions that provide a narrative frame that lends centripetal force to the contents of the book: the two opening chapters focus on gods, males, and destructive images such as death; the closing chapters accomplish the very opposite: one deals with a happy, productive occasion – Bao-Bao's wedding – and the other, "Sorrowfree," focuses on the construction of a female, not a male, identity.

In "Bao-Bao's Wedding" Winnie's big secret eventually comes out and Pearl finally realizes that her biological father was not the good-hearted minister Jimmy Louie, but the heartless rapist Wen Fu. Winnie's fear has not been so much the exposure of the secret itself as the concern that her daughter would develop her biological father's bad characteristics. Winnie comments on the development of a child's character:

> "Of course, every baby is born with *yin* and *yang*. The *yin* comes from the woman. The *yang* comes from the man. When you were born I tried to see whose *yang* you had. I tried to see your daddy. I would say, Look, she has Jimmy Louie's smile. I tried to forget everything else. But inside my heart I saw something else."
>
> . . . . . "You looked like Mochou. You looked like Yiku. You looked like Danru, Danru especially. All of them together." (709)

Yiku and Danru, Winnie's second and third child by Wen Fu, both died in childhood. Their names, like Mochou's, are symbolic and harbor Winnie's painful memories. While Yiku was being born in the hospital, her father Wen Fu was raping their servant girl at home. Winnie's name for Yiku, "pleasure over bitterness" (455–6), may either sarcastically refer to Wen Fu's lustful pleasure with other women over her own suffering, or express her wish that her daughter would grow up happy, unaware that she would die before even reaching adulthood.

Wen Fu's indifference toward the birth or death of Yiku, his daughter, contrasts starkly with his tenderness toward Danru, a son; in fact, he treasured him *because* he was a male descendant of his: a son would carry on his family's name, insuring the continuity of the male side of the family clan and fulfilling a Confucian expectation of filial piety by giving his family a male offspring. Winnie on the other hand again took up the role of a namer[10] and named the son with Taoistic resignation and indifference – Danru: "nonchalance" (474). The birth of Danru was followed by the arrival of Min, the real-life counterpart of the woman farmer Zhang brought home before he was made Kitchen God. The son, whom his mother wanted to protect – perhaps superstitiously – with a symbolic name, survived infancy but was killed in an epidemic carried by rats caused by chemicals left by the Japanese during the eight-year-long war, precisely the number of years Winnie's marriage with Wen Fu lasted. The 1945 ending of the Sino-Japanese war coincided with the *de facto* dissolution of their ill-matched marriage. Their married life was therefore implicitly likened to a long, devastating war.

As the war ends and the marriage dissolves, the novel draws to a close and the narrative returns full circle to its point of departure: accepting an invitation to Bao-Bao's wedding in chapter one, and attending it in chapter twenty-five; in between are the historical events that lead up to the formation of family secrets that require disclosure called for by the narrative closure. But Pearl's revelation of her MS is not the final disclosure of all secrets,[11] for Helen has one of her own to share, that is, she does not have a brain tumor: the tumor has been her own fabrication prompted by her declining health. Since Helen is privy to both Winnie's and Pearl's secrets, her possible death would mean taking those secrets to the grave, and yet she does not want to die and forget to thank Winnie for her friendship. Because of the sharing of secrets, mother and daughter are brought closer, for which Helen attempts to claim credit. But she wants to perfect her accomplishment with a new secret: she tells Pearl that curing her brain tumor was the original reason that they were planning a trip to China where she would be treated, but now that she is sure she has no tumor she wants to keep Winnie from knowing the real reason for the planned trip so that they can still go and pretend that the magic spring in China cured her – the same medicine that, according to Helen, can cure Pearl of her MS. The trip to China will therefore benefit all three women both psychologically and therapeutically, accompanied by a firm belief that a return to the root (the homeland) of the problems would help solve them as well.

The sentimental ending of *Kitchen God* is reminiscent of *Joy Luck*, where the daughter Jing-mei takes an emotional trip to China on behalf of her late mother. *Kitchen God* does not dispatch such a trip but offers instead a detailed itinerary of one. Apparently the trip to China will be just for Pearl's MS, but it will also be a trip with a goodwill mission to further cement their friendship and female bonding. This part of the novel is the least Orientalistic, even Occidentalistic: regardless of what medical research may say, Pearl's MS cannot be efficaciously treated with Western medicine – implying a lack of trust in it – and even though Chinese traditional medicine is legally listed as a last alternative, it is a welcome solution, deeply rooted in belief, to Winnie and Helen, two elderly Chinese women who grew up believing in the healing power of Chinese herbs. In their hearts, Pearl's MS is curable only in China, where the roots of their problems are, as well as the roots of their ethnic identity.

The framing events of the novel – Auntie Du's death and funeral, Bao-Bao's wedding, and the sharing of secrets – now help frame the messages, feminist, anti-Confucianist, and reconciliatory. The friendship of Winnie and Helen is strengthened, and the mother-daughter bond between Winnie and Pearl is renewed and deepened. This happy and celebratory atmosphere wafts into the final chapter, "Sorrowfree" – named for Mochou – which represents the turning over of a new leaf and focally describes the naming of a new identity. "Sorrowfree" again utilizes Winnie as narrator. The daughter begins the story and the mother ends it. Such a collaborative narrative tactic not only simulates the inseparability of mother and daughter but also reaffirms the importance of relationships. Helen, on the other hand, seems to have finally matured and gained self-knowledge in her advanced years. Wen Fu dies around the time of Auntie Du's death, suggesting the end of an abusive era and the dawning of a new one, and symbolically marking the death of Kitchen God, with whom he has shared one evil identity, as well as the beginning of real freedom for Winnie. When Winnie realizes the marathon she has been running to achieve freedom and happiness is undoubtedly coming to an end, and after learning of her daughter's MS, she is angry and sad and finally takes action:

And then I saw that picture of Kitchen God, watching me, smiling, so happy to see me unhappy. I took his picture out of the frame. I put it over my stove. "You go see Wen Fu! You go to hell down below!" I watched his smiling face being eaten up by the fire. . . . But then I listened again. And I knew: This was not Wen Fu's ghost. This was like a bingo blackout. This was like a Reno jackpot. This was Kitchen God's wife, shouting, Yes! Yes! Yes! (734)

This iconoclastic act occurs in one of the most revealing passages of the novel. One may recall how farmer Zhang betrayed his wife and became

Kitchen God by the decree of the Jade Emperor. Winnie's first husband embodies, in flesh and blood, the cruelty and depth of evil, and now she realizes the only way to get even with him is to destroy Kitchen God by purging Wen Fu of her life as well as of her memory. She subverts her earlier story of farmer Zhang in which he ascended and was made a god, and exacts her revenge by burning Kitchen God in effigy and telling him to join Wen Fu. This is the point where Wen Fu and Kitchen God merge into one and are punished as one, and where Kitchen God's wife separates herself from her husband to create her own identity. The destruction of old, bad, male gods calls for the creation of new types of divinities. As the principal victim characters are all women oppressed by men and gods, Winnie finally decides that she needs a goddess – a divinity of her own sex – to represent herself and her daughter. Therefore on a shopping trip she buys a porcelain statue that is special and represents women.

Kitchen God both opens and closes its narrative with the image of a store, a place for transactions and change. In the store that sells statues, Winnie finds all kinds of statues but none that she wants for Pearl. She wants a goddess that nobody knows, so she ends up buying a "mistake" – a nice statue on the bottom of whose chair the factory forgot to write down a name. This oversight on the part of the factory conveniently – and perhaps intentionally on the part of the novelist – provides an opportunity to Winnie who, for the fifth time in her life, exercises the power of naming. This opportunity and the power attendant on it hold a great deal of political significance for her. While the statue is a present meant for Pearl, Winnie's description of it seems a proper commentary on her own newfound self: "Look at her hair, how black it is, no worries. Although maybe she used to worry. I heard she once had many hardships in her life. So maybe her hair is dyed" (737). This description seems to have sprung from a newly obtained peace of mind and psychological freedom made possible by the death of Wen Fu; it also invokes Mochou who never had a life and whom Winnie is determined to remember in her own way – by naming the porcelain statue Lady Sorrowfree. In this act of naming, Winnie achieves the power of a Jade Emperor while displacing him with a female identity, a goddess who understands English and who listens and washes away sad things with her tears. The statue is thus uniquely Chinese American and represents a Chinese American female subjectivity.

All her life, Winnie has been subjected to the despotic commands of men – father and husband – and has had limited freedom as a woman. To undo the victimization and become a victor, to alleviate the pain she has suffered,

Winnie fights her past by investing in the present. Instead of burning down the house as Bertha Rochester did in Brontë's *Jane Eyre*, or drowning herself in the sea as Edna Pontellier did in Chopin's *The Awakening*, or drowning herself in the family well as No Name Woman did in Kingston's *The Woman Warrior*, or walking out on her husband as Nora Helmer did in Ibsen's *A Doll's House*, Winnie, like Hester in Hawthorne's *The Scarlet Letter*, is resolved to succeed in raising Pearl, also Wen Fu's biological daughter, to be entirely her own, by assuming the role of a namer and creator of goddess. The novelist, on the other hand, in this explicitly feminist, anti-sexist work, indicts Wen Fu and Kitchen God, while taking jabs at Confucius and the male hegemony.

Confucius's contributions – in education, morality, ethics, government, law, and philosophy – are towering, but his overt sexist discrimination against women is subjected to vigorous critique in Tan's novel, where power differentials between men and women are scrutinized. In men's mistreatment of women Confucius has played a conspicuously powerful role. So, subverting texts such as *King Lear* (Lear), *The Awakening* (Edna's father), and *A Doll's House* (Nora's father) where the man survives the wife, Tan's *Kitchen God* has the wife survive the husband and endows her with creative power so she indeed becomes a winner in the end. And Tan, in having a woman pull down Kitchen God, also incriminates Confucius, one of Chinese culture's greatest gods.

NOTES

1. See Tan's "Lost Lives of Women."
2. In defining God, god, and goddess, I referred to *Webster's New Universal Unabridged Dictionary* (New York: Barnes & Noble, 1996) for their basic denotations and connotations. The dictionary provides seven meanings of God as a noun: 1. the one Supreme Being, the creator and ruler of the universe; 2. the Supreme Being considered with reference to a particular attribute: the God of Islam; 3. (l.c.) one of several deities, esp. a male deity, presiding over some portion of worldly affairs; 4. (often l.c.). a supreme being according to some particular conception: the god of mercy; 5. Christian Science. The Supreme Being, understood as Life, Truth, Love, Mind, Soul, Spirit, Principle; 6. (l.c.) an image of a deity; an idol; 7. (l.c.) any deified person or object (817). Three fundamental meanings are given for goddess: 1. a female god or deity; 2. a woman of extraordinary beauty and charm; 3. a greatly admired or adored woman (818).
3. Winnie's marriage to Wen Fu was arranged and therefore she did not choose her own husband. Her acquaintance with Jimmy Louie affords her an opportunity to love and eventually marry him.

4. "Taonan," used as an adjective by Tan, is a verbal phrase in Chinese. "Tao" literally means escape or avoid, and "nan" refers to disasters, ordeals, and hardships, especially war and famine. In *Kitchen God*, "taonan" refers to desperate efforts to avoid the war by escaping to safer, more affluent places.

5. "New woman", "modern woman", and "liberated woman" are often interchangeable synonyms.

6. The theme song of the drama, also very popular for a half century, opens with these lines: "March on, march on! Heavy is soldiers' onus and deep is women's suffering. Just as there was Hua Mulan in ancient times, there is an army of women today." The song became common knowledge and remains familiar to many today.

7. This notion is occasionally still echoed axiomatically on the lips of some twentieth-century men: "Virtuous is the woman who has no talent" (*nuzi wucai bian shi de*).

8. Lau's translation. An alternative translation could read, "I do not distinguish between the kinds of people I teach."

9. Another example of Confucius's extreme bias against women is a comment he made in response to King Wu's statement that he had ten "capable officials": "With a woman amongst them, there were, in fact, only nine" (95). Confucius denied that a woman can be a capable official so he unapologetically discounted her.

10. It should be noted that Wen Fu as father of four children named none of them while Winnie gave each of them a name, indicating that she has the power of naming.

11. Three major secrets can be found in the novel: Winnie's secret from Pearl that Wen Fu is Pearl's biological father; Pearl's secret from her mother that she has MS; and Helen's secret from Winnie that she does not actually have a brain tumor.

WORKS CITED

Barlow, Tani. "Theorizing Woman: *Funu, Guojia, Jiating* [Chinese Women, Chinese State, Chinese Family]." *Genders* 10 (Spring 1991): 132–60.

Chin, Frank. "This Is Not an Autobiography." *Genre* 18 (Summer 1985): 109–30.

Chopin, Kate. *The Awakening*. New York: Avon Books, 1972.

Confucius. *The Analects*. Trans. D. C. Lau. London: Penguin Books, 1979.

Hawthorne, Nathaniel. *The Scarlet Letter*. New York: Penguin Books, 1983.

Hawthorne, Nathaniel. *The Blithedale Romance*. Ed. William E. Cain. Boston: Bedford Books, 1996.

Ibsen, Henrik. *A Doll's House. The Riverside Anthology of Literature*, 2nd ed. Ed. Douglas Hunt. Boston: Houghton Mifflin, 1991. 1197–1261.

Kingston, Maxine Hong. *The Woman Warrior: Memoirs of a Girlhood Among Ghosts*. New York: Vintage International, 1989.

Lowe, Lisa. "Heterogeneity, Hybridity, Multiplicity: Marking Asian American Differences." *Diaspora* 1.1 (Spring 1991): 24–44.

Morrison, Toni. *The Bluest Eye*. New York: Washington Square Press, 1972.

Nguyen, Viet Thanh. "The Remasculization of Chinese America: Race, Violence, and the Novel." *American Literary History* 12.1–2 (Spring 2000): 130–57.

Tan, Amy. *The Joy Luck Club*. New York: Ballantine Books, 1989.

Tan, Amy. *The Kitchen God's Wife*. Thorndike, ME: Thorndike Press, 1991.

Tan, Amy. "Lost Lives of Women." *Life* (April 1991): 90–91.

Wong, Sau-ling Cynthia. "'Sugar Sisterhood': Situating the Amy Tan Phenomenon." *The Ethnic Canon: Histories, Institutions, and Interventions*. Ed. David Palumbo-Liu. Minneapolis: University of Minnesota Press, 1995. 174–210.

CHAPTER 7

Realigning and Reassigning Cultural Values: Occidentalist Stereotyping and Representations of the Multiethnic Family in Asian American Women Writers

Tamara Silvia Wagner

The popular two-plot or multi-plot novel that connects culture clashes not only to generation conflicts but also to gender issues by juxtaposing the "exotic" past of an earlier immigrant generation with predominantly sentimental, yet frequently self-ironic, representations of cross-cultural relationships and family structures in the United States, has become a recognizable and vehemently criticized subgenre of Asian American fiction. Despite the recurring criticism of its promotion of stereotypes, its neatly streamlined sets of dualities, and its deliberate marketing of what can all too easily lapse into self-exoticization, however, it has not been subjected to the rigorous critical analysis it requires, and in fact deserves, as an important literary development. The functions of occidentalist stereotyping have been almost completely ignored. Yet, occidentalism as the counterpoint, or mirror-version, of orientalism structures the majority of domestic plots in these multi-plot novels. Value systems are negotiated and realigned precisely by being assigned to specific ethnic types. The eccentric and embarrassing Chinese-born mother or old auntie, the embarrassing non-Asian boyfriend or husband, the difficult hybrid offspring – and, it is almost routinely suggested, difficult because hybrid – figure as embodiments of places, ethnicities, and cultural problematics. Often paired with a neo-orientalist repackaging of ethnicity, occidentalist projections of exoticism on non-Asian family members negotiate the impasses, but also the new potentials of ethnic minority fiction. In taking a closer look at a range of recent novels by Asian American women writers, this chapter seeks to cast a different light on the ways in which the multiethnic family is being imagined and embodied.

The main emphasis will rest on the changing ways in which representations of domesticity and specifically "ethnic" food are inflected by hybridity within the family. First of all, a brief analysis of the influence exerted by Maxine Hong Kingston's controversial *The Woman Warrior* and Amy Tan's *The Joy Luck Club* on more recent fiction will help to outline recurring *topoi* or clichés that at times undoubtedly indicate a certain sameness, but have become increasingly central as subjects of critical dissection, even self-parody. In a series of close readings, together with a discussion of neo-orientalism and Asian American occidentalism, I will focus specifically on the typecasting of ethnic communities and the representation of cross-cultural experience within the family, yet with additional emphasis on the marketing of cultural hybridity as a popular plot device. The following analyses will further explore the micropolitics of embarrassment that dominate the representations of the multiethnic family in the domestic plots or subplots of the analyzed texts. Tan's later novels will be shown to transcend the most overused methods of cultural stereotyping. They lead Asian American fiction to new heights, as an almost self-parodying irony circumvents much of the criticized sensationalism and sentimentality.

Such revisionist works dismiss easy polarizations to address the burdens as well as potentials of cultural hybridity. As they expose both orientalist and occidentalist preconceptions as discursively constituted conceptualizations, the value and composition of different ways of understanding authenticity are, in fact, usefully drawn into question. In what is perhaps one of the most revealing, even ironic, self-referential passages in recent Asian American novels, two protagonists of Tan's *The Kitchen God's Wife*, for example, discuss the popularity of "exotic" victimization. Helen's advice to her friend Winnie capitalizes on the appeal wartime China has for an American audience, often including the victims' own children: "They'll understand. Maybe they'll be happy to know something about their mother's background. Hard life in China, that's very popular now."[1] Like Helen, Winnie is an aging Chinese immigrant whose sensationalized past is poised against a thin frame story that details the daily realities of her Asian American daughter's multiethnic family. Throughout the novel, comic descriptions of interlinked generation and culture clashes disrupt the harrowing evocations of World War II in a doubly remote Far East of the past. That a hard life in China is "very popular now" forms a self-ironic comment on the embedded lists of suffered atrocities that is at once disturbing and refreshing.

The novel's exploitation of exoticized, subaltern women is precisely what many diasporic novels have been accused of – the somewhat lopsided juxtaposition of past and present plots for which Tan, Kingston, and authors following in their wake have become most notorious. Tan's novels, in fact, increasingly revise the clear-cut dichotomies between past and present that characterize her early stories, and yet her attempts to dovetail the cultural hybridity of her Chinese American heroines with a reworking of their mothers' (or mother-figures') legacies of atrocity have irrevocably become just what her readership expects and hence wishes to buy. Nevertheless, the growing awareness of the past's marketability and, as a result, the desire to shatter expectations, to rework clichés critically and more creatively, has begun to displace a mere juggling with ready-made clichés. Helen's comical self-referentiality in *The Kitchen God's Wife* therefore provides a good point of entry to a new analysis of these clichés.

While there undoubtedly still are a number of newly emerging authors who continue an exoticizing typecasting as they feed on the steadily growing market for exotic afflictions, this movement towards a greater self-referentiality is without doubt the most interesting and also most promising development in Asian American fiction. As we shall see, many recent novels, apart from Tan's own, deliberately dissect and dismantle popular ways of typecasting to refine, redirect, but also intriguingly to redeploy the exotic appeal of previous publishing successes. The Malaysian-born Asian American writer and academic Shirley Geok-lin Lim, for example, has reworked some of the most persistent clichés of American multiculturalism and the problems of ethnic as well as cultural hybridity in her first novel, *Joss & Gold*. In aiming to shatter expectations, it strives to counteract not simply the prevailing stereotypes of beautiful Asian women encountering white males, but specifically the twofold repackaging of ethnicity that characterized the very marked marketing of her autobiography in the mid-nineties.

The memoir's two sets of subtitles, in fact, meaningfully externalize the ways in which complementary book markets are targeted through the growing popularity of marginality: *Among the White Moon Faces* was published as *An Asian American Memoir of Homelands* in New York, and as *Memoirs of a Nonya Feminist* in Singapore and Malaysia. It fed at once on and into a craze for multicultural autobiographies in America and a new interest in minority communities in Southeast Asia. The Baba-Nonya, or Peranakan ("locally-born"), community in Singapore and parts of Malaysia forms a unique culture that has grown out of intermarriages between Malays and immigrant Chinese over the centuries. Recently, its rapidly vanishing heritage has received renewed attention in the region, and Lim clearly speculated on that. By contrast, the community's uniqueness was largely erased from the ways in which "Asian Americanness" was marketed in the States.

Joss & Gold was likewise published simultaneously by Times Books International in Asia and the Feminist Press at the City University of New York; its recent publication similarly testifies to the marketability of minority writing both on the global marketplace and in the region. However, the novel negotiates a more critical awareness of the expected plots and clichés. Symptomatically, it starts with a description of racial conflicts in Southeast Asia in the late sixties and then stretches into the eighties, focusing first on an upmarket neighbourhood in New York and then detailing a returning American's brief sojourn in Singapore. After having been a long time in the making, it does not progress further than the eighties with their new ideals of multiculturalism, which are admittedly finely critiqued, yet no alternatives are offered. Instead, in a straightforward alignment of values, Li An's men serve to externalize her cultural hybridity. It is repeatedly stressed that she is "like a Western girl – bold, loud, and unconcerned about her reputation," and thus she is sandwiched between "such a China-type" (her husband) and a "hairy and sweaty" foreigner (her lover), an occidentalist stereotype of the bumbling "Westerner."[2] Most pointedly, her hopes of a multiethnic Malaysia are exposed in a tongue-in-cheek way as essentially foreign, "Western," the outgrowth of American neo-imperialism: "'Give us a few more years and we'll be a totally new nation. No more Malay, Chinese, Indian, but all one people.'" "'Hey, Lee Ann,' Chester [the bumbling American] said, beaming, 'you almost sound like an American.'"[3]

Most importantly, as it swerves away from a mere fictionalization of memories or mediated accounts, the novel circumvents the controversy about autobiography, authenticity, and fictionalized life-stories that has been central in the criticism of Asian American writing by women ever since Kingston's notorious "reuse" of Chinese myths in *The Woman Warrior*. In fact, as we shall see, in the wake of Kingston's autobiographical fiction and the "domestication" of her themes in Tan's sentimental interiors, the *Bildungsroman* of the female – frequently feminist – Asian (primarily Chinese) American has made the stories of the multicultural American hybrid first immensely popular and then common. The replication of favorite plot devices, including the pairing of past and present, domestic and exotic, and the central mother-daughter conflicts that cut across various generations, however, features alongside the leaning towards self-parody that has fascinatingly informed Tan's fiction from the beginning. The full-scale exploration of the writing and "ghost-writing" of inherited stories in her most recent fictional work, *The Bonesetter's Daughter*, is of course very far removed from the tentatively self-referential hints in her early works, and yet their presence casts an intriguing light on the absence of self-referentiality (not to say self-irony) from many imitative novels.

The following analyses will draw on a range of texts so as to reassess literary developments in the Asian American "female" novel with all its potentials and problems. If the majority of selected authors are ethnic Chinese as well as women writers, then this is by no means the result of a conscious exclusion. Instead, it has to do with the popularity of the domestic two-plot novel among female Chinese writers in the United States (as well as beyond), on which Kingston and Tan have perhaps expectedly exerted the most extensive and lasting influence. In addition – and this is surely significant – a rather disturbing tendency to subsume ethnic backgrounds has led to the inclusion of Southeast and North Asian writers. In this, they are in obvious opposition to ethnic American writers of Indian origins, most pervasively in their exclusion. Yet, it is precisely this self-subsuming conflation of "Asian" ethnicities that becomes increasingly critiqued. In *Joss & Gold*, for example, a performance of Puccini's *Madam Butterfly* triggers a chain reaction of guilt and renewed desire for the exotic in Chester. Ignorant of his orientalist dalliance, his American partner Meryl fails to understand his sudden obsession: "She could not see that a Japanese woman's suicide over a jerk like Pinkerton was in any way related to the Pentagon or to the boat people. It was a stretch, something academics invented for lack of more significant work."[4]

By contrast, in Lim's 1977 short story "A Pot of Rice," Su Yu's Asian alterity neatly re-merges as she cooks rice for an offering to her dead father in her New York apartment. She is locked in the "cold indifference of American winter," confronted with her confused non-Asian husband and her own conflation of Asian origins: "With her father's death there was no longer any reason to leave the city from whose harbour the Statue of Liberty seemed to gaze across the oceans to Singapore as if towards a giant Chinatown ghetto."[5] It is this erasure of specificities that readers in Asia as well as in various Asian diasporas (including the United States) object to most strongly when Asian American writing comes to be marketed globally. Residing in New York during her writing fellowship, Singaporean Hwee Hwee Tan, for example, made her novel *Mammon Inc.* play right into East-West dichotomies and the issues of Chinese American cultural hybridity. The clichés fail to be successfully counterpoised by the introduction of globalized urban Singapore later in the plot. Before I examine the representation of multiethnic families, together with their micropolitics of embarrassment, in various recent novels, I will therefore start with an outline of the problematics of self-exoticization in this growing subgenre of Asian American fiction.

MARKETING MULTICULTURALISM AND THE ENDS OF NEO-ORIENTALIST SELF-EXOTICIZATION

As Lim's choice of subtitles for her memoir adroitly repackages the author's identity, it all too beautifully exemplifies what Graham Huggan has recently termed "the alterity industry" in more than one sense.[6] The doubling of identities externalizes hybridity; its twofold naming is successful marketing. Significantly, Huggan's critique of a "postcolonial exotic" is directed against the common conflation of multicultural "exotic" fiction in both cultural studies as well as the book market. Hybridity as a new form of cosmopolitanism and a metaphor for postmodern writing – the hybrid genres of hybrid writers – has thus proliferated, reduplicated in critics' puns on doubling and halving. Nikos Papastergiadis has termed it a "multi-purpose globalising identity kit" that functions as "one of the most useful concepts for representing the meaning of cultural difference in identity."[7] Late twentieth-century diasporic, including Asian American, novels have as expected made much of this promising "identity kit" and its easy repackaging as "exotic" fiction. More recent literary criticism condemns precisely this selling out of identity politics. The revelation of the marginal alone is no longer enough. On the contrary, self-exoticization is increasingly regarded as dangerously involved in a marketing of alterity that can impel a disconcerting absorption of "exotic" marginality in mainstream neo-orientalism.

In a seminal examination of cultural value(s), Gayatri Chakravorty Spivak refers to the impasses of "alternative" canon formations that are after all premised on varieties of or variations upon old, realigned or simply inverted standards.[8] Ania Loomba similarly raises the pivotal question whether terms like "ethnic" and "postcolonial" have become "shorthand for something (fashionably) marginal," yet she does not engage further with the problems created by this marketing of the marginal.[9] In fact, in emphasizing what he terms the "postcolonial exotic," Huggan has perhaps accurately diagnosed an upcoming "alterity industry" built on "mechanics of exoticist representation/consumption."[10] His critique of postcoloniality's market-driven value critically re-examines the selling of alterity, including the diasporic writer's internalized sets of hybridized otherness.[11] Such critiques have become increasingly prevalent in recent years. As they focus on postcolonial literature's fluid boundaries, they extend their analyses to immigrant, or diasporic, fiction as well. As Bruce King puts it in his introduction to *New National and Post-Colonial Literatures* in the mid-nineties, it is necessary to establish a vital distinction between the writings of Commonwealth postcolonialism and those emerging from new diasporas, yet he simultaneously cautions against simplifying binaries that fail to account for significant developments.[12]

The newly created market for vaguely "multicultural" fiction that stretches across (and consequently tends to lump together) diasporic and globally distributed postcolonial literature has of course further contributed to a growing sameness in the selling of exoticized otherness. Literary criticism that praises authors first and foremost for their inclusion of maximum alterity, as it were, at the exclusion of other criteria, has helped to exacerbate this tendency. Published by Orion Press in London, *The Teardrop Story Woman* by the Singaporean novelist Catherine Lim, for example, was advertized as a version of Jung Chang's *Wild Swans: Three Daughters of China*.[13] Apart from an interest in the institutionalized, or commercialized, suppression of women (bondmaids in colonial Malaya and concubines in imperial China), there are very few similarities between the two novels. Such conflations of course facilitate the absorption of postcolonial products as generally "exotic" writing. Conversely, recent diasporic novels have capitalized on the postcolonial's growing popularity. An exotic backdrop can easily be mediated (perhaps most notoriously in the figure of the Chinese-born mother in Kingston's or Tan's novels). This "domestication" of past migrations in contemporary frame stories or subplots brings exoticism home, seemingly enriching the multicultural imaginary, while inadvertently promoting (self-)exoticization and even "ghettoization." As the main protagonist of *The Bonesetter's Daughter* remarks, the political correctness of cultural sensitivity, which diasporic fiction often not only seeks to promote but feeds on as a marketing device, can feel very much like the racial "ghettoization" that ethnic minorities have so long tried to overcome. In a hospital waiting room, Ruth Young is ill at ease as she notices the embarrassingly overt distribution of ethnicity: "Ruth saw that all the patients except one pale balding man, were Asian. . . . The balding man was glancing about, as if seeking an escape route."[14]

The drawbacks of such categorizations, together with their implicit conflation of alterities, have themselves become the subject of fiction. In Fiona Cheong's *Shadow Theatre*, Shakilah Nair returns temporarily to Singapore: pregnant, with no husband, but with a novel-in-progress that has, in her publisher's words, "too many voices."[15] She wishes to avoid using a Singaporean publisher, yet in order to sell her story in America she will have to capitalize on a targeted marketing of Asia's "exotic" stories: "Tell your editor this is how we tell stories. . . . Ask her to look at a piece of batik. Ah, that's what you should do, show her a piece of batik, how complicated and interwoven everything is."[16] Still, her efforts are carefully contrasted with those of the curious foreigner trying to cash in on exotic details to make himself more interesting abroad: "All he wanted was fodder for his letters home. . . . Using our own stories against us, . . . the foreigner thinks he can sound interesting to other people."[17] Yet, this is exactly what ethnic minority writers are regularly accused of as well.

In *Beyond Postcolonial Theory*, E. San Juan situates postcolonialism within the frameworks of the structural crisis of international capitalism to show the ways in which practices of consumerism inflect the multicultural imaginary more generally.[18] The "fashionable celebration of U.S. cultural diversity," he provocatively points out, is "mimicked if not surpassed by 'the united colors of Benetton,' the Body Shop's opportunism regarding indigenous peoples, and the 'strategic essentialism' of certain postcolonial celebrities."[19] His reading of *Redefining American Literary History*, edited by A. L. Brown Ruoff and Jerry Ward, partly anticipates Huggan's critique of the "postcolonial exotic." Shirley Lim's contribution, "Twelve Asian American Writers: In Search of a Self-Definition," San Juan suggests, is "[v]itiated by paltry essentialisms and indulgence in the Euro-American immigrant syndrome."[20] This "immigrant syndrome" connects diasporic fiction to the issues of postcolonialism, yet the revamping of stories of migration as part of multi-plot novels indicates at once their additional mediation (hence frequent allegations of inauthenticity) and, at times, their more imaginative (precisely because more distanced) engagement with the same *topoi*.

The subgenre of the domestic, "female," multi-plot Asian American novel, in fact, already forms the outgrowth of a twofold revision of ethnic canon formations in the post-assimilation multiculturalism of the United States. It is thus much more than simply a reaction to Anglo-American mainstream fiction. In her preface to Jessica Hagedorn's anthology *Charlie Chan Is Dead: An Anthology of Contemporary Asian American Fiction*, Elaine

Kim refers to her earlier study *Asian American Literature: An Introduction to the Writings and Their Social Context* as a crucial attempt to revise the canonization of exclusively male and ethnic Chinese American authors that was, by the early nineties, already in need of further revision. "A generation ago," Kim remarks, "I attempted to define Asian American literature as work in English by writers of Chinese, Filipino, Japanese, and Korean descent about U.S. American experiences. I admitted at the time that this definition was arbitrary."[21] She particularly deplores her exclusion of many Southeast Asian writers – a prevailing omission that has been remedied only recently by consciously specialized anthologies. As Shirley Lim and Cheng Lok Chua put it in *Tilting the Continent: Southeast Asian American Writing*, the specific multicultural histories imported by immigrants from variously, even multiply, colonized Southeast Asian nations tend to be submerged not only by mainstream cultures, but also by "the consciousness of the ethnic community now recognized as 'Asian Americans.'"[22] The recognition of their similar specificities constitutes a very recent phenomenon indeed, one that forms an important part of current reactions against the clear-cut dichotomies that have so far structured fictions of Asian American hybridities. However, before Kim, among others, endeavoured to bring out those women writers who promulgated this commonality, the Asian American novel had been canonized as the "frontier" novels of (in Kim's words) "dead yellow men," such as Carlos Bulosan's *America Is in the Heart*, John Okada's *No-No Boy*, and Louis Chu's *Eat a Bowl of Tea*.[23]

In sharp contrast to their negotiation of fixed masculinist Asian American identity, the final decades of the last century have brought forth explorations of migratory, hybrid, and fluid identities with all the paranoia and schizophrenia that emerge in their often self-consciously postmodern narratives. They bring gender problematics to the fore. Almost routinely couched in either culture or generation conflicts (usually both), they let familial issues assume center stage. Racial and other politics become reduced to a backdrop. By 1993, Kim was significantly able to exult over the onslaught of "dysfunctional families that bear no resemblance to the Charlie Chan version of 'Chinese family values,' tragic stories of suicide, incest, and child abuse, as well as bittersweet songs about aging, love, and death."[24] It was particularly the nineties, with its growing interest in "politics of identity" and hybridity as a newly appreciated "identity kit" for an age of globalization, that provided a fostering environment for the growth of ethnic American fiction. At the same time, the growth of Third World feminism created new interest in subaltern women. Consumers of mainstream fiction in the nineties looked for ethnic and/or feminist stories. The centrality of women in Chinese diasporic writing satisfied both demands.

Yet, as Asian American women writers set out to do something radically new, they also rediscovered long neglected works. Canonization could be rewritten. Most intriguingly, these resurrected narratives prefigured many preoccupations of the nineties – or at least, that was the way they were interpreted and marketed. Thus, Diana Chang's 1956 novel *The Frontiers of Love* was reissued in paperback in 1994. In her introduction to the new edition, Shirley Lim emphasizes Chang's anticipation of "themes, characters, actions, and stylistic textures [that] appear strikingly contemporary."[25] A novel about Eurasian women in wartime Shanghai, it foreshadowed the proliferation of "unnamed hybrids," "survivors of a colonialism that was fast becoming as antique as peace," as well as disillusioned comments on "the surface values of both East and West, and . . . the exoticism of the West."[26] In its emphasis on an ethnic hybridity that is not merely racial but also cultural, involved in a confusion of emulative and hostile occidentalism – an idealization of the exotic West and a condemnation of its imperialist ventures, *The Frontiers of Love* prefigured perhaps the most popular genres in a growing market of "exotic" fiction. Lim terms the novel at once an "analogue" and a "precursor" that addressed the "most contemporary debates on biculturality and biraciality."[27]

In a markedly similar vein, Shirley Lim's autobiography – published in the mid-nineties – has been read together with Janet Lim's 1958 *Sold for Silver*. The latter is the autobiographical narrative of a woman who was sold as a bondmaid and exported from China to colonial Malaya, where she lived through World War II. Shirley Lim's much later pictorial narrative of selfhood, by contrast, takes the reader from postwar Malaya (now postcolonial Malaysia) to American academia. At first sight, the two books have nothing in common apart from their representation of Southeast Asia for a "Western," primarily Anglo-American, audience. In juxtaposed close readings of both works, Wong Soak Koon, however, suggests that they negotiate identity in similar ways. They use, Wong argues, multiple discourses to construct women as "culturally recognisable subjects," and in the process, seek to dismantle both colonialist and nationalist perspectives on Southeast Asian histories.[28] Wong's feminist reading highlights ways in which the focus on women's stories lets alternative discourses emerge. In the fifties, the works of Janet Lim and Diana Chang were undoubtedly important pioneers in this field. By the nineties, however, the foregrounding of the subaltern struggles of Asian women against historical cataclysms had become a common strategy with its own canonization, typecasting, and impasses.

Asian American fiction by women writers in the new millennium has become clearly bifurcated: (1) imitative novels have continued to capitalize on the two- and multi-plot novel that has grown out of the autobiographical "exotic" narrative; (2) more intriguing reworkings have found new ways and plot developments to represent Asian American identities. In a review of *Wild Ginger* by Anchee Min, Hwee Hwee Tan terms the onslaught of deliberately "exoticizing" novels about Chinese womanhood "Chinese Chick Lit": a feisty, exotically gorgeous woman faces political/patriarchal adversity in Communist China in a sensationally marketable plot, with which Tan contrasts her own novels about contemporary urban Singapore and globalizing America.[29] Novels that fit the bill hail with telling titles like Natasha Pang-Mei Chang's *Bound Feet & Western Dress*, Adeline Yen Mah's *Falling Leaves: The Memoir of an Unwanted Chinese Daughter*, or the latter's second novel, *Chinese Cinderella: The True Story of an Unwanted Daughter*. The exotic is unearthed, made tangible, as a "re-searched" family history. It is framed by the subsequent generations' identity conflicts: American Asians endeavor to come to terms with the imported, strangely exotic, past.

Chang's novel, for example, opens with the literal opening of an ancient family trunk that contains the whole of mysteriously exotic China: "The carved mahogany trunk from China still stands in the living room of my parents' home in Connecticut. . . . There is everything in this trunk: the secrets of China, the smell of camphor and clothing, dresses of another time and place."[30] The turbulent story of the first-person narrator's great-aunt in prewar and wartime China is framed by the details of the narrator's own story of growing up Chinese and female in the United States. Her teenage identity crises are at once deflected and reflected by her search for cultural belonging – a juxtaposition that has become the expected norm in Asian American novels ever since the influential works of Kingston and Tan: "A teenager at the time, I felt caught in the middle of an acute identity crisis. As the first generation of my family born in the States, I was torn between two cultures. Chinese-American, I longed for a country I could call my own."[31]

Such narratives are often autobiographical, when they do not feed on the previous generation's mediated suffering. They are always targeted towards an audience hungry for exotic atrocities and ignorant of the re-represented histories. They lack the self-irony that has been with Amy Tan's novels from the beginning, even when it is at times submerged by a sensationalized foregrounding of female suffering in Communist China. In short, the central contrast of past victimization and Asian American engagements with multi-culturalism and hybridity as the "identity kit" of the nineties has become the central cliché that, endlessly replicated, has unfortunately lost some of its initial edge. When the American-born narrator of Chang's novel sets herself against her "classmates, most of whom were American" in her search for an exotic China that fails to resonate within her, the schizophrenia of the cultural hybrid becomes poignantly overt. Nothing is ever made of this unanalyzed dichotomy of Chinese Americans and ethnically unmarked "Americans" in the novel. Instead, the frame story vanishes into the margins of mediated past adventures. It is an unhappy slip, to say the least.

Furthermore, it sharply contrasts with Tan's comical treatment of such conflations of nationhood and ethnicity. The first-person narrator of *The Kitchen God's Wife*, for example, in a tongue-in-cheek way reports that "Bao-bao's two former wives were what Auntie Helen called 'Americans,' as if she were referring to a racial group."[32] Helen's occidentalist simplicity is clearly ridiculed, while her self-exclusion from American identity politics negotiates a chilling disillusionment as to the limits of a multicultural imaginary. Occidentalist exclusivity is relegated to the older generation. It epitomizes their inflexibility, but also a seeming stability of identity for which the cultural hybrid secretly longs. This nostalgia for stable dichotomies is routinely buried under a contemptuous façade. Invariably, from Kingston's narratives onwards, the Chinese-born mother embodies this mixture of self-exoticizing nostalgia and paranoid self-hatred. She externalizes the hybrid's dilemma. Yet as China and the Chinese-born are reduced to walking embodiments, the authenticity of their representation is rightly drawn into question.

When *The Woman Warrior* was published in 1976, it was notoriously steeped in controversy.[33] Its promotion and consequent interpretation as an autobiography and not a work of fiction were clearly at the root of the problem. Kingston was at once critiqued for selling an exoticized, neo-orientalist China to American readers in search of fictionalized alterity and for muddling the details in her reuse of Chinese myths. Mimi Chan deplored Kingston's tendency to "overwrite," a criticism that she partially extends to Tan's fiction: "Many Hong Kong Chinese I have talked to, or even recent immigrants to the United States – all 'Westernised' Chinese – tend to see Kingston as exploiting her Chineseness, selling out her country and her people. She wallows in accounts of barbarism and unspeakable horror."[34] In an attempt to counter the cultural misreadings of her American target audience, Kingston complains that reviewers tended to "praise the wrong things" "against the stereotype of the exotic, inscrutable, mysterious oriental."[35]

American and increasingly European readers, however, refused to be defrauded of what they consumed as authentic alterity, creating more food for Asian critics in the United States and elsewhere. In an important study of Kingston's reception, Yan Gao reassesses not only American "mis-readings," but also questions raised by sinologists in both Asia and America. Criticized for strategically deploying trivial Chinese substance as an exotic "treat" for the Euro-American reader, Kingston's books are on the whole unfavorably contrasted with Tan's *The Joy Luck Club* with its more authentic rendition of Chinese American families.[36] Novels that focus on Asian American families rather than on the mediated exotic terrains of a Communist China of the past generally fare better in recent critical analyses. The book market, however, does not reflect this. Instead, the marketability of "Chinese Chick Lit" with their relish in Communist atrocities suggests the contrary.

However that may be, it is important that the shift towards Asian American neo-orientalism has become a prevailing approach in recent criticism. Critics' preference for *The Joy Luck Club* with its neatly structured juxtaposition of the mothers' past in China and their daughters' American lives is located precisely in Tan's "domestication" of Kingston's themes. The Asian American family with its focus on gender and generation problems moves into the foreground. The mothers' "exotic" backgrounds serve mainly to provide insight into what their daughters misread as mere eccentricity, as alien idiosyncrasy, divorced from the realities of past suffering. The book's reception and even more pointedly, its adaptation into a movie have of course inverted this emphasis. Tan's second novel, *The Kitchen God's Wife*, once again relegates the presence of the contemporary multiethnic family to the margins of the narrative to display a bloodcurdling list of atrocities in wartime China. In an article on the semiotics of "China narratives," Yuan Yuan analyzes novels by both Kingston and Tan to show that the "nativeness" of ethnic American literature is essentially ambiguous. Their China plots "emerge in the 'other' cultural context informed by a complex process of translation, translocation, and transfiguration of the original experiences in China."[37] In a more recent article, Ma Sheng-Mei likewise provides an interesting analysis of the construction of the "primitive à la New Age" in Tan's next novel, *The Hundred Secret Senses*.[38] Once again, Tan's fiction is criticized for selling the "exotic."

The vaguely evoked Asia of Tan's novels is without doubt a literary, even orientalist, landscape. While they are concerned with the East or more specifically, with the meeting of East and West, their China plots remain exotic and remote. They are emphatically "other," but this is precisely the point. Asian Americans are shown to be divorced from the earlier generation's China. When the hybrid heroine of *The Hundred Secret Senses* visits rural China to research exotic culinary delights for a glossy magazine, it is made abundantly clear that the Asian American protagonists are not at home in China. In their encounters with "exotic" eating habits, repulsion predominates. What is important to note here is the self-reflexive emphasis on the distortion implicit in the presentation, not to say reportage, of the exotic. Olivia Bishop, the half-Chinese heroine, and her half-Hawaiian (ex-)husband Simon take pictures of a villager slaughtering a chicken. Puzzled by the lengthy and brutal process, Olivia questions the woman only to expose the process's enhancement. Shamefacedly, Olivia prefers to clad it once more in an exoticizing pastiche:

> "After I have enough blood, I usually cut off the head right away. But this time I let the chicken dance a bit." "Why?" "For you!" she says happily. "For your photos! More exciting that way, don't you agree?" her eyebrows flick up as she waits for my thanks. I fake a smile. "Well?" says Simon. "It's . . . Well, you're right, it's not kosher." . . . "It's more of an ancient Chinese ritual, a spiritual cleaning . . . for the chicken."[39]

The Hundred Secret Senses is the only one of Tan's novels that moves away from the popular plot device of framing the mother's experience in China with her American daughter's attempts to come to terms with her own as well as the family's past. Instead, it replaces the popular juxtaposition with a historical plot that evokes the British presence in nineteenth-century China. As a result, the novel is the first to depart from the simple dichotomies that split *The Joy Luck Club* and *The Kitchen God's Wife*. It is also the only one of Tan's novels that contains a lengthy return to China in its present-day plot. Most importantly, it substitutes an embarrassing half-sister, imported as an adult from rural China into a very American and very dysfunctional family, for the pivotal mother-daughter relationship that has become a hallmark of Tan's novels. *The Bonesetter's Daughter* admittedly reintroduces the clichés of the seemingly erratic, embarrassingly eccentric, aging mother who harbors secrets of the past, yet it also offers an intriguing postmodern exploration of the nature of reading and writing, adroitly linking ghosts and ghost writers. The symbolism is almost obtrusive, spiced up with self-ironic references, and yet what most readers immediately zoom in on is again the negotiation of heredity through mother–daughter conflicts.[40]

Ironically, it is precisely the clichéd dichotomies revolving around dualities of mother–daughter, China–America, past–present, and exotic–familiar that have had the most decisive impact on the production as well as promotion of ethnic minority fiction. In her study of Asian American women writers, Sau-ling Cynthia Wong calls the narrator of Fae Myenne Ng's short story "A Red Sweater" and second-generation protagonists in Tan's *The Joy Luck Club* "cousins of Maxine, fellow children of Necessity."[41] At the center of this repetitiveness is the "classic form of American modernity versus Asian traditionalism" embodied by immigrant mothers and their American daughters.[42] Predating the publication of Tan's second novel, Mimi Chan's essay likewise pinpoints a certain sameness: a sense of *déjà vu* overtakes the reader of *The Joy Luck Club*.[43] This uncanny experience of *déjà vu* is endlessly multiplied, not only in America but also at the international book market.[44] More recently, Wendy Ho has included Ng's novel, *Bone*, in her analysis of mother–daughter dualities. Suggesting that Tan must have drawn inspiration from *The Woman Warrior* just as Ng has to be considered in the context of Kingston's and Tan's novels, Ho emphasizes that there "was a consumer market for Tan's mother–daughter text."[45] This is not to say that such repetitiveness results only in pot-boilers, but it is this repackaging of an increasingly familiar alterity for mainstream consumption that many Asians resent, and which has become an even more poignant point of criticism after the film adaptation of *The Joy Luck Club* in 1993 and the plethora of imitative "Chinese Chick Lit" it has inadvertently spawned. Increasingly, however, the selling of marginality as a consumer product is self-ironically examined. A close look at the meeting of occidentalist typecasting of non-Asian alterity and neo-orientalist self-exoticization that characterizes the genre's most interesting exponents will show how self-irony works against the notorious sensationalizing. That food plays such a crucial role in their micropolitics of embarrassment expunges ethnic sentimentality.

RE-REPRESENTING ALTERITY: MICROPOLITICS OF EMBARRASSMENT IN THE MULTIETHNIC FAMILY

In a section of *The Joy Luck Club* that is particularly rife in embarrassments, a family dinner turns into a phantasmagoria of mutual humiliation. The American-born daughter, Waverly Jong, has invited her non-Asian boyfriend and sees him exposed, dissected, feasted on as an unwelcome intrusion of occidentalist exotica over dinner: "I couldn't save Rich in the kitchen. And I couldn't save him later at the dinner table."[46] His inept use of chopsticks is only the beginning of a series of humiliations. He fails to read the secret signs that structure the family. To him, they really remain inscrutable, so much so that he is never even aware of his blunders. To them, he is the occidentalist stereotype of the equally inscrutable, bumbling, pathetic (a word that indeed recurs to characterize him) non-Asian, usually male, addition to the diasporic family. When the mother disparages her own cooking to compel praises, he falls into the cultural trap: "This was our family's cue to eat some and proclaim it the best she had ever made."[47] Rich instead helpfully proceeds to spice up the dish with soy sauce, pouring "a riverful of the salty black stuff on the platter, right before my mother's horrified eyes."[48] At first sight, his blunders are comical, yet there is something very sinister in the occidentalist exclusion practiced in the dysfunctional family. And, exotic preconceptions turn out to be just as damaging as cultural ignorance:

> "You don't understand. You don't understand my mother."
> Rich shook his head. "Whew! You can say that again. Her English was *so* bad. You know, when she was talking about that dead guy showing up on *Dynasty*, I thought she was talking about something that happened in China a long time ago."[49]

With consummate irony, the mother's expected narrative is something "that happened in China a long time ago," not a preoccupation with American soap operas. The framed list of past atrocities has of course remained one of the most popular elements of ethnic minority fiction as reader expectations have been repeatedly reaffirmed from *The Kitchen God's Wife* onwards to *Bound Feet & Western Dress* and *The Bonesetter's Daughter*. The stories' specificities have moreover been lost in generalizations made for the doubtful benefit of the putatively ignorant reader. The self-reflexivity of their mediation has long been ignored, noticed only when it becomes almost crudely overt. *The Woman Warrior*, in fact, already questions the ethnic slots which Chinese Americans and their audiences create as well as play into: "What is Chinese tradition and what is the movies?"[50] *The Joy Luck Club* even draws the new "fashion" of all things Asian into debate, anticipating the side remarks on the marketability of old-world China in *The Kitchen God's Wife*. In a section aptly titled "Double Face,"

Waverly feels that it would now be fashionable to look Asian. Having grown up against the backdrop of "melting-pot" assimilation, she wishes to fit the new multiculturalism. Her mother comments: "My daughter did not look pleased when I told her this, that she didn't look Chinese. . . . But now she wants to be Chinese, it is so fashionable."[51]

The cliché of the inscrutable meal stands at the center of such reactions against "exotic" multiculturalism. The absence of any nostalgia or feeling of community in the representation of its consumption is strikingly conspicuous. Instead of engendering any commonality, ethnic identity, cross-cultural exchange, or even longing for lost homelands, family meals are the site of exclusion, repulsion, and humiliation. Their deliberately off-putting descriptions range from the quirky humor with which the narrator of *The Woman Warrior* describes the four- or five-day leftovers, "the blood pudding awobble in the middle of the table" and the revulsion of visitors – "Sometimes brown masses sat on every dish. I have seen revulsion on the faces of visitors who've caught us at meals"[52] – to the disastrous profusion of soy sauce in *The Joy Luck Club*, and the absence of ethnically "marked" food that makes the hybrid family of *The Hundred Secret Senses* "modern," "American," and "like everyone else" until the half-sister appears from China: "We were a modern American family. We spoke English. Sure, we ate Chinese food, but take-out, like everyone else."[53] Ironically evoked exoticization through food and eating habits indeed becomes multiplied in the novel. Kwan, the half-sister, for some time works at a Chinese restaurant without identifying the food produced there as Chinese. The non-Chinese mother, Louise Kenfield, born in Moscow, Idaho, describes herself as "American mixed grill, a bit of everything white, fatty and fried" in an evocation of melting-pot consumption that beautifully ridicules the food metaphors that are routinely thrown up as one of the putative virtues of multiethnic societies. The display of "exotic" food for American magazines in China only takes this collapse of "exoticizing" multiculturalism to its logical conclusion.[54]

The Hundred Secret Senses, in fact, most ruthlessly dismantles ideologies of multicultural idylls and their consumption. The non-Asian mother's proclivity to become involved with "foreigners" manifests itself not only in her marriage to her Chinese-born husband, but also in her choice of her second husband, an Anglo-Italian whom she took for a Mexican, and a list of similarly "exotic" boyfriends: "Mom thinks that her marrying out of the Anglo race makes her a liberal."[55] The introduction of her first husband's grown-up daughter from a previous marriage, imported to America after his death and comically unable to become the grateful "Chinese Cinderella" the American mother has in mind, maps out a failure of familial as well as other forms of integration. Kwan instead becomes a mother-substitute in a stereotypically dysfunctional "American" family. We have seen Kim's exultation over the onslaught of dysfunctional families in Asian American fiction.[56] With their proliferation of divorces, half-sisters, step-parents, and failed parenting, both *The Hundred Secret Senses* and *The Bonesetter's Daughter* push this demand for fragmented families to parodic extremes. Tan's novels have notably been called "postfeminist" in their implied reaffirmation of domesticity, family structures, and a happy marriage.[57] After all, they sensationally expose the detrimental effects of their absence. Unlike in Kim's analysis, dysfunctional families are hardly celebrated, even when they supply most of the comedy.

Thus, the failed family dinner becomes symptomatic of both dysfunctional relationships and the intrinsic desire for an essentially conservative restitution. Throughout Tan's novels, eating is embarrassing and even sickening, part of a power struggle that can, but need not be involved in self-exoticizing processes of exclusion. In ways that anticipate *The Hundred Secret Senses*, food serves as a structuring metaphor in Lena St. Clair's narrative "Rice Husband" in *The Joy Luck Club*. Lena's non-Chinese father is the only one in the story who enjoys his food: "My father was not Chinese like my mother, but English-Irish American, who enjoyed his five slices of bacon and three eggs sunnyside up every morning."[58] This comes right after we are told that he died of a heart attack at the age of seventy-four. The story then moves on to a retrospectively remembered child bent over her rice bowl. The Chinese mother admonishes her for not finishing her food: "your future husband have [*sic*] one pock mark for every rice you not finish."[59] Lena stops eating to punish this future husband in advance and blames herself when a hated boy, aptly called Arnold Reisman ("rice-man"), dies of complications from measles five years later. While the refusal to eat is to call punishment upon her, gorging is her chosen self-torture: she forces down spoonfuls of ice cream only to vomit it back into the container. This disgusting childhood episode later throws up important insights into her unhappy married life. Lena meets her husband while they are working in the same restaurant design and development division and they proceed to set up a company that specializes in "theme eating." They split all restaurant bills, keep a list of shared items on the fridge, and it is the ice-cream on this list that discloses dysfunctional relationships. Eating and refusing to eat are part of a power struggle between mother and daughter, husband and wife. In sharp contradistinction, ethnic food is the concern of marketed "theme eating." The story refuses to accommodate a hunger for the exotic or ethnic nostalgia.

Instead, throughout the book, any kind of "clan gathering," including the Jordans' family picnic, to which Rose Hsu is invited by her non-Asian boyfriend, is first and foremost a tableau of exclusion.[60] Mrs. Jordan uses the opportunity to suggest that Rose's ethnicity disqualifies her as a suitable daughter-in-law: "She assured me she had nothing whatsoever against minorities; she and her husband, who owned a chain of office-supply stores, personally knew many fine people who were Oriental, Spanish, and even black."[61] It is the reverse of Rich's reception in Waverly's narrative. Not all intrusions of non-Asian characters into Chinese family dinners (and vice versa) are as comically pathetic as Rich's juggling with chopsticks, slippery squid, and liberal helpings of soy sauce. Their description instead becomes more and more sinister as eating as a power struggle takes over relish in ethnic exotica, and means and motives of exclusion become multiplied across different "clan gatherings" of immigrant communities.

Shirley Lim's "A Pot of Rice" is on the other hand comparatively straightforward. The Chinese woman in New York cannot eat her husband's American rice and rather naively blames all their differences on their food habits: "She could not eat the gritty grains he served. Their food habits made them strangers to each other while most Americans, she thought sadly, held hands over slices of toasted Wonder Bread."[62] Hwee Hwee Tan's novel *Mammon Inc.* is instead very sarcastic in its evocation of "ethnic" food. When globetrotting Chia Deng returns from New York to stay with her former college housemate in England, she invites her sister from Singapore. Offered fish and chips, the "very Chinese" sister responds "I hate potato," and they ultimately resort to Chinese take-away, although "Chia Deng says the sweet-and-sour pork from our local Chinese take-away isn't real, whatever that means."[63] A meal with Chia Deng's parents in Singapore is even comically gruesome. A heated discussion about AIDS as a "Western" disease is camouflaged as a debate on oriental food. The parents refuse to share dishes with the potentially polluted occidental; the visitor innocently swallows explanations of culturally specific preoccupations with food: "'Oh nothing, we're just arguing over what food to order,' I told Steve in English. 'Perfectly friendly bickering about the relative merits of laksa and stewed chicken feet.'"[64] Multiple exclusions become the norm in dysfunctional family reunions. The East-West split of *Mammon Inc.* is perhaps particularly blunt. On each occasion, one "exotic" intruder breaks into an alien world, epitomizing the stereotyped hybrid's dilemma.

By contrast, the multiply bifurcated American family is increasingly riveted by overlapping patterns of exclusion. In *The Bonesetter's Daughter*, Ruth organizes a family dinner to celebrate the Full Moon Festival. It sharply brings out the divisiveness of Chinese and non-Chinese family members. Ruth's partner's ex-wife invites herself, her new husband, their two sons, and her former in-laws instead of simply sending the two daughters who alternately live with her and their father. This rather forced inclusion of questionable family members externalizes broken descent and entangled relationships. Multiple patterns of exclusion negotiate an uncomfortable clash of xenophobic family structures. Ruth's relatives become marginalized by her partner's overdressed parents and their sets of grandchildren, as their exotic consumption displaces the planned culinary nostalgia trip engineered for the aging Chinese-born mother:

> "What's that?" Ruth heard Boomer ask at the other table. He scowled
> at the jiggling mound of jellyfish as it swung by on the lazy Susan.
> "Worms!" Dory teased. "Try some." "Ewww! Take it away! Take it
> away!" Boomer screamed. Dory was hysterical with laughter. Art
> passed along the entire table's worth of jellyfish to Ruth, and Ruth felt
> her stomach begin to ache. More dishes arrived, each one stranger
> than the last, to judge by the expressions on the non-Chinese faces.[65]

The expression on the non-Chinese faces is one of uniform revulsion, hurting more stomachs than their own. Different forms of "otherness" are played out, as methods of deliberate exclusion are directed against the "other" family and specifically the "other" woman. Multiculturalism and xenophobia are multiplied as Ruth remains an outsider at her own dinner, reminding her that heirlooms and family feelings are bestowed on the ex-wife as the more "suitable" daughter-in-law, "now and forever the mother of the Kamens' granddaughters . . . [They] had given her the family sterling, china, and the mezuzah kissed by five generations of Kamens since the days they lived in the Ukraine."[66] In this, Tan's most recent fictional work to date, the micropolitics of embarrassment and exclusion are at once doubled and bifurcated, tying in with the occidentalist typecasting fostered by self-exoticization and countered by clashes of tightly knit communities of both Asian and non-Asian origins. Such rerepresentations of twenty-first-century multiethnic American families might negotiate a disturbing disillusionment, yet it is primarily in the contexts of such deliberately self-ironic and self-reflexive takes on clichés that explorations of multiculturalism with all its impasses as well as new potentials achieve the most effective realization.

NOTES

1. Amy Tan, *The Kitchen God's Wife*, 80.
2. Shirley Lim, *Joss & Gold*, 15, 9, 38.
3. Ibid. 45.
4. Ibid. 236.
5. Lim, *Life's Mysteries: The Best of Shirley Lim*, 57.
6. Graham Huggan, *The Post-Colonial Exotic: Marketing the Margins*.
7. Nikos Papastergiadis, *The Turbulence of Migration: Globalisation, Deterritorialisation and Hybridity*, 169, 14.
8. Gayatri Chakravorty Spivak, *In Other Worlds: Essays in Cultural Politics*, 154.
9. Ania Loomba, *Colonialism/Postcolonialism*, xii.
10. Huggan, *Post-Colonial*, vii, x.
11. Ibid. 6.
12. Bruce King, *New National and Post-Colonial Literatures*, 10.
13. Catherine Lim, *The Teardrop Story Woman*, book-flap; Jung Chang, *Wild Swans: Three Daughters of China*.
14. Tan, *The Bonesetter's Daughter*, 56.
15. Fiona Cheong, *Shadow Theatre*, 21.
16. Ibid. 24.
17. Ibid. 65.
18. E. San Juan, *Beyond Postcolonial Theory*, 1.
19. Ibid. 134.
20. Ibid. 179. Compare A. L. Brown Ruoff and Jerry Ward, eds., *Redefining American Literary History*.
21. Elaine Kim, *Asian American Literature: An Introduction to the Writings and Their Social Context*, viii.
22. Lim and Chua, Introduction, in Lim and Chua, eds., *Tilting the Continent: Southeast Asian American Writing*, xii.
23. Kim, x.
24. Ibid. xiii. Compare Sylvia Watanabe and Carol Bruchac, eds., *Home to Stay: Asian American Women's Fiction*.
25. Shirley Lim, Introduction, in Diana Chang, *The Frontiers of Love*, v.
26. Chang, *The Frontiers of Love*, 86–87.
27. Lim, Introduction, ix.
28. Wong Soak Koon, "Reading Two Women's Narratives: *Sold for Silver* and *Among the White Moon Faces*," in Mallari-Hall and Tope, eds., 161. Compare Janet Lim, *Sold for Silver*.

29. Hwee Hwee Tan, "Ginger Tale."
30. Natasha Chang, *Bound Feet & Western Dress*, 1.
31. Ibid. 4–5.
32. Tan, *Kitchen God*, 32.
33. Cynthia Wong, *Maxine Hong Kingston's* The Woman Warrior: *A Casebook*, 3.
34. Mimi Chan, "'Listen, Mom, I'm a Banana': Mother and Daughter in Maxine Hong Kingston's *The Woman Warrior* and Amy Tan's *The Joy Luck Club*," in Chan and Harris, eds., 67.
35. Kingston, "Cultural Mis-reading by American Reviewers," in Amirthanayagam, ed., 55.
36. Compare Liu Shaoming, "Cong Tang Tingting dao Tan Enmei: meihua xiaoshuo xin qidian" (From Tang Tingting to Amy Tan: The New Beginning of the Chinese American Novel) *Sinorama*, April 1992, cited in Yan Gao, *The Art of Parody: Maxine Hong Kingston's Use of Chinese Sources*, 47.
37. Yuan Yuan, "The Semiotics of China Narratives in the Con/texts of Kingston and Tan".
38. Ma Sheng-Mei, "'Chinese and Dogs' in Amy Tan's *The Hundred Secret Senses*: Ethnicizing the Primitive à la New Age."
39. Tan, *The Hundred Secret Senses*, 264–65.
40. Kingston's *To Be the Poet* (2002) and Tan's *The Opposite of Fate: A Book of Musings* (2003), are non-fictional "books of musings." Kingston's *The Fifth Book of Peace* (2003) is a postmodern narrative that marginalizes the autobiographical to address American involvements in global wars.
41. Sau-ling Cynthia Wong, *Reading Asian American Literature: From Necessity to Extravagance*, 40.
42. Ibid. 40.
43. Chan, "Banana," 68.
44. In a note at the end of *Women in Men's Houses*, Singaporean writer Wee Kiat speaks of Tan as an important inspirational source for her neatly split narratives. Ironically, the form of *The Joy Luck Club* was more accidental. See E.D. Huntley, *Amy Tan: A Critical Companion*. 43. On the impact of Asian American women writing on diasporic writers in Southeast Asia and Australia, see Tamara S. Wagner, "'After another round of tissues': 'Bad Time' Fiction and the Amy Tan-Syndrome in Recent Singaporean Novels," *Journal of Commonwealth Literature* 38.2 (2003): 19–39, and chapter 4 in *The Financial Straits: Occidentalism in Fictions of Singapore and Mala(si)a, 1800–2003*, forthcoming.
45. Wendy Ho, *In Her Mother's House: The Politics of Asian American Mother-Daughter Writing*, 44.
46. Tan, *Joy Luck Club*, 177.
47. Ibid. 178.
48. Ibid. 178.
49. Ibid. 179.
50. Kingston, *The Woman Warrior: Memoirs of a Girlhood Among Ghosts*, 6.
51. Tan, *Joy Luck*, 253.
52. Kingston, *Woman Warrior*, 92.

53. Tan, *Secret Senses*, 6.
54. Ibid. 3.
55. Ibid. 4.
56. Kim, Preface, xiii.
57. Jeannette Batz Cooperman, *The Broom Closet*.
58. Tan, *Joy Luck*, 150.
59. Ibid. 152.
60. Ibid. 117.
61. Ibid. 118.
62. Lim, "Rice," 57.
63. Hwee Hwee Tan, *Mammon Inc.*, 153, 155.
64. Ibid. 222–23.
65. Tan, *Bonesetter's Daughter*, 83–84.
66. Ibid. 80.

WORKS CITED

Brown Ruoff, A. L. and Jerry Ward, eds. *Redefining American Literary History*. New York: MLA, 1990.

Chan, Mimi. "'Listen Mom, I'm a Banana': Mother and Daughter in Maxine Hong Kingston's *The Woman Warrior* and Amy Tan's *The Joy Luck Club*." *Asian Voices in English*. Eds. Mimi Chan and Roy Harris. Hong Kong: University of Hong Kong Press, 1991.

Chang, Diana. *The Frontiers of Love*. Seattle: University of Washington Press, 1994.

Chang, Jung. *Wild Swans: Three Daughters of China*. New York: Simon & Schuster, 1991.

Chang, Natasha. *Bound Feet & Western Dress*. New York: Doubleday, 1996.

Cheong, Fiona. *Shadow Theatre*. New York: Soho Press, 2002.

Cooperman, Jeannette Batz. *The Broom Closet: Secret Meanings of Domesticity in Postfeminist Novels by Louise Erdrich, Mary Gordan, Toni Morrison, Marge Piercy, Jane Smiley, and Amy Tan*. New York: Peter Lang, 1999.

Ho, Wendy. *In Her Mother's House: The Politics of Asian American Mother-Daughter Writing*. Walnut Creek, CA: AltaMira, 1999.

Huggan, Graham. *The Post-Colonial Exotic: Marketing the Margins*. London: Routledge, 2001.

Huntley, E. D. *Amy Tan: A Critical Companion*. Westport, CT: Greenwood, 1998.

Kiat, Wee. *Women in Men's Houses*. Singapore: Landmark Books, 1992.

Kim, Elaine. *Asian American Literature: An Introduction to the Writings and Their Social Context*. Philadelphia: Temple University Press, 1982.

King, Bruce. *New National and Post-Colonial Literatures*. Oxford: Clarendon, 1996.

Kingston, Maxine Hong. "Cultural Mis-reading by American Reviewers." *Asian and Western Writers in Dialogue: New Cultural Identities*. Ed. Guy Amirthanayagam. Hong Kong: Macmillan, 1982.

Kingston, Maxine Hong. *The Woman Warrior: Memoirs of a Girlhood Among Ghosts*. New York: Vintage, 1989.

Koon, Wong Soak. "Reading Two Women's Narratives: *Sold for Silver* and *Among the White Moon Faces.*" *Texts and Contexts: Interactions Between Literature and Culture in Southeast Asia.* Eds. Luisa Mallari-Hall and Lily Rose Tope. Diliman: University of the Philippines, 1999.

Lim, Catherine. *The Teardrop Story Woman.* London: Orion, 1999.

Lim, Janet. *Sold for Silver.* London: Collins, 1958.

Lim, Shirley and Cheng Lok Chua. Introduction. *Tilting the Continent: Southeast Asian American Writing.* Eds. Shirley Lim and Cheng Lok Chua. Minneapolis: New Rivers Press, 2000.

Lim, Shirley. Introduction. *The Frontiers of Love.* Diana Chang. Seattle: University of Washington Press, 1994.

Lim, Shirley. *Joss & Gold.* Singapore: Times Books International, 2001.

Lim, Shirley. *Life's Mysteries: The Best of Shirley Lim.* Singapore: Times Books International, 1995.

Loomba, Ania. *Colonialism/Postcolonialism.* London: Routledge, 1998.

Ma Sheng-Mei. "'Chinese and Dogs' in Amy Tan's *The Hundred Secret Senses*: Ethnicizing the Primitive à la New Age." *MELUS* 26.1 (2001): 29–44.

Papastergiadis, Nikos. *The Turbulence of Migration: Globalisation, Deterritorialisation and Hybridity.* Cambridge: Polity, 2000.

San Juan, E. *Beyond Postcolonial Theory.* Basingstoke: Macmillan, 1998.

Spivak, Gayatri Chakravorty. *In Other Worlds: Essays in Cultural Politics.* New York: Methuen, 1987.

Tan, Amy. *The Joy Luck Club.* New York: Ivy Books, 1996.

Tan, Amy. *The Kitchen God's Wife.* New York: G. P. Putnam's Sons, 1991.

Tan, Hwee Hwee. "Ginger Tale." *Time,* 27 May 2002.

Tan, Hwee Hwee. *Mammon Inc.* London and New York: Michael Joseph, 2001.

Watanabe, Sylvia and Carol Bruchac, eds. *Home to Stay: Asian American Women's Fiction.* Greenfield Center, NY: The Greenfield Review Press, 1990.

Wong, Cynthia. *Maxine Hong Kingston's* The Woman Warrior: *A Casebook.* Oxford: Oxford University Press, 1999.

Wong, Sau-ling Cynthia. *Reading Asian American Literature: From Necessity to Extravagance.* Princeton: Princeton University Press, 1993.

Yuan Yuan. "The Semiotics of China Narratives in the Con/texts of Kingston and Tan." *Critique* 40.3 (1999): 292.

Perspectives on Language and Culture

"I Love My India": Indian American University Students Performing Identity and Creating Culture on Stage

Vincent H. Melomo

PROLOGUE: INDIA NIGHT

The scene is a spring night in North Carolina at a local university's main theater. For one night the space on this mostly white campus is radically transformed. The theater is packed with people of Indian descent, and with memories and imaginings of a distant land. "Yes, ladies and gentlemen, this is India, the land of the *bhangra*, *garba*, *bharat natyam*," an Indian American student announces, listing the names of dances included in the evening's program, the pieces of culture that move easily across national borders. "India, the mysterious land of snake charmers, elephants, tigers, doctors and engineers," a white American performer continues, revealing the often stereotyped locations of India and Indian immigrants in the American imagination. Throughout the program the sounds and sights of the Indian diaspora fill the stage as the students perform routines they have rehearsed for months. Their proud, devoted, and demanding parents watch with approval, and some curious non-Indian others watch and learn a little more about their classmates, friends, and lovers. As the show winds to a close, a grand success, the final song and dance performance of the evening begins. The song is introduced with the proclamation, "and wherever we are, whoever we are, we love our families, and we love our India!" Family and nation are merged as one in the second generation's imagining of the ethnic community. A group of children enter the stage waving Indian flags, followed by dancing young women dressed in colorful saris, and the hit

Bollywood movie song titled "I Love My India" begins to play.[1] The night is India Night – a night of Indian American students, loving their parents and their India, performing identity and creating culture, on stage.

INTRODUCTION

This chapter is based on observations I made of the cultural programs put on by Indian and South Asian student organizations in the Triangle Area of North Carolina while doing ethnographic fieldwork for my dissertation in the late nineties. More specifically, I was trying to understand how issues surrounding dating and marriage became caught up in issues of ethnic identity – an identity intersected by gender, class, race, religion, and nation.[2] Through my research, I came to appreciate the significance of the cultural programs of second-generation Indian Americans as a public presentation, construction, and negotiation of ethnic identity and culture. These cultural programs are put on by Indian and South Asian student organizations at many larger universities in the US. They can most simply be characterized as a kind of variety show, primarily including songs, music, and dances, and sometimes fashion shows and skits. I will discuss the significance of these cultural programs as public performances of ethnicity by the second generation. I will explore some of the meanings of the programs for the performers and their audiences, while addressing how through these programs the second generation constructs their vision and version of an Indian American culture.

In a volume on Asian American literary studies a discussion without well-known authors and texts is likely to seem a bit out of place. There is no shortage of popular writers portraying the experiences of Indians and other South Asians in America, perhaps the most notable of these including Meena Alexander, Bharati Mukherjee, Abraham Verghese, Chitra Divakaruni, and Vikram Seth. Additionally, a number of anthologies present an even greater diversity of South Asian American literary voices and concerns, including *Contours of the Heart: South Asians Map North America* (1996), and *Our Feet Walk the Sky: Women of the South Asian Diaspora* (1993).[3] While much of this literature is concerned with similar topics as this chapter – questions surrounding dislocation, diaspora, identity, hybridity, marriage, and gender – with few exceptions, South Asian American literature has not been written by and about the second generation. Little attention has been paid to their everyday experience, and the complexity of the identities and culture they struggle to create.

It is important to remember that the texts that Indian Americans and other Asian Americans create and give meaning to are not all written, printed, or even electronic. They include the dramatic performances of the everyday occurring on the figurative stage of life. They include performances of identity in interactions within ethnic communities, with families and friends; and they include performances of identity with and for people outside of those communities. Occasionally, these performances of identity by Asian Americans even occur on the literal stage. The dreams and struggles enacted in everyday life are performed in a different way, self-consciously put on display for diverse audiences. The cultural programs of second-generation Indian Americans are such performances, such creations of texts, for a diverse group of readers. These programs exist in the space where dreams and reality mix. They include portrayals of real struggles and performances of imagined traditions and hoped-for identities. The production of and participation in cultural programs are also part of the drama of life itself, one of the everyday ways in which ethnic identity is performed and ethnic culture created.

The cultural programs of the second generation are thus lived experience, models of life, and models for life, all at the same time. It is for these reasons that cultural programs deserve further study. They are important forums for the construction of ethnic identity not just for Indian Americans, but for other Asian Americans and ethnic groups as well. Academic writers have typically given much more attention to the published texts arising from Asian American and Asian diasporic writers.[4] However, as significant and insightful as these texts and their interpretations may be, they are only one of a variety of cultural products that are created and consumed by Asian American communities. They are also inevitably more elitist and exclusive than the everyday texts created through performance, such as the cultural programs. This study thus draws upon one of the most significant contributions of Cultural Studies, by bringing greater attention to an important youth and popular cultural phenomenon (Hebdige 1979).

SITUATING INDIAN AMERICANS IN NORTH CAROLINA

Second-generation Indian Americans construct their identities in the context of late modernity.[5] In late modernity, the world has become increasingly characterized by movements of people and media, and a resultant

complicated portability of culture and identity (Appadurai 1989, Breckenridge and Appadurai 1989, Gupta and Ferguson 1992). The globalizing
forces of media and migration move images and people across the landscape,
giving individuals a puzzling diversity of imaginative resources from which
to construct their identities and lifestyles. This global condition has forced
anthropologists and other students of society and culture to more closely
examine how culture and ethnic identities are reproduced and reshaped in
new environments and in new ways. In the Americas, the local has been
shaped by the global since the first Europeans came to these shores, and continues to be so with new immigrants. Hall writes that we see in the New
World "the beginning of diaspora, of diversity, of hybridity and difference"
(235). In tracing the context of Indian Americans in North Carolina we can
see how local and global histories intersect and shape their experiences, con-
tributing to new forms of culture and new constructions of difference.

While North Carolina has not always been a center of international migration, it has for several decades been a growing area, noted for its economic
opportunity and quality of life, making it an attractive destination for new
settlers from within the US and abroad. Since the mid-sixties, when large-
scale Indian immigration began, the South has been undergoing social and
economic transformations that have led to the shaping of a "New South"
(Escott 12). The immigration of Indians coincided with the development of
a more high-tech, service-oriented, post-industrial economy, which called
for the kind of well-educated professionals who were coming from India at
the time (Powell 531). As populations increased and the Southern economy
grew, a variety of other business opportunities became available for Indian
Americans. Most notably, Indian Americans invested in the hotel/motel
sector, bringing them into many of North Carolina's smaller towns.

This economic development in the American South followed popular
movements for civil rights and official policies of racial integration (Powell
530). However, while the civil rights era has come and gone, the South is
still deeply segregated. The United States generally, and especially the
South, is divided by a racial discourse of black and white. When Indian
Americans settled in North Carolina, there were few other Asians, and until
recently, few Latinos – there was only black and white.[6] Indians are typically viewed as "different" by members of either group, and typically do not
see themselves falling easily into either of these categories. To begin to
understand the meaning of the cultural programs to second-generation
Indian Americans, it is necessary to understand that as neither black nor
white, and mostly non-Christian, Indian Americans stand outside the dom-

inant Southern categories of difference. The meanings of the cultural programs to the second generation arise in part from these locations in the
South – as children of a small, middle-class, geographically dispersed,
minority group. The struggles of the second generation derive from these
locations in two ways: one, in dealing with pressures from their parents who
are interested in reproducing their culture and their class position; and two,
in dealing with being accepted by Southern American peers who view them
as different. By understanding these struggles we can better understand the
meaning and content of the cultural programs.

THE PARENTS' IMMIGRANT DREAM

The role of imagination, of imagined futures, selves, and communities, is
especially important in considering the lives of the second generation.
Children are perhaps human beings' most tangible dreams, carrying visions
and hopes for the future into the next generation. The act of migration is
also about dreams of the future and hopes for a better life. The lives of the
second generation are shaped by these dreams of their parents, and by the
dreams of the nations they are tied to by history. In this context, the second
generation creates their own dreams of whom they want to be, and how they
want to live their lives. These dreams, however, do not always easily fit with
the dreams of their parents, their communities, or their nations.

To understand perhaps the most significant meaning of cultural programs to Indian American college students, it is necessary to understand
how the second generation embodies their parents' immigrant dream. This
dream is of two closely interrelated parts, one part more material and one
more moral. The dream is a product of the parents' own experience of dislocation, of their hopes and ambitions, and losses and regrets. In being in
the US, many immigrant parents feel that they have made a kind of compromise. This compromise is based on a similar one constructed in India,
one that is common in modernity. Although in being in the US Indian
immigrants may have a greater degree of financial success and material
wealth and a greater status that follows, they may also feel or fear that there
is something they have lost along the way. What they fear they have lost is
something moral, familial, or spiritual – something they feel is tied to Indian
culture, and is distinctly not American.

In order to stave off the feelings of loss which may come from immigration, many immigrant parents struggle to achieve what has been called

"accommodation without assimilation" (Gibson 1988). That is, they may try to compartmentalize (Singer 321) their American/work and their Indian/home lives, happily accommodating themselves to the dominant society, while struggling against being fully assimilated by resisting the adoption of some dominant American values. Through their family relations, social networks, ethnic organizations and religious centers, as well as frequent visits to India if possible, immigrant Indians have struggled to negotiate this compromise and maintain a sense of "being Indian" on a new landscape. They seek to enjoy some of the material benefits and satisfactions of American society, while trying to hold onto aspects of their culture and values. These often include essentialized ideas about family, marriage, gender, and religion, the fossilized remains of a more complex and dynamic Indian culture they left behind.

For many immigrant parents, the real success of their dream, and the wisdom of their decision to move to the US, is felt to be contingent upon the behavior of their children. In raising their children in the US, in creating a new generation, the immigrant parents struggle to keep their dream alive and try to retain or regain the cultural or moral aspect they fear they have lost or may still lose. In order to fulfill their parents' dreams, Indian American children are often expected to do the same as their parents: to achieve financial success and security in the US, while also still maintaining an Indian culture and identity. The parents' hope is that their children will grow up in America, without becoming fully "Americanized."

In order to maintain an Indian identity, the second generation is expected to have an attachment to India, things Indian, and other Indians, and most importantly, to display what are considered to be "Indian values." These values emphasize identification with and affinity for the family, as well as proper relations among family members according to generation and gender. These values center on having a proper Indian marriage, as well as on reproducing gender roles that place the greater burden for maintaining an Indian identity on women (Bhattacharjee 1992, Dasgupta and Das Dasgupta 1996, Gupta 1999). If the children are successful and a positive Indian identity is maintained, then the parents' anxieties over the potential cost of their decision to immigrate are not realized, and the parents feel that they have achieved the material success of the West without having lost what is perceived to be their Indian spiritual or moral essence. The cultural programs of second-generation Indian Americans are significant in that they both satisfy the parents' immigrant dream and contest key aspects of it as well.

GROWING UP INDIAN IN AMERICA

However, the struggles of second-generation Indian Americans are due as much to feeling like a kind of outsider in American society and culture as to the pressures from their parents. As Fischer has noted, much of the difficulty of being part of a second generation is that there may not be any specific models for behavior, and people with whom one can easily identify (196). There may be plenty of available models for being Indian, or for being American, but few, if any, models for being Indian American. While certainly not all second-generation Indian Americans feel conflicted about their identities or their experience, at some point in their development they are likely to have some conflict with their parents, their Indian or non-Indian peers, or within themselves. This conflict may bring them to question their identities as Indians and as Americans, and may be seen as a struggle to reconcile what are often experienced as "two worlds." As the children of immigrant parents, most second-generation Indian Americans feel that they grow up in two worlds, a world of Indian culture and a world of American culture. Analytically, both historically and in the present, the boundaries between these worlds are quite porous; however, many second-generation Indian Americans experience these worlds as separate and distinct. They may feel that to "be Indian" and to "be American" are not easily reconcilable. The second generation often acts differently and feels differently in these worlds, and the people they know in either may have only limited insight into the other.

The world of Indian culture is generally experienced as a more private world, primarily including the home and the family, but also the public ethnic spaces that the parents have tried to create in American society. The Indian world can be a warm and familiar one, but it can also be experienced as unfair and restrictive. The world of American culture more typically includes their school, their peers, shopping malls, and popular culture. The American world may be a more fun place for the second generation, and they may find their more American identity to be liberating. However, the American world can also be an alienating and racist one, a lonely world in which the second generation may sometimes be victimized and made to feel embarrassed about being Indian. As the second generation grows older and enters college, their complex relationships to these two worlds are often reworked in interesting ways.

For second-generation Indian Americans, as for most middle-class Americans, college is a rite of passage, a time for intense enculturation, gaining independence from parents, and exploring and reworking their identities in transition to adulthood (Moffatt 1989). For many second-generation Indian Americans, college is a particularly important time for reworking their identities as Indian Americans. College is a time when they can create an Indian (or South Asian or Asian) community, culture, and identity on their own terms, rather than through their parents.

The interaction of Indian Americans on college campuses is facilitated by the presence of Indian or South Asian student organizations at most large universities. This emphasis on a regional South Asian or national Indian identity helps complicate narrower definitions of identity for the second generation. At the same time, however, the more numerous Hindus tend to dominate such organizations, and aspects of Hindu identity and culture are more emphasized. This is partly due to the merging of identities that can occur in an immigrant context, particularly in the US, where national-ethnic and religious-ethnic identities are both part of public discourse, and where religious centers are often arena for ethnic community building. However, this merging of identities also mirrors constructions of Indian identity promoted by Hindu nationalists in India, as well as their organizations overseas. Nevertheless, while the boundaries of religion are real for the second generation, the emphasis in the student organizations is more often on the secular and nationalist aspects of identity, both Indian and American, rather than the religious ones.

However organized, these major student organizations perform a variety of functions, providing an opportunity for second-generation Indian Americans to organize various social and cultural functions over the course of the year, and occasionally to inform about and mobilize over political issues. Most importantly, however, these allow second-generation Indians and South Asians to see and meet more people like themselves, together forging an identity and culture. The most anticipated events of these student organizations are the semesterly or annual cultural programs.

CULTURAL PROGRAMS: MEANINGS, CONTENT, AND STRUCTURE

Stuart Hall writes that identity is constituted through representation, and that cultural representations should not be thought of as "a second-order mirror held up to reflect what already exists, but as that form of representation which is able to constitute us as new kinds of subjects, and thereby enable us to discover places from which to speak" (236–37). The cultural programs of the second generation are a key means by which second-generation Indian Americans constitute themselves as new subjects on an American landscape and in a diasporic Indian community. The cultural programs are an important place from which the second generation speaks and are thus a key site for the construction and performance of their identity and culture.

The significance of these events to Indian American students lies in the variety of audiences to whom they speak, to whom they are able to showcase their talents and perform their Indian American identities. Most significantly, the programs serve to bridge the gap between their Indian and American worlds, and thus their Indian and American selves. To their parents, they show that the immigrant dream has not been lost. The programs reveal that although their children have grown up in America, and although they may have moved out of the family home to go away to school, they are still good Indian children, they still love their family and their India. The programs also give the second generation the opportunity to share their culture with non-Indian others and to create a space in their American world that is neither black nor white, a space to proudly proclaim their difference. Finally, the programs also provide an opportunity for the second generation to perform for their Indian American peers and for themselves, showing that they are not too American, and not too Indian, but hopefully an attractive balance of both.

By looking more closely now at the structure and content of these cultural programs we can see some of these various meanings more clearly, as well as gain insight into the complexity of second-generation Indian American culture and identity. I will discuss the performances that typically made up a cultural program in my study area in the late 1990s. My discussion does not completely cover the variety that I observed then; however, it addresses several threads that were common among them. In the following sections I will consider the significances of the Indian American culture and identity that is constructed through these programs, and how the second generation reproduces and challenges the constructions of their parents' generation.

Introducing the Programs: Raj and Rani

The programs typically began with an introduction, a kind of statement of purpose that explicitly positioned the presentations that followed. The stated purpose was to display the continuity of their parents' culture into their generation, and to share this culture with a broader universe of others, thus addressing the key components of their audience. One cultural program I attended presented the night's performance as a chapter in a story, the story being that of their parents' immigration from India, and the new chapter being the students performing that night, continuing the immigrant dream of balancing Indian and American culture. However, the balancing that they proposed revealed that an Indian American identity is often constructed in specifically gendered ways.

As discussed by Partha Chatterjee (1989), Indian nationalists struggled with the problem of how to achieve independence and become a modern nation without reproducing the Western state. The nationalists struggled to place India among the great nations of the world, while still having a distinctly Indian national culture and identity. They resolved their dilemma by constructing a national identity that stood in opposition to the West, relying upon the dichotomies of the spiritual and material, inner and outer, home and world. The materialist business and politics of the modern state, associated with the West, became the responsibility of men, whereas a pure spiritual essence, thought to be distinctly Indian, became the preserve of women. In this new middle-class form of patriarchy the woman would maintain India's spiritual essence in the household, primarily by taking care of her family.[7] The family and the home would become the private world where traditions are maintained, and where the polluting effects of modernity are kept at bay.

While the writings of Indian nationalists from over fifty years ago seem to have little impact on the lives of the second generation in America, the strength of this nationalist construction of gender and family was revealed in the program's introduction. Through a brief performance introducing a cultural program, the second generation showed their understanding of the gendered nationalism of their parents, and revealed their willingness to reproduce that relationship, although in somewhat modified ways. A male student and a female student who were emceeing the program narrated the story that follows: In India there once lived a man named Raj (ruler) and a woman named Rani (queen), who were very different from each other. They were different in that the man was interested in politics and business, and the woman was interested in dance, music, and heritage. However, despite their difference, they fell in love, became married, and decided to move to the US. They came to the US in pursuit of opportunity, yet they, and especially the wife, also wanted to preserve their heritage. They stayed in the US and raised a family, and their children were said to represent the next part of the story. The "moral of the story," as told by the storytellers, was that it is possible to balance Raj's "love of change" with Rani's "love of heritage," and the evening's program, performed by the second generation, stood as evidence of this balance.

The story of the parents' union was presented as a model for the second generation constructed by themselves to themselves, and also to their parents in the audience. The story suggested that in the same way that their parents balanced their differences, both their parents and the second generation can balance their experience with American and Indian culture. Through their performances on stage that night, the second generation provided evidence that despite their parents' engagement with American culture, their children were still able to perform Indian culture. However, what went unsaid, but was more than implicit in this story, was that according to the gender images portrayed in the skit, in America the responsibility for the preservation of Indian identity would fall differently on women. Struggling with the nationalist problem fifty years later and in a new continent, the woman becomes positioned as the guardian of the "traditional" world of Indian culture, while the man engages the "modern" changing world. The two emcees for the evening embodied these gender distinctions, with the woman wearing clothing more typically marked as Indian throughout the program, and the young man wearing clothing more typically marked as Western for the first half of the program, later changing into Indian clothes.

"Classical" Forms

Following the introductions, the programs typically began with a "classical" dance, usually *bharat natyam*. This form of classical dance is learned by many young Indian American women from an early age for the purpose of performing in public. There are many teachers of the dance in the US and some young women even visit India to train. This classical dance is among the most respected forms of Indian culture, and is presented as being "ancient," and thus in some sense the most "purely" Indian performance of the night (Katrak 15). The dance allows the students to make a claim to their inheritance of the historical greatness of Indian culture, tying their performances in the present into the timelessness of the Indian cultural past. This dance is also presented as a form of prayer, as it is said to invoke the god of dance, and often portrays scenes from the great Indian epics

Mahabharata and *Ramayana*. As such, the performance of *bharat natyam* makes clear the association of woman with the spiritually and culturally Indian. By opening the cultural programs, the dance is in a sense used to sanctify the space and content of the program, and reveals the event as a kind of act of devotion, to their parents perhaps, as well as to a god. The opening dance also helps to legitimize the rest of the performances of the evening, which as the event progresses might be considered more modern, and whose authenticity or purity might more easily be called into question.

Folk/Regional Performances

The cultural programs also usually include a variety of performances that are said to be specific to different regions of India. These dance and musical segments are offered as examples of traditional folk styles, falling somewhere between the classical cultural forms and the more popular forms I will discuss next. These forms are more likely to be performed by immigrant college students, but some varieties are also popular among second-generation Indian Americans. They are learned by the second generation at weddings or other social events, and are used in the programs to illustrate the diversity of India and of Indian Americans. The borrowing of folk forms by choreographers for the Bollywood movie industry also adds to their popularity and adaptability to the cultural programs.

Some of the most prominent of these folk forms are the group dances of *garba* and *dandia ras* associated with the western Indian state of Gujarat; and *bhangra* of the northwestern state of Punjab, which will be discussed below.[8] The state of Gujarat has been a major source of immigrants to the US, and Gujaratis have been very successful in organizing their own cultural and religious organizations and events in North Carolina and the US, and dominate many of the pan-Indian organizations. The Gujarati dances are most typically performed each year in Indian American communities in the fall, during the season of *Navratri*. This nine-night celebration pays homage to the Hindu goddesses, but is also a time of more secular fun.

While Gujaratis are the dominant group engaging in the celebration, the prominence of Gujaratis in the US has to some degree shaped this into a pan-Indian American function. Through the cultural programs, Gujaratis as well as other Indians consume the *garba* and *ras* as part of the diversity that comprises an Indian national identity. As Benedict Anderson (1983) has reminded us, all nations are imagined into being, and this is perhaps especially true of the incredibly diverse India, which Rushdie has characterized as a mass fantasy (125). By including different regional styles in the program, from Gujarat, Punjab, Tamilnadu, and Bengal, the second generation takes their part in the fantasy, and tries to create an India (or South Asia) that is united on stage, if more fractured elsewhere.

Bollywood

The most common performances in these programs are choreographed dancing to Bollywood film-songs. The name Bollywood refers to the globally popular productions of the Indian film industry centered in Bombay (Mumbai). The movies typically produced there are a kind of epic musical, loved for their dramatic stories and song and dance sequences. Many second-generation Indian Americans grow up watching Bollywood movies at home or in local theaters, and listening to the film-songs on tapes or CDs. These media products are available in virtually any Indian grocery store, and are now easily purchased online. Watching these videos is something of a family ritual in many households and can be a key aspect of the second generation's Indian identity that they share with their parents. Over several decades there has been little variation in the themes and dramatic content of Bollywood productions, allowing them to be enjoyed by both younger and older Indian Americans.

The film-song dances, although wildly popular, are also generally considered by India's educated classes as a less authentic or pure cultural form than the classical dances.[9] Not surprisingly, these dances are also considered more fun, and are more easily performed. They provide an opportunity for virtually all second-generation Indians to be on stage participating in the performance of Indian culture. Through these dances, young women and men who were raised in America are able to temporarily recreate themselves as the Bollywood stars they see on video. On stage, they are able to become cool, attractive, famous and desired, as Indians.

Although the message of the Bollywood songs lies more in the medium of the performance than in the content, it is interesting to consider the significance of the content too. Many of the Bollywood songs performed by the second generation are about love and desire, albeit often frustrated. While in college, many young Indian Americans are themselves struggling with issues of desire, love, and marriage. While they may keep their dating relationships a secret from their parents, they may have the satisfaction of publicly expressing their desire for a loved one through a Bollywood song or dance. In dancing to these songs then, they are able, in some sense, to depict their own struggles as second-generation Indian Americans, using an Indian idiom.

Some of these film-song dances also include hybrid versions of Indian culture that speak to the second generation's experience. Bollywood has for a long time incorporated music, dance, and dress styles from Hollywood, as Hollywood has also been influenced by Indian culture. As a result, in performing dances to some Indian film-songs, the students are also performing the mix of culture that is familiar to them growing up as Indians in the US. This mixing of things Indian and American was also sometimes done more self-consciously. Occasionally, dance performances were conducted to music remixes created by Indian American deejays. As stated in one program, "Our generation is always trying to find a balance between Indian and American culture, and these remix versions symbolize just one of the many ways we incorporate both 'cultures' into our lives."

Bhangra

Whereas the cultural programs typically began with a classical dance piece, considered to be the most ancient and pure Indian cultural form, they often ended with the opposite, dances that are new, youthful, and hybrid. Several of the programs I observed ended with a music and dance form known as *bhangra*. *Bhangra* is an especially energetic and flexible art form which has in recent decades been spread throughout the South Asian diaspora and has been much transformed in the process. *Bhangra* originated in the Punjab, an agricultural region lying on the border of India and Pakistan, which was divided with the partitioning that created these countries. In response to the changing political landscape brought by the partition, hundreds of thousands of Punjabi Hindus and Sikhs in Pakistan fled to India, and Punjabi Moslems in India fled to Pakistan, resulting in one of the world's largest historic migrations and massacres. This massive dislocation played a significant role in the migration of Indians abroad, particularly to England.

In England in the 1970s, *bhangra* became mixed with disco sounds and emerged as one of the first diasporic cultural forms to be popular with second-generation youth, and which had cross-over appeal (Banerji and Baumann 1990, Gopinath 1995). *Bhangra* has more recently become mixed with hip-hop and reggae beats, gaining global popularity in youth culture (Jones 2003, Lipsitz 129–32). While *bhangra* is a dance form that is often positioned as more masculine, during my research there was one very popular group of mostly female *bhangra* performers. They called themselves *Bhangra* Elite, and reflecting the hybridity of the music, they also included white and black American dancers. In a flyer for a performance, the women stated that through their *bhangra* they were offering an alternative vision of woman to that portrayed in many of the Bollywood dances in the program. They wrote, "*Bhangra* Elite will show you the many facets of a woman, from the soft and seductive, to the strong and independent."

By ending the programs with *bhangra*, the second generation has come a long way from portraying their culture as pure, ancient and timeless, and instead finishes with an expression of culture as youthful, vigorous, and changing. Beginning with *bharat natyam*, through Bollywood, and ending with *bhangra*, the programs work their way through the classical and the popular, the pure and the hybrid, the traditional and the modern, all in an Indian vein. The performances seek to create on a stage in North Carolina the dream of India. They seek to create a coherence and unity that is still very often just imagined, and often contested. They seek to unite the geographical and the historical diversity of the nation, moving across different regions, and from the ancient past to the diasporic present. In including all of these performances, the second generation makes a claim to this diversity as part of their own identity, as part of their own culture. However, within this performance of diversity, as in their own lives, the fractures of religion are often elided, and the Hindu norm is typically assumed.

CULTURAL PROGRAMS: LEARNING, CHALLENGING, AND CREATING CULTURE

The cultural programs of the second generation are not, however, just performances of fossilized or hybrid culture that provide statements of identity to parents and peers. They are also a means by which the second generation reflexively produces and learns their own culture. They create and learn the culture through the discussions, negotiations, and rehearsals that go into putting together a performance. In one cultural program this reflexivity was made explicit when the emcees were cast as two confused second-generation Indian Americans who were learning about Indian and South Asian culture and history through each of the night's performances. After seeing the dances and listening to the speakers all night, the emcees finished by saying, "I learned so much. . . . I feel totally culturized!"

Although cultural programs are designed primarily just to entertain, through the use of skits the second generation also sometimes addresses issues and concerns that are more relevant to their daily lives, providing models for identity and behavior. These skits may challenge the normative behavior expected by their parents, while also struggling to negotiate a compromise. These skits reveal that the cultural programs are not just about referencing India, but are also about representing the struggles of growing up as Indian children in America. Following from their parents' immigrant dream, the second generation struggles most with pressures for educational success, and with concerns about marriage and gender. In the following sections I will use examples from these cultural programs to illustrate how second-generation Indian Americans negotiate these struggles, and how they are constructing their culture and identity in the process.

Negotiating Major and Career Choice: Ajay's Dilemma

Following from their immigrant dream and middle-class aspirations, Indian American parents generally place great emphasis on their children getting a good education in order to have access to secure professional positions, most typically in medicine, engineering, and business. We can see how these pressures are negotiated by the second generation by looking at one of their skits. The skit was a comedy, enacted in several segments, providing a vehicle for the rest of the performances in the program. The drama was introduced as an "epic saga" about a student named Ajay. Ajay introduced himself as "an all-around Indian," which was described in the skit as meaning that he was a good student whose parents expected him to be premed. The drama was constructed around Ajay's conflict over his desire to be a "social dance major" rather than pre-med.

While the choice of a social dance major may have been simply because of its comic appeal, other meanings should be considered as well. The social dance major represents a sociability, an interaction with others, which is often compromised by the competitive isolation of pre-med or engineering coursework, and which stands in contrast to the stereotypical "geekiness" of these other majors. Social dance also represents an expressive freedom with the body, in contrast to more controlled, disciplined presentations of self. Many Indian American students I spoke with felt that their behavior is closely monitored by other Indian Americans, both of their parents' generation and their peers, and thus feel restricted in their actions in public. So in other ways, not just in terms of career ambitions, social dance could be seen to represent a choice of major that provides freedom from the pressures of being Indian.

The skit began with Ajay telling his parents of his desire to be a social dance major. They reacted wildly, with his mother screaming and his father falling to the ground. In a subsequent scene Ajay approached other Indian students who were stereotypically portrayed as geeks. Even after explaining his struggle, none of them understood why Ajay wanted to be a dance major. Unable to find a sympathetic ear, an alienated Ajay continued his journey. In the final scene, while walking down a hallway Ajay smelled incense coming from behind a door with the name "Buddha" on it. After engaging "the enlightened one," Ajay asked what he should do about his dilemma. The Buddha said that he too faced a similar dilemma, "to be a cardiologist or to dance the dance of love." The Buddha said that he chose to dance, and the skit ended with the Buddha jumping up from meditation and dancing alongside Ajay. As in a scene from a Bollywood film, Ajay is able to live out his fantasy in dance. Ajay's struggle over career choice thus seems to be resolved by using an Indian idiom to find a solution to an Indian American problem.

However, as it is constructed on the stage, the solution really does remain in the realm of fantasy. By positioning social dance as the alternative major to pre-med, the second-generation performers are making the choice to be farcical and ludicrous. In reality, many second-generation Indian Americans I spoke with struggled over whether to choose from a variety of majors in the humanities and social sciences, including those with a South Asian focus. For example, for some second-generation Indian Americans the study of South Asian religions was a satisfying intellectual avenue for exploring their identity. By not considering more realistic options and instead turning the issue of choice of major into a farce, a catharsis occurs. The anxieties of the students can be satisfactorily relieved, while the conventional ambition of the students is not really challenged. In fact, the boundaries of major and career choice are in a sense strengthened because to not be pre-med or engineering is now seen to be a social dance major.

In this skit, we see the second generation representing their culture to themselves and an observing and listening audience of others. They enact struggles and scenes from their lives, providing models for identity and behavior. At the same time, these models make clear what the boundaries of those identities and behaviors are. Through the skit, the students express the frustrated desires that follow from the pressures of educational success. However, they do so in a way that presents the fulfillment of these desires as ludicrous, the linking of these desires with an Indian identity as unlikely, and thus actually reinforce the normative aspirations of their parents. The boundaries of an Indian identity in the US, shaped by class, are thus effectively maintained.

Negotiating Marriage

More significant to the second generation than educational pressures are the issues of dating, marriage, and gender, which lie at the center of the family values considered so central to an Indian identity. The dominant discourse on the marriage process in the Indian American community places the second generation in the difficult position of having to mediate conflicting views about marriage, dating, and sexuality in terms of their ethnic identity. As they are growing up, second-generation Indian Americans are exposed to a variety of discourses about whom they should marry and how they should marry. These messages come from their parents, relatives, Indian peers, non-Indian peers, religious figures, as well as American and Indian media. Although these messages are in fact quite complex, both their Indian and American communities tend to essentialize them into an oppositional discourse. According to this dominant discourse, dating, premarital sex, and relationships with non-Indians are associated with being "Americanized"; while not dating, abstinence prior to marriage, and having relationships with other Indians, are considered to be more appropriately "Indian" behaviors (Bhattacharjee 1992, Leonard 1999). These dichotomies often cluster around the issue of having an "arranged" marriage, which is considered to be distinctly Indian, as opposed to a "love" or "choice" marriage, which is considered more American.

Like the Indian American organizations dominated by their parents, the second generation often chooses to place marriage at the center of their own public displays of Indian ethnicity. However, the second generation tries to use these programs to challenge a traditional model of the marriage process and to negotiate the dichotomous constructions of Indian and American identity. One young woman I interviewed, Arti, told me that the first cultural program that the Indian student organization at her university ever performed centered on a skit about an Indian wedding. She said that the students chose to simulate a traditional wedding ritual so that they could learn more about what they might expect in their own lives. At the time, few of the students had ever attended an Indian wedding, and few second-generation Indian Americans had yet reached marriageable age and had experiences that would serve as an example for their younger peers to follow.

The students consulted the local Hindu priest in putting together the staged ritual and tried to present it as a "traditional" one. However, Arti said that the students scripted the wedding couple to meet each other on their own, without their parents' assistance. In this onstage depiction of a "traditional" Indian wedding, the students were struggling to negotiate a compromise with their parents' expectations. In doing so, they created a model for their parents and themselves, a mixing of traditional weddings with self-selected spouses, which in time came to reflect the actual experiences of many second-generation Indian Americans. By using the cultural programs as a creative means of representing their hopes for a future reality, they were able to create a model for themselves and their community that inevitably helped to shape that reality. The students taught the parents that they can have the satisfaction of a more traditional wedding ritual in an American context, if their children are allowed to negotiate the choice of spouse.

In another skit performed at a second-generation cultural program, the Indian American students contested the criteria for marriage emphasized in the Indian marriage model and the arranged marriage process. In the skit, a young man and woman stood on opposite sides of the stage with their backs turned to each other, and then strolled backwards to the center of the stage, taking turns speaking. The young woman began by reading criteria from Indian marital ads placed by parents for their children, speaking with a stereotypical Indian accent. The young man followed, doing the same. Then having dropped the accent, the young woman talked about what qualities she wants in a mate, saying that an MD is not important, but that he should believe in her and help her to become whom she wants to be. The young man read a poem, saying that he desires a "soul mate" to make him complete. The two then bumped into each other, apparently finding their soul mates. Through the skit, the students challenge parental expectations and interests in the marriage process, and replace them with their own. They take the criteria that they associate with an Indian model of marriage and replace it with a more American one. At the same time, they provide a new romantic model for second-generation Indian Americans that they hope is acceptable to their parents. It is significant that in stumbling along in the skit they each found another Indian American. Offstage, when the second generation resists their parents' expectations about marriage they often stumble into non-Indians, a drama that would have been far more troubling to many of the parents in the audience. Through these skits the students are expressing and dealing with their own anxieties about their future. They are trying to create something that is Indian and American, reflecting their own experiences and concerns, and they are hoping that they are doing so in a way that is satisfying to their parents and their community.

Negotiating Gender

The issues surrounding dating and marriage are of course intersected by gender. The responsibility for preserving Indian identity in America has greater implications for women than simply having to wear Indian clothes and perform Indian dances. As the embodiment of Indian identity, young Indian American women learn that their behavior is much more circumscribed than their brothers and male peers. Indian American young men are usually given much more freedom than their sisters. Parents are more likely to allow young men to spend time away from the home and family to socialize with their peers, and perhaps even to date. This double standard was portrayed in a skit written and performed by a second-generation Indian American student.

The skit can thus be read as an act of resistance to both the dominant gender positions called for in the story, as well as the typical representation of young women in cultural programs. The skit, entitled "Ladies Night," began with a young Indian American woman in "American" clothes standing alone on the stage, talking on the phone to her girlfriend about a fraternity party that they wanted to attend that night. She got off the phone, called her mother onto the stage, and asked her if she could go to the party. Her mother said that she was not allowed to go, and asked her why she would not want to stay home and spend time with her parents like "a good Indian girl." The young woman challenged her mother's decision by saying that her brother is allowed to go out all of the time without any comment or objection. Her mother replied, "That is different, he is a boy and you are a girl, do not compare." The mother made clear that in Indian families, young men and women should not expect to be treated the same.

Her brother then entered the stage smiling, and affectionately touched their mother while complimenting her on her appearance. Their mother smiled and laughed, obviously very pleased by her son's presence. The son then told their mother that he would be going out to a couple of parties. She offered no protest and instead encouraged him to have a good time. While the mother was responding to the son, he confidently winked at his sister, showing his awareness of his privileged position in the family and the greater freedoms that follow from it. The son then left the stage, and the mother and the daughter went to opposite corners of the stage, and each spoke to the audience in turn. In speaking to the audience, the young woman questioned why her parents do not trust her, and explained that she knows how to take care of herself. She pleaded her case with the audience, which in large number included the parents of the students on stage, and said, "Just because I want to go out doesn't make me a bad daughter." Drawing on a more American model of development based on individual experience and self-determination, she added that her parents have to be willing to let her make her own mistakes, since learning from mistakes is part of growing up. Her mother, pleading the parents' case to the audience, said that she trusts her daughter but not other people, who in the context of a fraternity party, would mostly be non-Indian Americans. The mother added that she is concerned about her daughter's safety and well being, and wishes her daughter would be more understanding. The daughter then concluded the skit by asking the audience, "Will this ever change?" The audience, and most notably the male voices in the audience, responded with a loud "No!" exhibiting perhaps both agreement with the realistic depiction, as well as an interest in maintaining these unequal relations.

The skit ends without resolution and without critique. Rather than contesting the mother's position and her unwillingness to restrict her son's behavior, the mother's view and the daughter's view are simply presented as irreconcilable. Although a language of purdah, dangerous sexuality, or virginal purity, was not used in the skit, the patriarchal concerns are clear, as it is the daughter, not the son, who is at risk and in need of protection outside of the home in a non-Indian environment. This skit intelligently reveals the struggles of second-generation women who are raised with vestiges of patriarchal traditions that are tied to images of nation. The young women, embodying the Indian identity, are perceived to be in need of protection in an immigrant context. Great demands are placed on their behavior as they are expected to uphold family values and to follow their mothers' example, focusing their attention and energies on the home and on the family. If they do not wish to do so, and they express other interests, they are subject to interrogation, and their identity as good Indian daughters is called into question. As seen in the story of Raj and Rani discussed earlier, second-generation culture and identity is often tied to reproductions of such gender inequalities. However, through skits such as this, as well as through formal organizations and informal relationships, many young Indian Americans also actively challenge these constructions.

CONCLUSION

The culture and ethnic identity of second-generation Indian Americans, like all cultures and identities, are created through interactive performance.

In these cultural programs, this performance is much more visible and self-conscious. However, these programs are only part of second-generation performances of culture and identity that occur for a variety of audiences in a variety of contexts. The primary significance of the cultural programs for the second generation perhaps lies in the public nature of this performance to a combination of these audiences. If all goes well with the programs, all audiences are satisfied. Their parents leave the event proud of their Indian children and perhaps more sympathetic to their struggles, their American friends leave more intrigued with their Indian friends, and the second generation leaves impressed by each other and more secure in their own identity. If all goes well, through songs and dances and skits, they have successfully expressed what it means to be a second-generation Indian American, and in doing so have created a distinctly second-generation Indian American culture. Through these programs we can see ethnicity as described by Fischer, as not "simply a matter of group process (support systems), nor a matter of transition (assimilation), nor a matter of straight-forward transmission from generation to generation (socialization)," but as a search for identity, an "effort of self-definition" (197). We see second-generation Indian Americans using these performances as a way to explore the contours of their experience, to define themselves, largely through references to and negotiations of Indian culture, but experienced through and in relation to an American context. These references to Indian culture are both essentialized and hybrid, revealing the complexity of the culture created by the second generation, and the complexity of their identification with India. As Maira writes, "The experiences of Indian American youth call for a theory of identity in cultural practice that transcends old binaries of essentialization and hybridity, while still being able to encompass both possibilities as aspects of the lived realities of social actors" (195).

As a result of this complexity, the culture and identity created through these cultural programs are not likely to be fixed. Second-generation Indian American culture is a continuing negotiation, a continuing adoption of and resistance to things Indian and things American, both real and imagined. Second-generation culture and identity are likely to continue to change as the context changes both in India and in the US, and with the changing interactions between the two states. Their culture and identity will likely change as the second-generation Indian American population grows, as the India that their parents knew becomes more liberalized, as opportunities for new racial formations and new cultural mixes arise in the US, and for other reasons as well. Some of these possibilities for change were made clear to me when I attended a more recent cultural program while working on this project.

EPILOGUE: INDIA NIGHT 2004

The scene is now a familiar one; a local theater in North Carolina, filled mostly with Indian Americans turning out for the student organization's annual cultural program. The printed guide to the event still celebrates the program as a showcase of "India's cultural traditions and heritage," and asserts that "keeping these Indian traditions alive in the United States illustrates the uniting and harmonizing of these two different cultures." To begin the program, both the Indian and the US national anthems are sung, ritually reasserting the second generation's ties to these dual nationalisms. However, despite these claims of identity and purpose, much seems to have changed over the past few years since I first conducted my research.

The program was still a way for the second generation to create and perform their ethnic identity; however, the cultural references they drew upon were decidedly different. The displays of ethnic identity appeared less concerned with heritage, traditions, and nation, and were more likely to emphasize local identities in the US, popular American media culture, and fusions of Indian and American song and dance. While these references were not entirely absent from the programs I attended in the late nineties, their prevalence in the more recent program was distinct. Students were less likely to draw upon folk dances and movie songs to construct the content of their performances, and were more likely to draw upon break-dancing and American television shows. Students were less likely to state their love for India, and more likely to send shout-outs to themselves and chant the name of their university. In the recent India Night, the boundaries of race, religion, and region became erased not in the dreams of a unified nation, but in the celebration of self, peers, university, and pop culture.

Still, Indian references were by no means entirely absent from the program. The skits that ran through the program drew their humor from familiar Indian American stereotypes and cultural references. However, these were channeled through popular American television shows, such as "Newlyweds," "The Bachelor," and "American Idol." Most notably, throughout the skits there was little portrayal of struggle or of conflict for the second generation. Their negotiation of Indian and American cultures was presented as virtually seamless in the landscape of American television.

An even more dramatic change was the number of performances including hip-hop music, dance, and dress. In drawing on hip-hop, the performers were more directly referencing American, and more specifically Black American, youth culture. These hip-hop song and dance numbers were also often mixed with a *bhangra* style. In the past few years the ever-flexible music of *bhangra* has been successfully reworked by young deejays in the Indian diaspora, giving the music a wider appeal. *Bhangra* dance competitions showcasing blends of American and Indian music and dance have also become an increasingly popular arena for second-generation displays of identity and culture.

The emphasis on hip-hop and American television seems to mark a distinct shift in the cultural references employed by second-generation Indian Americans. Whether this program was an exception or represents more persistent changing identifications among the second generation remains to be seen and deserves further study. However, with the contours of both Indian and American society and culture changing, it is likely that whatever identity and culture second-generation Indian Americans construct, it is likely to continue to be shifting and contested terrain.

NOTES

1. The name "Bollywood" refers to the globally popular productions of the Indian film industry centered in Bombay. The song "I Love My India" is from the 1998 hit movie *Pardes* that located its characters in the diaspora and focused on how middle-class Indians in diaspora struggle to maintain constructions of Indian culture abroad.
2. I use the terms ethnicity or ethnic identity to refer to the various ways in which the people of the world are often identified by others and identify themselves, based on perceptions of difference in nation, religion, culture, race, region, tribe, language, or caste. I am sympathetic to Hall's use of the term which is intended to marginalize or exoticize non-dominant groups, but rather, to suggest that we all speak out of a particular history, culture, place, and experience. Also, as Lisa Lowe reminds us of Asian American subjects, though the same can be said of any subject, one "is never purely and exclusively ethnic, for that subject is always of a particular class, gender, and sexual preference" (32).
3. For a thorough critical review of South Asian American literature see Katrak (1997) and Srikanth (2004).
4. A notable exception is Mukhi's *Doing the Desi Thing: Performing Indianness in New York City*. Her focus is on the South Street Seaport Indian Festival in New York City and does not specifically address the second generation. Maira also discusses these programs, but has given them limited attention (120–26).
5. I borrow "late modernity" from Anthony Giddens as a general term to characterize

our contemporary age and condition. Anthony Giddens and Arjun Appadurai discuss late modernity as being characterized by the increasing dialectical interplay of the local and the global in ways which intersect with the personal.

6. According to the 2000 Census for North Carolina, whites made up 72% of the total population, blacks/African Americans 21.6%, Hispanics/Latinos 4.7%, Asians and Pacific Islanders 1.4%, and Asian Indians 0.3%. For Hispanics/Latinos and Asians, these percentages were a significant increase over the 1990 census, with Hispanics/Latinos making up only 1.2%, Asians and Pacific Islanders 0.8%, and Asian Indians 0.15% of the total population. In 1980, Hispanics/Latinos made up 1%, Asians and Pacific Islanders 0.4%, and Asian Indians 0.08% of the total population. According to the census, there were 26,197 "Asian Indians" living in North Carolina in 2000, and approximately 10,891 living in the study area, making them the largest of all Asian groups. They made up about 1% of the total population in the study area, with a concentration of as much as 3.5% in one town. This is compared with 0.3% statewide, and 0.6% nationwide.

7. Hansen discusses how Hindu nationalists have linked motherhood to nation in similar ways, creating a new "patriotic motherhood."

8. For a vivid description of these performances, see Divakaruni.

9. Maira and Mukhi argue that these more popular or vernacular forms of Indian culture are looked down upon as not being "purely" or "authentically" Indian, but for most second-generation Indian Americans Bollywood film-songs are quite fully Indian.

WORKS CITED

Anderson, Benedict. *Imagined Communities*. London: Verso, 1983.

Appadurai, Arjun. "Global Ethnoscapes, Notes and Queries for a Transnational Anthropology." *Recapturing Anthropology*. Ed. R. Fox. Santa Fe, NM: School of American Research Press, 1989. 191–210.

Appadurai, Arjun. "Fieldwork in the Era of Globalization." *Anthropology and Humanism* 22.1 (1997): 115–18.

Banerji, Sabita, and Gerd Baumann. "Bhangra 1984 – Fusion and Professionalization in a Genre of South Asian Dance Music." *Black Music in Britain: Essays on the Afro-Asian Contribution to Popular Music*. Ed. Paul Oliver. Philadelphia: Open University Press, 1990. 137–52.

Bhattacharjee, Anannya. "The Habit of Ex-Nomination: Nation, Woman, and the Indian Immigrant Bourgeoisie." *Public Culture* 5.1 (1992): 19–44.

Breckenridge, Carol, and Arjun Appadurai. "On Moving Targets." *Public Culture* 2.1 (1989): i–iv.

Chatterjee, Partha. "Colonialism, Nationalism, and Colonialized Women: The Contest in India." *American Ethnologist* 16.4 (1989): 622–33.

DasGupta, Sanyantani, and Shamita Das DasGupta. "Women in Exile: Gender Relations in the Asian Indian Community in the US." *Contours of the Heart, South Asians Map North America*. Eds. S. Maira and R. Srikanth. New York: Asian American Writers Workshop, 1996. 381–400.

Divakaruni, Chitra Banerjee. "The Garba." *Our Feet Walk the Sky: Women of the South Asian Diaspora*. Ed. Women of South Asian Descent Collective. San Francisco: Aunt Lute Books, 1993. 50–51.

Escott, Paul D. "The Special Place of History." *The South for New Southerners*. Eds. P. D. Escott and D. R. Goldfield. Chapel Hill: University of North Carolina Press, 1991. 1–17.

Fischer, Michael M.J. "Ethnicity and the Post-Modern Arts of Memory." *Writing Culture*. Eds. J. Clifford and G. E. Marcus. Berkeley: University of California Press, 1986.

Gibson, Margaret. *Accommodation Without Assimilation: Sikh Immigrants in American High Schools*. Ithaca: Cornell University Press, 1988.

Giddens, Anthony. *Modernity and Self Identity: Self and Society in the Late Modern Age*. Stanford, CA: Stanford University Press, 1991.

Gopinath, Gayatri. "'Bombay, UK, Yuba City': Bhangra Music and the Engendering of Diaspora." *Diaspora* 4.3 (1995): 303–21.

Gupta, Akhil, and James Ferguson. "Beyond Culture: Space, Identity, and the Politics of Difference." *Cultural Anthropology* 7.1 (1992): 6–23.

Gupta, Sangeeta R., ed. *Emerging Voices: South Asian American women redefine self, family, and community*. Walnut Creek, CA: AltaMira Press, 1999.

Hall, Stuart. "Cultural Identity and Diaspora." *Identity: Community, Culture and Difference*. Ed. J. Rutherford. London: Lawrence and Wishart, 1990. 222–37.

Hansen, Thomas Blom. "Controlled Emancipation: Women and Hindu Nationalism." *Ethnicity, Gender and the Subversion of Nationalism*. Eds. F. Wilson and B. F. Frederiksen. London: Frank Cass, 1995. 82–94.

Harvey, David. *The Condition of Postmodernity*. Cambridge, MA: Blackwell, 1989.

Hebdige, Dick. *Subculture: The Meaning of Style*. London: Methuen, 1979.

Katrak, Ketu H. "Body Boundarylands: Locating South Asian Ethnicity in Performance and in Daily Life." *Amerasia Journal* 27.1 (2001): 2–33.

Katrak, Ketu H. "South Asian American Literature." *An Interethnic Companion to Asian American Literature*. Ed. King-Kok Cheung. New York: Cambridge University Press, 1997. 192–218.

Kaur, Ravinder. "Viewing the West through Bollywood: a Celluloid Occident in the Making." *Contemporary South Asia* 11.2 (2002): 199–209.

Leonard, Karen. "The Management of Desire: Sexuality and Marriage for Young South Asian Women in America." *Emerging Voices: South Asian American women redefine self, family, and community*. Ed. S.R. Gupta. Walnut Creek, CA: AltaMira Press, 1999. 107–19.

Lipsitz, George. *Dangerous Crossroads: Popular Music, Postmodernism and the Poetics of Place*. London: Verso, 1994.

Lowe, Lisa. "Heterogeneity, Hybridity, Multiplicity: Marking Asian American Differences." *Diaspora* 1.1 (1991): 24–44.

Maira, Sunaina. "Identity Dub: The Paradoxes of Indian American Youth Subculture (New York Mix)." *Cultural Anthropology* 14.1 (1999): 29–60.

Maira, Sunaina. *Desis in the House: Indian American Youth Culture in New York City*. Philadelphia: Temple University Press, 2002.

Maira, Sunaina, and R. Srikanth, eds. *Contours of the Heart: South Asians Map North America*. New York: Asian American Writers Workshop, 1996.

Melomo, Vincent. *Immigrant Dreams and Second Generation Realities: Indian Americans Negotiating Marriage, Culture and Identity in North Carolina in Late Modernity*. Diss., Binghamton University, SUNY, 2004.

Moffatt, Michael. *Coming of Age in New Jersey*. New Brunswick, NJ: Rutgers University Press, 1989.

Mukhi, Sunita S. *Doing the Desi Thing: Performing Indianness in New York City*. New York: Garland, 1999.

Powell, William S. *North Carolina: Through Four Centuries*. Chapel Hill: University of North Carolina Press, 1989.

Rumbaut, Ruben G., and Alejandro Portes. *Ethnicities: Children of Immigrants in America*. Berkeley: University of California Press, 2001.

Rushdie, Salman. *Midnight's Children*. New York: Knopf, 1980.

Singer, Milton. *When A Great Tradition Modernizes*. New York: Praeger Publishers, 1972.

Srikanth, Rajini. *The World Next Door: South Asian American Literature and the Idea of America*. Philadelphia: Temple University Press, 2004.

Women of South Asian Descent Collective, eds. *Our Feet Walk the Sky: Women of the South Asian Diaspora*. San Francisco: Aunt Lute Books, 1993.

CHAPTER 9

Speaking Outside of the Standard: Local Literature of Hawai'i

Amy N. Nishimura

> What I got instead was a local experience, neither Chinese nor American, not a blending, not an egalitarian "multi-cultural" experience, where all ethnic groups contributed equally, but a complex experience of actively negotiated "bonds of meaning" among a multiplicity of conflicting forces. (Lum 15–16)

In a historical context, Hawaiian Creole English (HCE) is a language constructed out of business and empire – people of various ethnicities developed the language in order to communicate with one another on the plantations.[1] In many ways, the language is a tool that Local people utilize to claim their subjectivity.[2] Alternatively, those who use the language have been stigmatized by the dominant class – those who speak "Standard" or hegemonic English.[3] Because HCE is often stereotyped as "fractured," or "broken," speakers are often left questioning a crucial part of their self-identity: how their speech is perceived by others. Their dual or tri-lingualism has also resulted in a defensive posturing as Local people must validate their identity in circumstances in which the dominant language is privileged. Although historically, educators and administrators have regarded HCE as inferior, what many have overlooked are the ways in which fluency in HCE along with fluency in English has the capability of fostering creativity among people of different backgrounds and cultures. In essence, those who speak Pidgin actually speak two (or more) languages and are able to move within several discourses. By extension, this means they can demonstrate an understanding of one culture in one moment and an understanding of another in the next. As Darrell Lum writes in the epigraph cited above, this ability suggests that a careful negotiation and understanding can be fostered among speakers. In its creation, HCE served as a bridge for different groups, although one cannot see this status as unproblematic, for HCE also encompasses tensions and conflict among its speakers. Also, because it is an orally expressive language, Local people often perform their use of the language along with the use of body language. Thus, the language is demonstrative of expression that is not only intellectual but emotive as well. My discussion focuses on how HCE serves as a resistant tool used by Local people against assimilation, but at the same time, it is a tool that helps make visible the fractured identities that remain on the periphery of hegemonic culture.

In the past two decades, Local writers have drawn strong attention to Local immigrant experience and literature: the tensions involved among a polyethnic community, the stigmas that plague some speakers of Pidgin, the self-hatred and self-mutilation of those who struggle to define their identity, and the influences of popular culture on Locals who feel a desire to resemble pop culture icons. Some texts that illustrate such identities include Lois-Ann Yamanaka's *Wild Meat and the Bully Burgers*, *Blu's Hanging*, and Zamora Linmark's *Rolling the R's*. Lisa Linn Kanae's *Sista Tongue* provides historical and theoretical discussions that prompt readers to reconsider the use of Pidgin. These are only a few representations of Local literature; however, in the interest of discussing fractured identities, education, and language, I will focus on these particular texts.

The recognition of Local literature as a genre arguably began in the 1970s as *The Hawai'i Writers' Quarterly* published excerpts of Local writing. As those in the community have seen, Bamboo Ridge was the first small press to publish Local writing on a regular basis, beginning in 1978 with the first *Best of Bamboo Ridge*, a compilation of pieces.[4] The intent was to publish Local literature of Hawai'i and to show how its contexts made it different from what was, at the time, being studied under the rubric of Asian American literature. Local literature of Hawai'i has often been read as a genre separate from Asian American writing even though the work of many Local writers has been included in various Asian American anthologies. Despite the growing recognition of Local texts, it has been difficult for Asian American scholars to fit Local writers into specific political frameworks – primarily because they may not be familiar with identity politics in Hawai'i.[5] In "Postcolonialism, Nationalism, and the Emergence of Asian/Pacific American Literatures," Stephen Sumida discusses the complications of Local identity because of where it is situated – a group of islands where the people continue to suffer from colonialism. Therefore, even as Local Asians attempt to re-construct their identities in a postcolonial fashion, they are still "inheritors of a colonial history they have not escaped" (278). Sumida argues that because the Local Asian identity emerged out of "the sugar plantations" (277), even though they have been able to construct a literary agency through the use of Pidgin, they were in fact treated as "sub-alterns, not colonialists like the sugar planters" (277). Thus, the argument that Local Asians have constructed a sense of nationalism, a system that assumes they no longer bear the effects of colonialism, rings false. Precisely because they were treated as "othered subjects" and continue to be treated as such in an imperialistic "American" location, it is problematic to suggest that they are presently undaunted by their histories. Providing an example of how Local writers are reconstructing their identities, through a reading of a Lois-Ann Yamanaka poem, Sumida's discussion of HCE's usefulness as a tool to create "agency" for Local Asians suggests that the differences between the two literatures involve history, location, politics, and language. HCE or Pidgin was the fundamental component that Darrell Lum used to define Local literature in the 1970s: "The literature of Local writers has a distinct sensitivity to ethnicity, the environment (in particular that valuable commodity, the land), a sense of personal lineage and family history, and the use of the sound, of the languages, and the vocabulary of island people" (*Local* 4). Lum's writing has often been described as capturing the sound of Local people – more recent authors such as Lois-Ann Yamanaka have contributed to the multivocal sound of Local literature.

LOCAL WRITERS: CONSTRUCTING THEIR OWN PATTERNS

One reason Lois-Ann Yamanaka's *Wild Meat and the Bully Burgers* has received great attention is due to its ability to capture the tension between Local culture and American popular culture. Although the backdrop of the novel is an area that embraces distinct ethnic traditions, languages, and food, the characters are obsessed with images of pop culture. Shirley Temple, Donny Osmond, and Barbie dolls are mentioned repeatedly in the novel. These products bear no likeness to the characters, but they have greater appeal to Locals than the Asian faces they see when they look in the mirror. However, since the face of "Barbie" is perceived as the "norm" or normal, Lovey, one of the characters, and her friends feel alienated from the culture of the "mainland." In this way, Yamanaka comments on the duality and internal struggle that Local people experience both consciously and unconsciously. The desire to connect with Western culture while retaining Local identity is a theme she revisits in her second novel, *Blu's Hanging*. Because their Asian faces are not valued in Western culture, the Local characters in Yamanaka's text are not able to value their identities. Yamanaka comments on American pop culture's lack of ethnic representation through humor; however, the light-hearted references can turn to descriptions of self-destruction as demonstrated in *Saturday Night at the Pahala Theatre*. In *Saturday Night*, Yamanaka's book of poetry, the author introduces readers to an alter-ego, Tita, a Japanese girl who speaks with ferocious rabidity but whose rage indicates anxiety and a lack of self-confidence. While Lovey Nariyoshi begins to play with Barbie dolls and imitates Charlie's Angels, Tita takes the desire to look Caucasian further. In her portrayal of Tita, Yamanaka informs us of the self-destructive behavior of those whose likeness is not represented on television shows or other media. Symptoms that mark Tita's self-destructive patterns include self-degradation, teasing those who speak or act differently, and engaging in violent, "high-risk" behavior. She is a character who targets those who do not perform Local characteristics; she provokes those who do not speak HCE or those who are "well-behaved."

While self-hatred and the feeling of invisibility are consistent themes in the work of Yamanaka, one does not read this as an argument either for or against assimilation. Instead, the author points to the need to reevaluate the colonialist practices that seek to eradicate ethnic culture and language, and she suggests that Hawai'i, through the presence of certain stores (Starbucks, Tiffany's, and Neiman Marcus), demonstrates how the islands continue to suffer from colonialism. As Local people move between different languages, achieving a balance between the dominant discourse and HCE has not always proven successful. Berated for their use of the language, the characters in *Rolling the R's*, *Blu's Hanging*, and *Wild Meat and the Bully Burgers* cannot embrace the identity that speaks Pidgin and refuses to build an identity based on "Standard" English. However, by calling attention to this, Yamanaka addresses language and development of the "I," and encourages Local people to embrace their histories rather than reject them. The popularity of Yamanaka's novels among Local people is tied to this ability to capture experiences bound to language and identity. Her insistence on using the language is grounded in her awareness that people who live in Hawai'i need literature with which they can identify: "[t]he 'classics' of literature never included anything about Hawaii, much less Hilo or Kaunakakai. Darrell says that until you see yourself in literature, you don't exist. You have to see yourself reflected in what you read. That's how powerful words are . . . And that's why I decided to write in Pidgin" (11). Many scholars and writers agree with Yamanaka's insistence that "we got to" write and read literature written in HCE. Some authors have taken Yamanaka's insistence further. Lee Tonouchi is a scholar, writer, and activist who believes that Local people need to write and read in HCE so they can reclaim their identity rather than be told that their identity should adhere to dominant patterns. Writing out of his sense of activism, he writes his texts, from narrative to dialogue, entirely in HCE, whereas Yamanaka uses HCE primarily for dialogue.

Interviewed in 1999, by Kyle Koza, the "Pidgin Guerilla," aka Tonouchi, argues for schools that would emphasize the use of HCE. His model of education would invite children from the ages of five through eighteen to voice their thoughts in Pidgin; thus, they would be provided a positive environment where their Local identities are encouraged instead of repressed. While his view is more extreme than most who advocate the use of the language, he raises many interesting questions, one of which is why so many Local people speak in "Standard" English when the communities in which they work and socialize support the use of HCE. One could argue that Tonouchi's belief that Local people should always speak the language irrespective of occasion is radical and needs to be more balanced. Local people, despite their geographical and cultural location, are part of a larger community (United States) that enforces and rewards the use of "Standard" English. Furthermore, this issue is not unique to Hawai'i as debates regarding the use of Spanglish or Ebonics raise questions about the necessity to learn hegemonic English versus the necessity to speak the language reflective of one's culture. The Local community continues to define its own subjectivity, and this means experimenting with both frames of dialogue, "Standard" English and HCE, a point to which I will return later.

Although Tonouchi's view is extreme, his belief and intent are similar to that of Yamanaka and other Local writers: Local people, especially children, need to validate their own experiences as they see and feel them. Lisa Linn Kanae's *Sista Tongue* extends the view held by Tonouchi and Yamanaka by addressing the stigmas her brother faced because of his speech impediment. As she discusses the discrimination to which he was subjected, she equates the way he has come to label himself as "handicapped," paralleling his perception of self with the self-perception of those who speak HCE: "Hal had a real speech disorder. The plantation children did not, and yet, they were treated far worse than he. Hal's speech therapist simply wanted to get Hal to talk. The English School System tried to silence Local children. In many instances, they did" (50). Kanae, an editor for '*Ōiwi, A Native Hawaiian Journal*, has written several short stories and teaches at Kapiolani Community College, located on the island of Oahu. She also belongs to the same writing group as Tonouchi. They are friends and colleagues who often challenge one another's beliefs about what Local literature should *sound* like. In a conference on Local literacy in 1999, Kanae claimed that she is able to detect when someone is "faking" his or her linguistic ability to speak HCE. Tonouchi's reply was that because so many variations of the language exist, no one can determine whether or not there is a right or wrong way to speak the language.

Tonouchi's assertion supports the frame for the definition of Local literature: multiple voices that are representative of multiple experiences. Therefore, the different ways the language is represented, either orally or through writing, depend on the individual who is speaking or writing. Tonouchi broaches the fact that languages are complex in origin and history, and, as with many languages, usage and dialect vary from one location to the next, from one generation to the next. He also points out the many variations of HCE, which is used and spoken differently from island to island, city to city, and town to town. The frequent use of HCE is evident in Hilo, a town located on the Big Island, whereas the use of HCE in Honolulu, a city located on the island of Oahu, is often discouraged in favor of "Standard" English.

The language differs not only from a geographical standpoint but it differs from generation to generation. A relative informed the present author that while he lived in Pahala, a rural area on the Big Island, he often used words from different vocabularies. To this day, he uses many of those same words. An example of a sentence he uses frequently is: "oos mala you no stop kau kau my house olu timu?" The words "kau kau" are Hawaiian words for food or meal and the words "olu timu" are actually "all the time" but pronounced with a Japanese accent. A person from Honolulu would probably choose not to use the words "kau kau," "oos mala," or "olu timu." Instead, he or she might say, "You like eat or what?" or "What get for grind?" HCE has become popularized among the newest generation; however, many of them lack historical knowledge of the language. They are unaware of the humiliation that was tied into the language, and many are unaware of how difficult it was for Local authors to publish their work.

LOCAL LINGUISTIC IDENTITY BEGINS

While the most recent generation of Local writers has benefited from the support of fellow writers, workshops, mentors, and teachers, writers like Milton Murayama worked under harsh circumstances, and they did not gain the kind of popularity from which more recent writers have profited. Murayama found it extremely difficult to publish his first novel, *All I Asking for Is My Body*. Told to correct the grammatical flaw in his title, Murayama would not relent and finally published his novel in his garage, under the name Supa Press, named after his dog. In "Hau fo rait pijin: Writing in Hawaiian Creole English," Suzanne Romaine notes that "various publishing houses objected to the title since they regarded it as 'ungrammatical with its missing copula'" (21). Romaine's essay, through her discussion of Murayama's text, situates HCE as a reflection of complex diversities:

> While the book did not break radically from the expected
> conventions for the use of non-standard speech in the English novel
> more generally, it was in fact praised by some critics for reflecting
> the cultural and linguistic diversity of Hawaii through its use of
> language varieties ranging from Standard English to "pidgin." (21)

Despite the difficulties that Murayama encountered, his work is used in various classes that discuss Local literature and/or the Nisei experience in Hawai'i, and it is often heralded as one of the most important novels about the Nisei experience, perhaps because he was able to offer so many different perspectives within one narrative. This is symbolic of the author's ability to construct a novel that discusses not only issues pertaining to assimilation, but, as Stephen Sumida highlights in *A Resource Guide to Asian American Literature,* to issues that relate to "class struggle in relation to race and ethnicity; relationships among members of an immigrant generation and between that generation and the next; education and literacy; vernacular diversity and its functions" (135). Sumida stresses a crucial point about teaching a text like *All I Asking for Is My Body*. As he closes with an abundance of questions for educators to consider so that their students "reach beyond superficial and preconceived responses" (136), he implores educators not to simplify the text's themes.

While it has been thirty years since Murayama published his text (1975) and nearly ten years since Yamanaka published her first novel (1996), attitudes about HCE are still negative. Therefore, even though some time has passed since the movement to recognize HCE began, Yamanaka and other Local writers continue to fight prejudice about the language. In an interview with Yamanaka entitled "Pidgin Politics and Paradise Revisited," Renee Shea points out that discriminating attitudes and exclusionary tactics still affect those with different or marginalized voices. While Yamanaka has gained recognition and her work is published by respected publishing houses, she must still justify her use of HCE: "I am devoted to telling stories the way I have experienced them – cultural identity and linguistic identity being skin and flesh to my body" (Shea 32). In spite of her conviction and credibility, however, her use of language is questioned by one of the most powerful influences in the field of book reviewing. *The New York Times*'s review of *Blu's Hanging* referred to the "sometimes inscrutable stream of pidgin," and other reviewers have called for a glossary (Shea 33).

This veiled bigotry, however, is not exclusive to mainland publishers. Even more disturbing is that Yamanaka must combat prejudice in Hawai'i itself. In the same article where Shea discusses Yamanaka's use of HCE, both Shea and Yamanaka infer that those who have established a middle-class status in Hawai'i have, in the process, adopted a middle-class mentality, which often means striving for and adopting a lifestyle of material comfort. To achieve this, the middle class must lean toward thought and speech patterns that secure opportunity. In Yamanaka's words: "Even the governor came out and said: 'I don't know why teachers are insisting on pidgin in the classroom; their insistence is only going to make this worse.' And he spoke pidgin growing up! I think it's fear. As people move into the middle class, I hear their children saying that they don't talk pidgin" (33). People's fear of repercussions against those who speak HCE is converted, in Yamanaka's text, into fear used as a metaphorical character in some of her work, a three-dimensional character without physical form that attaches itself to Local people. The people who serve as vessels for fear, whether middle-class or working-class, either enforce assimilation or negotiate against it. In *Wild Meat and the Bully Burgers*, Mr Harvey believes that "Standard" English must replace HCE:

No one will want to give you a job. You sound uneducated. You will be looked down upon. You're speaking a low-class form of good Standard English. Continue, and you'll go nowhere in life. Listen, students, I'm telling you the truth like no one else will. Because they don't know how to say it to you. I do. Speak Standard English. DO NOT speak pidgin. You will only be hurting yourselves. (9)

Mr Harvey's insistence that his students speak "Standard" English reflects his own cultural position and his belief in a concrete border between "right" and "wrong." However, by referring to the language as "low-class," the text reveals here that educators like Mr Harvey overlook the fact that while the language has a working-class origin, it is now spoken by middle-class people. Thus, he demonstrates a lack of appreciation for the cultural significance of HCE. Mr Harvey is incapable of understanding that these kids are speaking a language that they learned from their own parents – who learned it from their parents and friends and so on. More disturbing are his feelings of contempt toward those who are not prototypically "American." As Lovey Nariyoshi, the heroine in the novel, responds to Mr Harvey's questions about her future, "When I grow up pretty soon, I going be what I like be and nobody better say nothing about it or I kill um," Mr Harvey's response is a "red-faced, 'OH REALLY,' he says. Not the way you talk. You see, that was terrible. All of you were terrible and we will have to practice and practice our 'Standard' English until we are perfect little Americans" (12). This stream of contempt turns to self-importance as Mr Harvey tells his students that "you need me more than I need you" (12) and that he will also have to "correct" their pronunciation and inflection. While Mr Harvey continues his posturing about the importance of "Standard" English, Lovey, who, on the surface, wears a defiant smile, actually struggles with feelings of shame.

Yamanaka refers to Lovey as a "little weirdo."[6] Chubby and pegged as a slow learner, Lovey is alienated not only from the white world but also from her family and peers. She is ashamed of everyone in her family, ashamed of the "can spinach and tripe stew" (9), ashamed of the car her father drives, the home they live in, and the clothes they wear because "sometimes we have to wear the same pants in the same week and the same shoes until it breaks" (10). She is even ashamed of her grandmother because the habits of her grandmother are alien to her: "Her whole house smells like mothballs, not just in the closets but in every drawer too. And her pots look a million years old with dents all over" (10). Caught between her ethnic heritage and an English class that instructs her to sound and think differently, Lovey sees nothing that resembles the English-speaking world that Mr Harvey preaches about: "And nobody looks or talks like a haole. Or eats like a haole. Nobody says nothing the way Mr Harvey tells us to practice talking in class. Sometimes I secretly wish to be haole" (10). Despite her wish, and despite the hopes of Mr Harvey, Lovey ultimately speaks in her Local tongue. As she thinks about how, at times, she is able to speak "Standard"

English, she also realizes that no matter how hard she concentrates, the words "always sound like home" (13).

Lovey's occasional "wish to be haole" is the by-product of a push-pull effect to negotiate an identity in a place where one must demonstrate ethnic legitimacy (embracing Local food, Local music, language) but strive for "American" principles. Early in the novel, Lovey is pulled to the side that desires "to be haole," and her thoughts parallel the goals of Mr Harvey for his students: that they become "perfect little Americans" who speak "well." Mr Harvey's belief in the phantasmic construction of what is acceptable and what is not is also a by-product of what he has learned.[7] He is after all a product of an educational system that has a history of repressing difference in order to produce a common nation and language. In addition, while he believes that his bellowing and method of humiliation will create products who resemble him, he fails to see that re-production of his image will not ensure a "good education" or a middle-class occupation for his students. The dilemma that his students face extends beyond simply learning another language; their dilemma is also steeped in the difficulty of understanding their identity according to hegemonic standards.

Tied into Mr Harvey's sense of urgency to reproduce students in his image is the issue of race and class. In "Standard English and student bodies: Institutionalizing race and literacy in Hawai'i," Morris Young offers a critical examination of language discrimination in Hawai'i. As he discusses the work of Marie Hara, Milton Murayama, and Lois-Ann Yamanaka, he problematizes questions about Local and "mainland" institutional thinking, arguing that even though some institutional standards are fading "from Hawaii's landscape, their discussions about language and identity remain near the surface" (430). As he discusses Yamanaka's "chubby little weirdo," his arguments further contextualize how "Lovey and her classmates are subjected to pressures of race and class in a situation – schooling and education – that is held up as the promise of American democracy" (428). Perhaps, then, what is "near the surface" or the surface of one's skin is how students like Lovey become targets for racialization by educators like Mr Harvey – who believes he is superior in his thinking and cultural training. Thus, as they are told to adopt American accents, Lovey and her friends are also being instructed to reject their cultural literacy.[8]

In Yamanaka's second novel, *Blu's Hanging*, the writer presents another educator who tries to enforce rules of "Standard" English on HCE speakers. She is a grade school teacher who shares Mr Harvey's feelings of contempt for Local children. However, while Mr Harvey is presented as a non-threatening caricature, spouting loudly to ensure his presence as "authority figure," Miss Owens is loathsome because she takes pleasure in humiliating the Ogata children:

> "Will your father be here soon?" Miss Owens asks without even looking at me.
> "No. Just me."
> "And why is that? Should we reschedule the conference for another day?"
> "No need. I mean, no can. My fadda no can come ever 'cause he gotta work. So he wen' send me for take his place. I here to talk with you about Maisie, then I gotta tell him."
> "Can we get a few ground rules – what's your name again? It seems to have *slipped* my mind."
> "Ivah."
> "Ivah, that's right. Unusual name. Well, dear, we need to speak to each other in standard English for the duration of this conference. I find the pidgin English you children speak to be so limited in its ability to express fully what we need to cover today. Am I clear?" Miss Owens turns her back to me and erases the chalkboard. She mutters something about "the darn lyin recruiter" and a "lousy teacher's cottage in paradise."
> I nod my head. (59–60)

Periodically, as Miss Owens complains about Maisie, Ivah silently questions why this teacher does nothing to help her sister. Her conclusion that Miss Owens takes pleasure in humiliating Maisie has Ivah seething with rage, but she is powerless and remains silent. In part, Ivah's anger toward Miss Owens is rooted in how she, her sister, and her brother are treated – like "low-class uneducated people" who do not understand the implications behind Miss Owens's words. However, Yamanaka, through her narration, makes an important distinction about HCE speakers. Although Ivah is only thirteen years old, Yamanaka suggests that she can be cognizant of Miss Owens's attempt at intimidation. As Miss Owens addresses Ivah without "even looking at her" and forgets Ivah's name, she establishes an artificial control of the situation. However, her attempt is flat and Ivah recognizes this: "She's show. All show. Acting like she's in control. With fists clenched and teeth gritted, I nod my head once. Tammy Owens smells scared, she can smell it herself, so she turns" (62). Reading body language and visual cues is part of the intricate matrix of oral languages, so as Ivah "reads" the actions of Miss Owens, Yamanaka offers evidence of the insights available by way of the defamiliarization offered by HCE.

When Miss Owens suggests that Maisie must be tested for "Special Education," Ivah knows that Maisie's silence is not because of a set of "social, emotional, psychological, and academic problems" (61). Miss Owens fails to recognize this, however, and this marks the inadequacies not only of the educational system but also of the system of language that Miss Owens believes to be superior. A text that contextualizes the prejudicial process that children such as Maisie experienced is Kanae's *Sista Tongue*. In a historical, sociological, linguistic, and narrative account, the author offers an overview and personal perspective on the treatment of Pidgin speakers and those who were labelled "handicapped," "mento," or "dummy":

> My little bradda not mento, so you betta stop teasing him all da time
> jus cuz you tink you can talk more betta dan him. Jus cuz you can go
> one regula-kine school – not da special-kine school whea da teacha
> clamp one rula-looking kine ting on your tongue. Wot? You no
> believe me? I saw yum fo real kine. I promise! I dunno why da teacha
> did dat to him. Jus cuz my litto bradda get hard time fo talk no mean
> he stupid. He no can – was dat word again – arteekcolate? (2)

Kanae, in her recollection of her little brother and the cruelty he endured, makes three important distinctions in her essay. First, she discusses the cultural label that her little brother reproduced for himself well into his late twenties. That is, she concludes that her brother suffered from a speech impediment and was not "handicapped," as many people told him and his family; however, because her brother was labelled by his entire community (friends, family, teachers), he came to believe he was "handicapped." Second, as we saw earlier, Kanae outlines the similarities and differences between labels attached to those who had "real speech disorders" (50) and those who spoke HCE. Her argument is that while those who spoke HCE did not suffer from a learning disability or speech impediment, they were treated as though they did. Discrimination by adults, as demonstrated by those like Miss Owens and Mr Harvey, shaped an inferiority complex with which many second-generation and third-generation immigrants have struggled.

Finally, by writing in HCE, Kanae reinforces an artistic and political resistance with which she and other Local writers are experimenting in their writing. The Local literature that she and fellow writers have produced helps heal "the inferiority complexes and self-loathing that was created by cultural elitists" (54). Therefore, as Local people read literature written in HCE, the language solidifies not only the manner in which they speak, but it reminds them that their experiences are valid, not unusual or abnormal. Furthermore, the literature not only affirms Local experience but calls attention to the different ways in which Local authors use HCE. Because the language does not adhere to a specific set of standards, writers are able to create their own nuances of the language. As seen above, Kanae's own writing demonstrates a natural rhythm and poetic quality.

Local poets and Local poetics are discussed by Rob Wilson who argues that Local writers are experimenting with language.[9] He describes the ways that writers such as Joe Balaz, Albert Saijo, Juliana Spahr, and Joseph Kinsella are experimenting with conventional boundaries: they might write in capital letters only, they might not write uniform paragraphs, and they might not use any punctuation in their texts. Also, even though Kanae's use of HCE does not demonstrate an ethnic vocabulary as displayed in the work of other Local writers, her intent still validates the unique form of language and calls attention to its complexity. That is, by choosing not to extract specific words from a given ethnic group or groups, Kanae indirectly argues that to affirm a conventional pattern of HCE is restrictive and ahistorical. Instead, she and other Local writers are shaping their own tapestries of the language, recognizing the importance of choice and difference. As she and other Local writers draw attention to language and education, her work, her reference to her brother, allow people in the community to rethink classroom policies that enforce a rigid "English only" standard.

TENSIONS OF INSIDER/OUTSIDER POLITICS

In contrast to characters like Miss Owens and Mr Harvey are characters who are seemingly well-intentioned. One such educator is Miss Ito – the kind yet aggressive Local Japanese teacher who relates to the Ogata family. Through her sense of compassion, Miss Ito helps Maisie to communicate with others. As she writes Maisie notes and asks the five-year-old simple questions, Maisie begins to break her silence. Even though Maisie's responses are written in HCE and break the rules of "Standard" English, she is not reprimanded for it; in fact, she is encouraged to communicate further. At first, Miss Ito resembles the stereotypical good-natured Asian

American teacher. However, Yamanaka complicates this notion when Miss Ito encounters Miss Owens:

> "You're so condescending, Tammy, it's pathetic. I'm a Jap to you.
> And my friends are all brownies. It's written all over your face every
> minute of every day. I've had to put up with your judgment of us
> and your snide remarks for months now. I'm no dummy, so don't
> you ever talk down to me, you undastand" – Miss Ito's pidgin
> English comes out. (128)

As Miss Ito talks to Tammy Owens with an aggressive tone and defiant posturing, Yamanaka constructs the ugly dichotomy that exists between Locals and those perceived as outsiders. As Miss Ito attacks Miss Owens, she reproduces several constructs of Local insider/outsider dichotomies.

At this point in the text, Yamanaka asserts that speaking in HCE allows Miss Ito and the children to reclaim their subject positions, enabling them to speak on their terms and "talk back" to those who repress rather than make room for their voices. On the surface, her use of HCE enables the Ogata children to speak the language with pride. However, Miss Ito's posturing in front of the children suggests that what she says and the intent behind what she says are commendable, and her actions can be reproduced. The text constructs a situation where the tension between an "insider" and an "outsider" escalates to the point where the children construct very rigid lines as to who their allies are and who their "enemies" are. By extension, vilifying Miss Owens only confirms Ivah's beliefs that she is the enemy, someone who cannot be trusted. The text seems to illustrate the basis for some of the stereotypes that were constructed against those who resemble Miss Owens – those who abused their positions of authority and were then labelled by the community. The ugly encounter between the two teachers contextualizes tensions between "haole" and "Local," academic English versus HCE in a manner that could make Local children reject one for the other.

Where Miss Ito's character is representative of an insider, Mrs Takemoto and Ms Takara in Linmark's *Rolling the R's* are "insiders" because of their non-white characteristics, but they are, paradoxically, treated as outsiders (by the children) because they expect Local children to conform to the expectations of "Standard" English and mainland ideals. They exemplify people who support a middle-class mentality and a set of values or standards that resemble the dominant culture. Mrs Takemoto and Ms Takara are educators who, because of their middle-class values and ideals, believe that Local children must shed their accent.

The intent of teachers like Mrs Takemoto and Ms Takara can be paralleled to ideas expressed in "The Banking Concept of Education" by Paulo Freire. Freire argues that students are often treated like containers that must be filled with specific information like commodities. However, in his opinion, many authority figures fail to recognize that they are not actually providing their students with knowledge that will help them interact and relate to others; rather, the teachers are merely fulfilling expectations of a hegemonic and capitalistic society that tells students to follow the rules, to learn the "correct" methods for speaking and writing, so that they may "grow up" and contribute to the economic machinery where wealth is valued over concepts of humanity. In this sense, people like Mrs Takemoto and Ms Takara are Japanese educators who are regurgitating standards related to hegemony.

In letters that detail the progress of each student, Ms Takara and Mrs Takemoto encourage parents to promote the practice of "Standard" English; thus, they prompt parents to prevent their children from associating with those who speak HCE: "Ms Takara and I also noticed that Mai-Lan constantly talks to Katherine Cruz while instructions are being given. Katherine Cruz only speaks pidgin, and Ms Takara and I think that she is the reason for Mai-Lan's inattentiveness and worsening study habits" (52). Mrs Takemoto and Ms Takara are, like Miss Ito, familiar with the struggles of language acquisition faced by Local children. However, unlike Miss Ito, they believe that there is one "right" language and attempt to leave their connection and understanding to HCE behind them. Like Governor Cayetano, Mrs Takemoto and Ms Takara probably grew up speaking HCE, but given their professional status and accomplishments, they believe it is not appropriate to speak the language in the classroom.

Linmark's portrayal of two Asian American educators who are kind on a superficial level provides a new perspective when considering the effects of assimilation. In Linmark's portrayal of Mrs Takemoto and Ms Takara, their beliefs or lack of them are not easily spotted. Ms Takara is regarded as young and "beautiful" (48), and most of her students believe in her good intentions. However, not all of the students believe she is actually concerned about their progress or education: "Florante thinks that Ms Takara is two-faced. A Japanese and an American wrestling in one mind" (48). While Yamanaka has provided portrayals that detail tensions between elitist thinking and rebellious practice, Linmark offers a different perspective on identity politics in Hawai'i through his portrayal of Ms Takara. Commenting on her Japanese and American mind, he suggests that she has accepted dominant patterns of thinking and has repressed her Local identity.

The dangers and proliferation of the model minority myth and how it is enacted by those like Ms Takara are potentially more frightening than hundreds of teachers like Miss Owens. Asians have been historically portrayed as the hard-working, studious, and obedient group that will amiably fit into American culture. Sometimes the myth influences those Asian Americans who believe they have acquired the right tools and insist that instilling them in others will prove valuable to people, especially children, who are culturally *like them*. In this context, then, Ms Takara is re-creating herself in the master's likeness and feels assured that she will be successful. Also, Ms Takara naively believes that she can help young children with their struggle of duality by helping them wear two faces – suggesting that the two cultures provide masks that are easily taken on and off. Finally, what is most frightening about Ms Takara is her muted denial of her own culture and her power to reproduce that denial in others. In the minds of her students, Ms Takara is an Asian American who conforms and fully assimilates into American culture. As a result, she helps perpetuate standards that destroy difference.

Linmark and Yamanaka comment on Local identity politics as it pertains to Local Asians who reveal their institutional and "mainstream" conditioning. As Local educators, these particular teachers have chosen to continue a historical racial bias against those who do not conform to dominant standards. In many ways, they represent Local Asians who suffer from a particular kind of fracture, perhaps a self-loathing that causes them to mistreat other Local people. This duality is symptomatic of the pressure that Locals feel to implement imperialist structures in order to gain acceptance in the mainstream culture. In *Writing Women's Communities*, Cynthia Franklin offers an engaging perspective about the duality of Local insider/outsider dynamics. As a white English professor at the University of Hawai'i at Manoa, Franklin discusses her pedagogy for teaching freshmen English. Her political and literary agenda involves enabling Pidgin speakers to construct their own agency. In one particular class, toward the end of the term, she had students put together an anthology of their work. As the students voted between various working titles, many of them in HCE, students voted almost unanimously for: "English 100 Is Like a Box of Chocolates" (194). Franklin's vote was one of two opposing voices. She had hoped to provide students with a sense of authority and a subject that mattered to them (195);

however, she discovered that many of them "felt cheated out of an education that would serve as a transport out of Hawai'i" (195). Here is a disturbing example of Local students who enacted not only a form of fracture, but a mentality where place, culture, and Local identity held little value to them. Her students' inability to grasp the importance of what she attempted to impart to them demonstrates how they had been seduced by "mainland" ideals. While they are concerned about their economic mobility, securing a job, the students failed to recognize the opportunity of combining their literary agency along with "Standard" English.

NOTES

1. I use HCE in reference to Hawaiian Creole English, a makeshift language of contact that enabled plantation workers of various backgrounds to communicate with one another, and the language used by second- and third-generation speakers as their native language. The more colloquial term, Pidgin, is used among Locals and Local writers. See Charlene Sato's "Linguistic Inequality in Hawai'i: The Post-Creole Dilemma."

2. Local can be defined as a negotiated privileged position. Locals are privileged because they have achieved economic and social power; at the same time, they must negotiate their identities because they speak two, or more, languages. They weave back and forth between speaking the language they are expected to (Standard English) and the language many of them are comfortable speaking, HCE. A rigid definition of the word is reductive since Locals embody and perform the word in different methods, ranges, and styles. Resisting simplistic definitions allows the community to rethink diversity and inclusion.

3. I place the word Standard in quotations or use the term hegemonic English since an actual "Standard" has never existed. Reflective of a changing culture, the language has changed according to power, class, and privilege.

4. Since its inception in the 1970s, Bamboo Ridge's readership, popularity, and authorship have grown substantially. It is a quarterly journal that has given authors a public space to publish their work. See also Stephen Sumida's *And the View from the Shore* where the author notes that Asian American literature of Hawai'i can be traced back to the 1920s.

5. See Sau-ling Wong's *Reading Asian American Literature: From Necessity to Extravagance.*

6. See Valerie Takahama's interview of Lois-Ann Yamanaka in *The Orange County Register*, "Controversial adventures in 'paradise': bully burgers and pidgin."

7. The phantasmatic provides understanding of the cultural construction of self. Those like Mr Harvey are not blamed in an individual sense since he is repeating what he has learned.

8. See Morris Young's "Standard English and student bodies: Institutionalizing race

and literacy in Hawai'i." The author further connects ideas of race and colonialism to issues of language discrimination.

9. See Rob Wilson's *Pacific Postmodern: From the Sublime to the Devious, Writing the Experimental/Local Pacific in Hawai'i*, in which the author argues that writers are experimenting with Pidgin Poetics:

> What I would claim is that, in such a poet, the postmodern Experimental play of language, identity role, and voice, and the Postmodern Local literature's struggle to express multi-constructed identity, situated history, and embodied poetics of place, can somehow come together, fuse, mix, and merge into something anti-lyrical, Asian/Pacific based, interesting, open, and new. (11)

WORKS CITED

Craig, Dennis R. "The Sociology of Language Learning and Teaching in a Creole Situation." *Language of Inequality*. Eds. Nessa Wolfson and Joan Manes. Berlin: Walter de Gruyter & Co., 1985. 272–83.

Franklin, Cynthia. *Writing Women's Communities*. Madison: University of Wisconsin Press, 1997.

Freire, Paulo. "The Banking Concept of Education." *Ways of Reading*. Eds. David Bartholomae and Anthony Petrosky. Boston: St. Martin's Press, 1996. 211–26.

Kanae, Lisa Linn. *Sista Tongue*. Honolulu: Tinfish Press, 2001.

Linmark, Zamora. *Rolling the R's*. New York: Kaya Production, 1995.

Lum, Darrell H.Y. "Fourscore and Seven Years Ago." *Growing Up Local: An Anthology of Poetry and Prose from Hawaii*. Eds. Eric Chock, James R. Harstad, Darrell H.Y. Lum, and Bill Teter. Honolulu: Bamboo Ridge Press, 1998. 63–70.

Lum, Darrell H.Y. *Local Genealogy: "What School You Went?" Stories From a Pidgin Culture*. Diss., University of Hawaii, 1997.

Murayama, Milton. *All I Asking for Is My Body*. Honolulu: University of Hawaii Press, 1988.

Romaine, Suzanne. "Hawai'i Creole English as a literary language." *Language in Society* 23 (1994): 527–54.

Romaine, Suzanne. "Hau fo rait pijin: Writing in Hawai'i Creole English." *English Today* 10 (1994): 20–24.

Sato, Charlene J. "Linguistic Inequality in Hawaii: The Post-Creole Dilemma." *Language of Inequality*. Eds. Nessa Wolfson and Joan Manes. Berlin: Walter de Gruyter & Co., 1985. 255–71.

Shea, Renee. "Pidgin Politics and Paradise Revised." *Poets and Writers Magazine* 26.5 (September/October 1998): 32–39.

Sumida, Stephen H. *And the View from the Shore: Literary Traditions of Hawaii*. Seattle: University of Washington Press, 1991.

Sumida, Stephen H. "Postcolonialism, Nationalism, and the Emergence of Asian/Pacific American Literatures." *An Interethnic Companion to Asian American Literature*. Ed. King-Kok Cheung. Cambridge: Cambridge University Press, 1997. 274–88.

Sumida, Stephen H. *"All I Asking for Is My Body*, by Milton Murayama." *A Resource Guide to Asian American Literature*. Eds. Sau-ling Cynthia Wong and Stephen H. Sumida. New York: MLA, 2001. 130–39.

Takahama, Valerie. "Controversial Adventures in 'paradise': bully burgers and pidgin." *The Orange County Register*, 15 February 1996: E1.

Tonouchi, Lee A. "Pidgin Guerilla: An Interview with Lee A. Tonouchi," by Kyle Koza. *Hawaii Review* 53 (1999): 173–80.

Wilson, Rob. *Pacific Postmodern: From the Sublime to the Devious, Writing the Experimental/Local Pacific in Hawaii*. Honolulu: Tinfish Press, 2000.

Wong, Sau-ling Cynthia. *Reading Asian American Literature: From Necessity to Extravagance*. Princeton, NJ: Princeton University Press, 1993.

Yamanaka, Lois-Ann. *Blu's Hanging*. New York: Avon Books, 1997.

Yamanaka, Lois-Ann. *Wild Meat and the Bully Burgers*. New York: Farrar, Straus, and Giroux, 1996.

Yamanaka, Lois-Ann. *Saturday Night at the Pahala Theatre*. Honolulu: Bamboo Ridge Press, 1993.

Young, Morris. "Standard English and student bodies: Institutionalizing race and literacy in Hawai'i." *College English* 64 (2002): 405–31.

CHAPTER 10

Staging Heterogeneity: Contemporary Asian American Drama

Christiane Schlote

I learned to make my mind large, as the universe is large, so that
there is room for paradoxes. (Maxine Hong Kingston)[1]

In a lively conversation that took place in New York in the early 1990s, the
musician, artist, and critic Fred Ho was adamant in pointing out that
Asian American drama and Asian American culture in general were by no
means limited to the visions of those Asian American artists whose works
happened to be in the public limelight at the time and which thereupon
eventually entered academic critical debates.[2] Instead, he insisted, these
works should be seen within the larger context of an Asian and Asian
American folk and art tradition, directly linked to Asian American community life. What Ho was referring to, among other issues, was a certain class
phenomenon which, in the field of Asian American drama, resulted in an
overwhelming number of plays dealing with personal identity crises and
only a few addressing a broader and more consciously historico-political
canvas. In a foreword to the anthology *But Still, Like Air, I'll Rise* edited by
Velina Hasu Houston, Roberta Uno, a veteran theater practitioner and one
of the foremost pioneers in producing, collecting, and publishing works by
Asian American women playwrights, emphasizes the issue of visibility with
a similar urgency. Recalling a question from a journalist regarding "major"
Asian American playwrights, whom that journalist defined as "those whose
works have been reviewed in major publications," Uno poignantly asks:
"*Whose* vision determines an Asian American playwright's work as major?
. . . What about those whose work is community-based? . . . while it is
important to look at the individual achievements of specific writers, it is

essential to provide a context for their writing and to look at the major work that has not been validated by the mainstream" (ix–x).

This chapter seeks to address some of the gaps in Asian American drama criticism as identified by Ho and Uno, through examining the staging of communal conflicts and heterogeneous communities in three plays by contemporary Asian American women playwrights. Although Asian American theater and drama has been strongly influenced and shaped by the work and initiative of Asian American women theater artists, it continues to be identified most often with the work of prominent male playwrights such as Frank Chin, Philip Kan Gotanda, and David Henry Hwang. Shifting our view from the highly acclaimed and important plays of these selected few, however, and consciously searching for Asian American plays that address broader public concerns, we find that Asian American women playwrights in particular began early on to investigate intra- and intercommunal conflicts in regard to Asian American and other communities on stage.

As Trinh Min-ha reminds us: "Multiculturalism does not lead us very far if it remains a question of difference only between one culture and another. Differences should also be understood within the same culture . . . To cut across boundaries . . . is to live aloud the malaise of categories."[3] Proceeding from the representation of culture and class differences and confrontations within a group of Japanese American women in Velina Hasu Houston's play *Tea*, moving on to the depiction of intercommunal conflicts between different segments of American society in Elizabeth Wong's documentary-like play *Kimchee and Chitlins* and, finally, examining the repercussions of an international war in Jeannie Barroga's play *Walls*, this chapter will trace the women playwrights' various strategies in staging heterogeneity and – bearing in mind Kingston's words from the above epigraph – in presenting the need to enlarge one's mind for the accommodation of various paradoxes. But we need to first situate the plays within the material and ideological context of Asian American theater and drama history.

LOOKING BACK IN GENDER IN ASIAN AMERICAN THEATER AND DRAMA

In his *History of the Theatre* the theater historian Oscar G. Brockett strongly emphasizes the importance of dramatic literature which feeds on more cultural sources than just the Anglo-American tradition and which is thus often unjustly neglected: "As a result most of us know little about the theat-

rical traditions of the various . . . groups that have contributed to the total-
ity of our cultural heritage."[4] One of the earliest collections on the so-called
ethnic American theater, Maxine Schwartz Seller's *Ethnic Theatre in the
United States* includes chapters on most European American theater traditions (for example, Irish, German, and Polish American theater) and even
on the development of African, Mexican, and Puerto Rican American
theater, but no chapter on the Asian American theater. In her preface Seller
attributes this absence to the lack of scholars working in Chinese and/or
Japanese American theater and drama.

The reason why Asian American theater entered the public limelight late
in comparison with other ethnic groups in the US must not least be sought
in Asian American immigration history. Whereas Hispanic theater had
already flourished north of the Rio Grande before the advent of Anglo-
American theater, Chinese and Japanese migrants arrived in the US much
later. It was almost exactly 300 years after the first documented performance
of Hispanic theater occurred in the US that the first Chinese theater opened
its doors in San Francisco in 1852.[5] Thus, the institutionally enforced
general "invisibility" of Asian Americans was inevitably reflected on
American stages. Misha Berson notes that any kind of theatrical employ-
ment was seen as financially unviable and morally deplorable within the
Asian American community, which is why the performers in the American
Chinese Opera houses were mainly members of guest theater companies
from mainland China.[6]

Moreover, what has remained relatively unknown is that the first Asian
American play was conceived by a woman playwright. *The Submission of
Rose Moy* (1924), written by Ling-Ai Li under the name of Gladys Li,
centers around the story of a Chinese woman who refuses to comply with
an arranged marriage. According to Uno, this first generation of Asian
American women playwrights developed their plays neither on the West
Coast nor on the East Coast but in Hawaii.[7] *The Submission of Rose Moy* premièred in 1928 at the Arthur Andrews Theatre at the University of Hawaii
in Honolulu.[8] It was at the forefront of the emergence of Asian American
drama in which women played an important role across the country. In an
updated version of her classic work *Look Back in Gender: Sexuality and the
Family in Post-War British Drama*, from which I borrowed the title for my
work here, Michelene Wandor writes: "Theatre lags far behind the novel
and poetry in being prepared to accept women giving voice, for reasons that
are related to long-standing gender taboos on public speaking which relate
back to the strictures on women in politics and religion."[9]

In general, Asian American theater artists benefited greatly from the establishment of the first Asian American theater company in 1965, the East West Players in Los Angeles, that paved the way for subsequent Asian American theatre ensembles nationwide.[10] The Chinese American playwright Genny Lim states: "If it hadn't been for the existence of East West Players and the Asian American Theater Company, I don't know if I would have gone ahead and written a play because there would have been no place to have it shown."[11] The unsatisfactory situation for Asian American theater artists eventually led to the establishment of one of the most important Asian American theaters on the East Coast, the Pan Asian Repertory Theater, founded in 1973 by the actress and director Tisa Chang. Nonetheless, Asian American drama had remained a kind of stepchild within the emerging field of Asian American Studies and until the early 1990s, had only been briefly mentioned, if at all, in the context of other critical works.

In the wake of the successful run of David Henry Hwang's Broadway hit *M. Butterfly*, the number of published anthologies of Asian American drama increased and it also began to receive greater critical attention.[12] Due to the initiative and invaluable efforts of Roberta Uno and her collaborators, the status of near-invisibility of the work of Asian American women playwrights has been improved considerably. In 1979 Uno founded the New WORLD Theater at the University of Massachusetts at Amherst, specializing in works by African, Asian, Latina, and Native American playwrights. Most importantly, Uno also initiated the Roberta Uno Asian American Women Playwrights' Script Collection 1942–present, which, apart from the play scripts, also includes photos, playbills, and interviews.[13] Misha Berson's anthology of Asian American plays, *Between Worlds* (1990), was followed by several play collections exclusively devoted to Asian American women playwrights: Houston's *The Politics of Life: Four Plays by Asian American Women* (1993) and Uno's *Unbroken Thread: An Anthology of Plays by Asian American Women* (1993). Works by Asian American women playwrights have also been included in other anthologies: Kathy Perkins and Uno's *Contemporary Plays by Women of Color* (1995), Houston's *But Still, Like Air, I'll Rise: New Asian American Plays* (1997), Brian Nelson's *Asian American Drama: Nine Plays from the Multiethnic Landscape* (1997), Roger Ellis's *Multicultural Theatre II: Contemporary Hispanic, Asian and African-American Plays* (1998), and Alvin Eng's *Tokens? The NYC Asian American Experience on Stage* (1999).[14]

In the introduction to Brian Nelson's anthology, Dorinne Kondo (among many other critics) notes that the term "Asian American" (or the increasingly used "Asian Pacific Americans") denotes "a historically specific, coalitional identity that embraces peoples of Asian origin . . . a strategic alliance, not an inert, monolithic category" and that the "anthological text is a medium particularly well-suited to the contradiction and multiplicities of Asian American identities."[15] As we will see in the following analyses, "the contradiction and multiplicities of Asian American identities" lie at the heart of the representations of internal and external communal conflicts in *Tea*, *Kimchee and Chitlins*, and *Walls*, thus providing us with a broad kaleidoscope of contemporary forms of Asian Americanness.

TEA AND SYMPATHY: INTRA-COMMUNAL CONFLICTS

The title of Houston's play is as deceptive as are its calming connotations. Even audiences not expecting any moderate slices of Asian American life, sweetened by memories of soothing traditional tea ceremonies, might be taken aback by the immediate climax in the opening scene of *Tea*, as we are confronted with Himiko Hamilton committing suicide through "a gunshot followed by a deafening atomic-like explosion" (Prelude 163).[16] This initial image directly links Himiko's personal tragedy – two years before her own suicide she had shot her abusive Anglo-American husband and shortly afterwards suffered the loss of her teenage daughter who was raped and murdered – to one of the twentieth century's greatest atrocities, the bombing of Hiroshima on 6 August 1945. When Himiko's body is found by Chizuye Juarez – one of the five Japanese women characters – Chizuye describes her thus: "there she was, paler and bluer than the sky over Hiroshima that strange August" (i, 169). While Himiko's death initiates and drives the play's narrative, it does so only in conjunction with the broader historico-political background, thereby emphasizing that any of the following experiences, as told and recalled by this group of Japanese women, are to be seen as firmly embedded in and partly caused by their historical context. As Margot Norris explains in reference to literary and filmic accounts of Hiroshima:

> Such openings themselves [beginning at the moment of the flash]
> represent a narrative rupture with significant implications for
> constituting Hiroshima as a historical and moral event, for they
> begin the story in medias res, by confounding the ending of a story

(the dropping of the atomic bomb, the ending of the Second World War) with a beginning (the survivor memoir).[17]

Although Himiko dies, through this narrative strategy Houston directs our gaze towards the survival skills of the other four Japanese women, who emerge not so much as passive victims (for a long time the stereotypical depiction of Asian women in mainstream American culture) but as survivors of various historical and personal tragedies. In that sense Himiko's suicide, particularly following her active part in dealing with her abusive husband, differs from what James Moy describes as the endless "list of suicidal Asian emperors, princesses, and soldiers . . . characters whose final act involved death preferably by their own hands" in early popular American cinema.[18]

Tea received its world première at the Manhattan Theatre Club in New York in October 1987. It is the last part of a trilogy, following *Asa Ga Kimashita* [*Morning Has Broken*] and *American Dream*, which is partly based on the life story of Houston's parents.[19] While the first play is centred around the life of her Japanese mother in Japan and her decision to marry an African American/Native American soldier, the second play charts the couple's arrival in the US and the problems and prejudices they are faced with.[20] Set in 1968, *Tea* departs from the autobiographical framework through a focus on the life of five "war brides": Himiko Hamilton, Chizuye Juarez, Setsuko Banks (whose character is based on Houston's mother), Teruko MacKenzie, and Atsuko Yamamoto, all of whom, after leaving their homeland Japan, settled with their American husbands (of various ethnic descents, as their last names indicate) in Junction City, Kansas, near the army base Fort Riley, and who, on this particular day, have gathered at the house of the deceased Himiko in order to perform a ritual farewell for her.[21] Their stories are partly gleaned from interviews Houston conducted with fifty of the international brides who moved from Japan to Kansas between 1946 and 1960 and who were among roughly 100,000 marriages between Japanese women and American soldiers during the occupation of Japan. As their history has been largely ignored and undocumented, *Tea* (dedicated to "the Japanese women of Kansas") represents Houston's attempt at preserving and staging their stories. As Atsuko puts it: "When we're dead, no one will remember there were Japanese in Kansas" (iv, 193). The urge to save and document one's ancestors' stories has always been of particular importance within the context of immigrant writing and presents part of the nexus between personal and public history. It is what Kondo in reference to Perry Miyake's play *Doughball* calls "an act of collective memory" and what Rosemary Hennessy describes as an essential part of feminist historiography.[22]

The rules of a traditional Japanese tea ceremony provide the structure for the play, divided into a Prelude (Invitation to Tea) and five scenes (The Art of Tea, Selecting Tea, Serving Tea, Cold Tea, Perfect Drinking Temperature). Japanese culture is conveyed synaesthetically through the use of music (traditional Japanese melodies), costumes (kimonos), props (tatami room, pile of zabuton [Japanese sitting cushions]), and food (o-shushi, furoshiki, sashimi, and so on). Yet, according to Houston, this "is not tea in the Japanese ceremonial sense, but the ritual of everyday life."[23] Starting in the opening scene, the stark aesthetics of the Japanese setting and any notion of a harmonious tea ceremony are contrasted with the harsh, tragic and shrill realities of the women's lives as exoticised aliens in the American Midwest and are thus far removed from Frank Chin's rhetoric of "food pornography."[24] From the first image of Himiko removing a pistol from her kimono sleeve, it becomes obvious that the atmosphere in Himiko's house, the play's claustrophobic setting throughout, is just as tumultuous inside the home as the political situation in 1968 outside. An overall surreal notion of time gone out of joint is enforced through Houston's use of realism and its continuous transcendence. The play's setting is representative of the two levels between which the narrative shifts: "a representation of the netherworld (in which time is elastic and the spirit can journey) and a representation of the home of Himiko," and the stage directions explicitly demand that "The reality is distressed" (162), allowing Himiko's spirit – which remains in limbo after her suicide – to wander between the other women and an unspecified sphere.

The women who have gathered at Himiko's house to clean it and have tea together did not do so out of friendship but rather out of duty, as, despite living in close proximity in a small community, they are not friends and have hardly been in contact before. Atsuko, the somewhat hypocritical head of the local Buddhist chapter and one of Himiko's sharpest critics, arrives first at Himiko's house. Atsuko considers Himiko a prostitute and is convinced of her insanity: "Something was not right inside her head. I mean, whoever heard of a Japanese shooting her husband with a rifle?" (i, 172). She despises Himiko's psychological instability while ignoring her situation as a battered wife, and criticizes Chizuye for her assimilated American ways (ii, 174). Instead, Atsuko continues to promote traditional notions of the subservient Japanese. By twice pairing Atsuko in an antagonistic character relationship (with Himiko and then Chizuye), Houston explicitly deconstructs any dreamy notions of communal alliances, regardless of gender, nationality or common experiences:

> ATSUKO: Just because I'm Japanese doesn't mean I have anything to do with her [Himiko's] life.
> . . .
> SETSUKO: Shame, ne! After all, this is a difficult occasion for us: the first time a member of our Japanese community has passed on.
> CHIZ: What "community"?
> HIMIKO: Yes, what community?
> . . .
> ATSUKO: It's obvious we're all from different neighborhoods.
> SETSUKO: But we are all army wives – and we are all Japanese.
> CHIZ: So what? That won't buy us a ticket to Nirvana. (i, 167, 171)

The great differences between their individual personalities are reflected in the way they bow and take their tea, the degree of their assimilation, the choice of their husbands, and the education of their children. Houston further addresses racial prejudices in both American and Japanese society, as well as the limbo-like position not only of Himiko but of all "war brides," who try to negotiate between the Japanese, American, and Asian American facets of their identities.[25] Thus Teruko observes: "Amerikans don't want us. Japanese Amerikans too busy feeling bad themselves. We can't go back to Japan" (iv, 196).[26]

Himiko's suicide, along with the fear it causes in the other four women, finally functions as a catalyst and forces the women to confront their situation, past and future. While the women's biographies are revealed during the course of the play (partly through the perspectives of their husbands and children, who are also impersonated by the five women), they also gradually begin to share their often traumatic experiences and anxieties which mark their life in Kansas. The motif of a family member who commits suicide and whose soul remains restless, thereby acting as a cathartic ghost-like figure for surviving family members and friends, is particularly common in Asian and Latino American fiction and drama.[27] Rick Shiomi's *Uncle Tadao*, a play about a Japanese Canadian family, also features a spiritual character (Tadao) shifting between two different spheres indicated by two stage levels. Drawing on Jacques Derrida's concept of "hauntology" (the study of ghosts and haunting), You-Me Park argues that the use of ghosts within what Park calls "minority women's writings" as "alternative modes of existence" is highly ambiguous, as ghosts only become powerful once they are removed from material life: "Thus when women's culture relies on women ghosts to escape patriarchal orders, it also risks the dangers of infinitely deferring women's empowerment."[28] However, this does not easily apply in Himiko's case, as she already assumed an autonomous status in shooting her husband before her suicide, which in turn was not directly triggered by her husband's but rather by her daughter's violent death. Ilan Stavans, on the other hand, recognizes Ambrose Bierce's definition of a ghost as "the outward and visible sign of an inward fear" as an appropriate description of Hispanic culture, where ghosts, visions, and apparitions play an important part in the negotiation of everyday problems.[29] Similarly, Tadao in Shiomi's play symbolizes George's most intimate fears, but he disappears as soon as George starts talking about his anxieties. Thus, while *Tea* starts with the violent, albeit self-determined, act of Himiko's suicide, it ends with the four women participating in a Buddhist chant, which suggests that their newly-found communication might not only release Himiko's soul from limbo, but even develop into a sort of alternative community for the remaining women, although Houston avoids a definite closure for the play.

What emerges as a true beacon of hope, however, is again drawn from Houston's own experiences as an Amerasian, which is how she describes herself and her own multiracial, multicultural background:

> Even though there were a lot of difficulties growing up, and even though I still face difficulties today because I don't really belong to any one ethnic community, I do think that as an artist it has been an advantage for me . . . because I feel, that I can see the perspective of more than one group.[30]

This utopian vision is reflected in Setsuko's daughter. Perhaps not surprisingly, the otherwise calm Setsuko, whom Chiz ironically calls "a social worker" (iii, 184), proves to be most determined and progressive in her pride of her Amerasian daughter:

> Back home, country papa-san says to me when my first is born, "Bring it here for me to see." He wants to see how ugly she is. But she's pretty, and the Japanese crowd and stare. She doesn't look Japanese, they say, and she doesn't look Negro. And I am glad

because I have created something new, something that will look new
and think new.[31]

URBAN TURF WARS: INTER-COMMUNAL CONFLICTS

While *Tea* is marked by haunting documentary details, often composed in
a poetic language, Elizabeth Wong's *Kimchee and Chitlins* utilizes various
dramatic genres and departs from a purely realist mode to stage a specific
incidence of intercommunal conflict and violence.[32] In her "Production
Notes" Wong explains that the "world of the play must be symbolic and
not literal. . . . Multi-layered platforms allow for fluidity of motion and
quick change of locale" (396). She insists on banishing all props (except
for one sign) and employs a black and Korean Chorus in addition to the
nine main characters and numerous smaller parts. *Kimchee and Chitlins*
premièred at the Victory Gardens Theatre in Chicago in 1993. In a
Brechtian manner Wong examines the media representation and distortion of a conflict between Korean Americans and African Americans in
New York City in the early 1990s, and perhaps more importantly, she also
focuses on the way the media are instrumentalized by both groups.[33] In
this particular instance, a Korean store owner (Grocer Key Chun Mak) in
Flatbush is accused by his African American customers for treating them
disrespectfully, culminating in an alleged attack of a Haitian woman,
Matilda Duvet (who has disappeared afterwards), in his store. The play
concentrates on the ensuing boycott of Grocer Mak's store by the black
community and it is set in various locations – newsroom, court, store,
streets – all significant in terms of shaping public opinions. The play's
central figure, Suzie Seeto, an ambitious, thirtyish Chinese American TV
reporter, is assigned to the story and is partly based on Wong's own jour-
nalistic experiences.

True to the spirit of a heroic journey, Seeto's quest for the "truth" behind
the conflict leads her to an ever more confusing array of different versions
of the story, but eventually to a self-discovery and transformation. In his *The
Hero with a Thousand Faces* Joseph Campbell describes the archetypal stages
of these epic journeys as "Departure," "Initiation," and "Return." In the
course of the play Secto transforms from "innocent cub reporter straight out
of J-school" (I, 398) via "one big story" (the coverage of the boycott) to the
much coveted anchor seat. But her way up the career ladder and her path of
gaining historical, cultural, and spiritual knowledge are strewn with obsta-

cles. While the play opens with the black and Korean Chorus narrating Seeto's first encounter (as a child) with an African American man and her fear of "the bogeyman" (I, 398), she later is accused by her boss, the news director Mark Thompson, and then temporarily suspended from her job for being too accommodating to the African American point of view (II, 446) in her reporting. Yet, at first angry about being the token "ethnic issues" reporter (Seeto: "Face it, Mark. It's the only kind of story you ever send me out on. If it's got Asians, Latinos, blacks, Jews, women . . . and/or cute fluffy animals, I'm your man" [I, 400]), her gradual transformation into a more informed and open-minded journalist reflects Wong's own experience: "I always used to blanch when they sent me to do the Vietnamese-arriving-from Vietnam story. I resented it. . . . I didn't make those connections that maybe I could . . . learn a different type of sensitivity."[34]

Wong addresses these entangled issues of racial and national identity politics in the format of a play-within-television news, complete with satirical commercial breaks and televised warnings, as the Black Chorus announces: "Warning! The following may contain material that may not be suited for . . ." (II, 429), before Seeto – in a parody of such classic muckraking accounts as *All the President's Men* – meets the African American activist Reverend Lonnie Olson Carter off the record in a café in the hope of attaining information about Duvet's whereabouts. Reverend Carter embodies a mixture of well-known black New York activists such as Reverend Al Sharpton and Sonny Carson, who played an important role during the Crown Heights Riots in 1991 (dramatized in Anna Deavere Smith's play *Fires in the Mirror: Crown Heights, Brooklyn and Other Identities*), and whom the Chorus describes as "the white man's dream . . . a white man's nightmare" (I, 407). As an experienced actor in the world of New York City race relations Reverend Carter knows how to feed the media. When Suzie overhears some of his demagogic and derogatory remarks about the Korean community during a protest rally, he is only too willing to comply when asked by Seeto to repeat them in front of the camera: "Korean monkeys, go back to Korea!" (I, 406). In terms of political rhetoric, Reverend Carter's direct counterpart, Grocer Mak, emerges as a weak opponent, whose English is rudimentary (Nurse Ruth Betty: "Is that guy speaking English? Sounds like gibberish to me?" [I, 403]) and who still believes in America as a place of equal opportunities: "I came to America to be a businessman. . . . That is my dream" (II, 439). It should be noted, however, that in terms of their male identity, Grocer Mak (who has an affair with a woman in New York while his wife still lives in Korea) comes across as strong and chauvinistic as Reverend Carter.

Wong shows the materialistic aspects of Seeto's and Reverend Carter's respective "missions." When asked by Seeto whether he is participating in the boycott to advance his career as an activist, he counters: "Are you doing this story to advance your career as a journalist?" (II, 434).

Despite this unsavory side of reputed public service, however, Seeto is forced to acknowledge Reverend Carter's talents in mobilizing the masses and in beating mainstream media at their own game. Wong's staging of the African American protagonists (apart from Reverend Carter there are the outspoken Nurse Ruth Betty and the less aggressive Barber James Brown) as the dominant and politically active characters of the play not only reflects vital periods of African American history but also locates it as an essential component of American history. As Reverend Carter puts it at a court hearing: "We rioted back in the 1960s, and we'll riot again. Black America, rise up and have a Boston Tea Party!" (II, 434). On her literary influences Wong says: "In African American literature . . . it's all about protest. It's about asserting the identity against the other . . . So I feel more of an affinity for writers like Langston Hughes . . . rebellious language."[35] The Korean American characters' relative marginality and inexperience in communal politics, on the other hand, mirrors their later arrival and entry into pan-Asian political activism. Like in *Tea*, it is a member of the younger generation, Grocer Mak's niece Soomi Mak, who points towards change: "I made a protest sign . . . just like them. [The sign reads: 'Yellow Is Beautiful'] . . . The teevee will see we mean business too. Don't I catch on fast? I know a protest song too" (II, 437).

At the end of the play, its visionary title remains a chimera. While the combination of a culinary staple of Black soul food *chitlins* (pig intestines) with the Korean cabbage dish *kimchee* (both with a very intense smell) proves a winning recipe with Barber Brown: "I put some of that kimchee into my chitlins, . . . it tasted good . . . cleared up my sinuses. . . . The wonder *food* or the wonder *drug*" (I, 411), it is no panacea for solving the communal conflicts. Moving beyond Houston's exposure of American and Japanese racist attitudes, Wong not only reveals what she calls the "deep-seated racial prejudice which we all have"[36] (Reverend Carter calling Koreans "monkeys," Grocer Mak calling Chinese people stupid), she also emphasizes their strategic use in public discourses, as brought to perfection by Reverend Carter: "A black man in America can never be a racist. To be a racist, you have to have power. And that, I most certainly do not have. I may be bigoted. I may be prejudiced. But I'm not a racist" (II, 431). Seeto, who finds herself caught between both parties and constantly forced to confront her own racial identity, tries to convince her boss that nothing is more important to her than "the race issue" (II, 446). Throughout the play Wong has Seeto collecting and providing contextual information to Thompson and the audience: about the causes of the economic differences between Korean and African Americans, about their respective and often traumatic histories, and so on. Thompson's laconic answer, "We're a news operation, remember? Not a race relations seminar" (II, 446), captures the key problem of accommodating complex issues in minute-long media soundbites.

The play's ending is appropriate in view of its overall reliance on epic theatre devices. With two alternative endings it can be viewed as an inter-textual reference to Luis Valdez's classic agit-prop play, *Zoot Suit*. In the first version, we see Soomi Mak making another sign (read "For Sale") and putting it on the store's door, and Grocer Mak telling his only African American friend Barber Brown: "You stay with your people. I stay with mine" (II, 449). The Chorus informs us, however, "reality is depressing. We would like to offer you a more cheerful solution" (II, 449). Thus we are presented with a second version, in which the relationship between Grocer Mak and Barber Brown continues as the only direct link of communication between the two communities and they leave the stage together for a meal of *kimchee* and *chitlins* after all. Although Seeto succeeds in finding Matilda Duvet, she realizes that talking to her "didn't make one hoot of difference," and Seeto and the audience are left with "her truth, your truth, their truth" (II, 441).

THE WRITING ON THE WALL: REPERCUSSIONS OF AN INTERNATIONAL CONFLICT

In a century dominated by monumental and controversial warfare, debates concerning the purpose and design of memorial architecture commemorating the unparalleled number of victims of some of the twentieth century's bloodiest conflicts have been equally controversial. One of the most notorious controversies grew out of the plans for the now most prominent American war monument, the Vietnam Veterans Memorial in Washington, D.C., dedicated on 13 November 1982. Co-founded by the veteran Jan C. Scruggs, the Vietnam Veterans Memorial Fund organized a competition for the memorial's design. Although the winning design convinced the organizing committee unanimously, the design itself and the background of the designer caused the controversy, which has surrounded the memorial from its very beginnings, to flare up again. The winner, Maya Ying Lin, then a 21-year-old undergraduate architecture student at Yale, had designed a modernistic monument in the form of a V-shaped wall, consisting of polished black granite panels, on which were engraved the names of the 58,000 casualties.[37] Not only did the veterans and others oppose the design because of its allegedly "unheroic" character, they also objected to Lin's age, gender, and Chinese American descent. Eventually – and without Lin's agreement – a flag and a sculpture of three American soldiers were added on one side of the monument. Over time, the memorial has become one of the most visited sites in the US and has been praised by veterans, protesters, and visitors alike.[38]

Jeannie Barroga's *Walls*, premièred at the Asian American Theater Company in San Francisco in April 1989, centers around this debate and its sensitive issues of loss, memory, and national identity.[39] It predates recent works of literary and cultural criticism in Asian American Studies, where critics began to re-evaluate the symbolic and material significance of the controversy and Lin's success.[40] Set between 1982 and 1984 with occasional flashbacks, and in contrast to the literal racket of *Kimchee and Chitlins* and in regard to its contemplative atmosphere, language, and cast of characters, *Walls* more closely resembles the stylized *Tea*. As such it partly succeeds in conveying the unique qualities of the memorial itself, described by one juror as "looks back to death and forward to life" and called by Lin "visual poetry."[41]

Walls was inspired by Jan Scruggs and Joel Swerdlow's book, *To Heal a Nation: The Vietnam Veterans Memorial*, with some of the characters clearly based on accounts from that book. The play opens with a group of people who are as varied as the casts of *Tea* and *Kimchee and Chitlins* and who are on a visit to the memorial with equally varied expectations. The cast of major characters includes Maya Lin, Jan Scruggs, Rich (representing the Vietnam Veteran's Memorial Fund), Tom Carhart, and a Suzie Seeto-like news reporter named Vi. Other characters are Terry (a white veteran), Dave (African American) and his friend Stu (Asian American) who have come to exorcise the ghosts that have been plaguing Stu (suffering from post-traumatic shock syndrome), the African American paraplegic Morris, the white anti-war protester Julie who is looking for the names of two of her fallen former classmates – Dan (Asian American) and Jerry (Anglo-American) – who appear as ghosts in fatigues, and Sarah, an African American nurse who came to look up one of her former colleagues with whom she served.[42] This multiethnic medley of women and men from various backgrounds and different places allows Barroga to present the audience with a multiperspectival view of the war and its aftermath and – in reference to the play's title – to examine the different types of walls separating people. Like Houston's international brides and their families, these characters have been marked for life by their war experiences; affected psychologically and physically (such as the paraplegic Morris); or like the ghost figures of Dan and Jerry who, as an ultimate consequence, lost their lives – euphemistically described as making "the supreme sacrifice" in military terms.[43] In that respect both *Walls* and *Tea* are dramatic analyses of war's repercussions and its gradual traumatic encroachment into everyday life, which Norris describes as follows:

> War invades the home front both at the time of its duration and in
> its aftermath, as veterans carry their wounds and their trauma home
> and infect their families. . . . When the home front became the arena
> of combat in the Second World War, the boundaries that separate
> war and peace became so thoroughly collapsed and confused that
> "total war" takes on a temporal as well as an operational dimension,
> its effects perduring into the future, and into the lives of ensuing
> generations.[44]

Scruggs and Swerdlow have observed that the "people back home had fought about Vietnam while their soldiers fought in Vietnam" and that the experiences and opinions of soldiers and civilians vastly differed.[45] Similar to Houston's and Wong's dramatic strategies, Barroga tries to express this cacophony of voices in the play's episodic structure. As in the other two plays, the collapse of the borders, framing private and public spaces, cannot be contained within a realist format and so Barroga resorts to a discontinuous time frame, flashbacks, a narrator figure, and the use of ghosts. What sometimes makes the play slightly confusing, on the other hand, contributes to its literary reflection of the monument's "message," which Lin has always emphasized to be psychological, not political, by refusing to dictate or privilege any point of view. The conversations and arguments between various constellations of characters throughout the play (the veteran vs. the nurse, the anti-war protester vs. the veteran, Maya Lin vs. the press, and so on) not only echo the question which proved to be the most contentious issue between Lin and the veterans during the planning phase of the monument – the question of who was in control of the memorial – but even more importantly, whose version of the events, whose perspective of the war dominates historical accounts, defines the public collective memory, and shapes the politics of remembrance:

> JULIE: Tell me what was going on? Was I wrong to want my friends
>   alive? Were you wrong to fight? Who's wrong here?
> TERRY: This is a twenty-year-old argument, lady –
> JULIE: Julie! I have a name. You have a name. We can both say them.
>   We're not reading the two of them off some wall either –
>   . . .
> DAN: The war's here, Jerry. It's still going on. (I, vi, 225)

Like *Tea*, *Walls* ends with a meditative gesture, as all characters come together to read the names on the panels until the lights fade. But Barroga leaves it open whether or not Lin's intention succeeds, of creating not a cheerful or happy piece but a place that brings out in people "the realization of loss and a carthartic healing process" (II, xii, 259); it succeeds at least within the confines of a play.

CLANGING NOISES AND SQUEAKY WHEELS

Tea, *Kimchee and Chitlins*, and *Walls* do not belong to the category of conventional immigrant family and Asian American kitchen-sink drama. Rather, they are dramatic experiments in capturing the paradoxes caused by the clash of public and private spheres. By necessity, their choice of topical subject matters entails the danger of didacticism, for example, in the form of embedded "history lessons," which to a certain degree occur in all three plays, and a reliance on the continuing importance of the issues discussed. By personalizing their topics, chosen from the broad canvasses of Asian American, Asian, and American history and politics, however, all three plays manage to examine the macro-level through a micro-level perspective, which, in turn, through its universal character, escapes sinking into irrelevance.

Stan Yogi's classification of Houston's work as postmodern Asian American literature is appropriate in the sense that she (and this also applies to Wong and Barroga) is at pains to point out that "there is no one monolithic Japanese [Asian] American experience."[46] All three plays are marked by the constant exposure of the necessity to maintain the fluidity of one's identity, not least as a means of survival (when Seeto is mistaken for a Korean by a gang of African Americans or when any Asian Americans are attacked during the Vietnam War). Most characters literally become other characters through the playwrights' device of double-casting and are thus – together with the audience – almost forced to adjust their perspectives (the Japanese women play their husbands and children, Seeto plays Duvet, and so on). A heterogeneous perspective is further achieved through a multilingual and multidialectical language (including Japanese, Korean, and Haitian Creole). Although no documentary plays (which are based exclusively on facts), all three plays address highly complex issues through an aesthetic mixture of docudrama (a blend of fact and fiction), social realism, epic theatre devices (directly addressing the audience, narrator figure, and so on), satire, and dream imagery. Their subject matters and stylistic experimentations are obviously marked by an attempt to overcome personal identity politics in favor of broader, material vistas. Houston, Wong, and Barroga foster a transnational perspective which, in the words of Setsuko, "makes us see – just once – beyond our tiny country and our tiny minds" (ii, 181–82). It also makes us realize, as Matilda Duvet tells Suzie Seeto during an interview in Haiti (where Seeto remains obsessed with the Brooklyn conflict and entirely ignorant of the Haitian dictatorship), that "the world is a bigger place than we are" (II, 440). Elizabeth Wong might thus speak for all three playwrights when she writes:

> In my plays I don't struggle so much with identity, as I struggle with the question of how you empower yourself, how do you as a person of color make yourself heard and be effective in the world . . . people always make you invisible. So you have to learn how to be very loud and make a lot of clanging noises. . . . I am trying very hard to be a very squeaky wheel.[47]

NOTES

1. Kingston, *Woman Warrior*, 29.
2. Thanks are due to Wesley Du and Lona Leigh of the Asian American Theater Company in San Francisco.
3. Trinh Minh-ha, *When the Moon*, 107.
4. Brockett, *History of the Theatre*, 714.
5. Hsu and Palubinskas, *Asian American Authors*, 13. The Chinese Opera House in Doyers Street in New York's Chinatown opened in 1893.
6. Berson, *Between Worlds*, x.
7. Frank Chin's *The Chickencoop Chinaman*, which premièred at the American Place Theater in New York in 1972, is often considered to be the first contemporary Asian

American play. While the play was received with mixed reviews, it has had an immense influence on subsequent generations of (particularly male) Asian American playwrights.

8. Perkins and Uno, *Contemporary Plays*, 4–5.

9. Wandor, *Post-War British Drama*, 134.

10. Theatre, just like Asian American literature, criticism, music and fine arts, was, to use Darrell Y. Hamamoto's words, "forged in the crucible of the passionate political struggles and counter-culture practices that attended the new social movements of the 1960s and 1970s." *Countervisions*, 1.

11. Uno, *Unbroken Thread*, 7.

12. *M. Butterfly* ran at the Eugene O'Neill Theatre from 1988 to 1990.

13. As Perkins and Uno note, material on Asian American women playwrights can also be found in the Hawaiian-Pacific Collection of the University of Hawaii and at the archives of the East West Players at the University of California at Los Angeles.

14. Recent Asian American drama criticism includes Josephine Lee, *Performing Asian America: Race and Ethnicity on the Contemporary Stage* (Philadelphia: Temple University Press, 1997); Roberta Uno and Lucy Mae San Pablo Burns, eds., *Color of Theater: Race, Ethnicity and Contemporary Performance* (London: Continuum, 2002), and Karen Shimakawa, *National Abjection: The Asian American Body Onstage* (Durham: Duke University Press, 2002). For an overview of Asian American theater and drama with a focus on New York City, see Schlote, *Bridging Cultures* and "Other Voices."

15. Nelson, *Asian American Drama*, ix, xi. For recent critical explorations of Asian American subjectivities, see Eleanor Ty and Donald C. Goellnicht, eds., *Asian North American Identities: Beyond the Hyphen* (Bloomington, IN: Indiana University Press, 2004); Kandice Chu, *Imagine Otherwise: On Asian Americanist Critique* (Durham: Duke University Press, 2003); Laura Hyun Yi Kang, *Compositional Subjects: Enfiguring Asian/American Women* (Durham: Duke University Press, 2002); Rachel C. Lee, *The Americas of Asian American Literature: Gendered Fictions of Nation and Transnation* (Princeton, NJ: Princeton University Press, 1999), and David Palumbo-Liu, *Asian/American: Historical Crossings of a Racial Frontier* (Stanford, CA: Stanford University Press, 1999). For an extensive bibliography of earlier works, see Cheung, *An Interethnic Companion*, 367–408.

16. The plays are referenced in the following order: Act, Scene, page. No references to Acts are given for *Tea*, as it is structured by Scenes only (including a Prelude). Likewise, no references to Scenes are provided for *Kimchee and Chitlins*, as it includes two Acts but no individual Scenes.

17. Norris, *Writing War*, 175.

18. Moy, *Marginal Sights*, 85–86. In *Kokoro* Houston dramatizes the Japanese concept of *oyako shinju* (parent/child suicide).

19. *Tea* has garnered numerous awards, among them the *Los Angeles Times* and DramaLogue Critics Choice awards, and the prestigious Susan Smith Blackburn Prize designating *Tea* as one of the ten best plays by women worldwide. Houston's other plays include *Kokoro*, *Necessities*, *The Matsuyama Mirror*, *Hula Heart*, *Ikebana*, *Waiting for Tadashi*, and *Shedding the Tiger*, all produced nationwide.

20. Even under more favorable circumstances than those of wartime Japan and post-war US, the subject of international relationships is represented as highly problematic in Asian American cultural expressions, particularly in connection with intergenerational conflicts. In Gotanda's *The Wash*, a young Japanese woman is alienated from her father because of her African American husband, and the heroine of Mina Shum's film *Double Happiness*, the daughter of a Chinese Canadian family, has to move out for dating a Canadian man. In Fae Myenne Ng's novel *Bone*, racial intolerance results in one of the female protagonists committing suicide, when she is forced to give up her Mexican American boyfriend.

21. Houston was born in 1957 in Tokyo and moved to Kansas when she was two years old. Apart from her work as a playwright she has also published poetry and essays and has been teaching courses in Playwriting and Dramatic Literature.

22. Kondo, "The Narrative Production," 110; Hennessy, *Materialist Feminism*, 137.

23. Uno, *Unbroken Thread*, 157.

24. See Wong's analysis in *Reading Asian American Literature*, 55–58.

25. These kinds of ambiguous identity politics are a recurring theme in Asian American writing. One of the earliest examples can be found in Hwang's first play, *FOB*, which focuses on the differences between ABCs (American-born Chinese) and FOBs (Fresh-off-the-Boat immigrants).

26. Whenever the Japanese characters in *Tea* use the word "Amerikan" (or any form of it), it is spelt with a "k" instead of a "c."

27. See, for example, Ng's novel *Bone*, Eduardo Machado's play *Broken Eggs*, and Bina Sharif's play *My Ancestor's House*.

28. Park, "Boundaries of Violence," 164–65.

29. Stavans, *Hispanic Condition*, 116–17.

30. Telephone interview with Velina Hasu Houston, 30 July 1993. Houston also contributed to the issue "no passing zone: the artistic and discursive voices of asian-descent multiracials" of *Amerasia Journal* 23.1 (1997), available at http://www.sscnet.ucla.edu/esp/aasc/aj/aj23_1.html.

31. See iii, 187; Houston's italics.

32. Among Wong's other plays are *Letters to a Student Revolutionary*, *China Doll*, *The Concubine Spy*, and *The Happy Prince*. She was part of the writing team for the ABC sitcom *All-American Girl* and has written several screenplays.

33. For an analysis of this continuous conflict, see Claire Jean Kim, *Bitter Fruit: The Politics of Black-Korean-Conflict in New York City*. New Haven, CT: Yale Universiy Press, 2003.

34. Uno, *Unbroken Thread*, 262.

35. Telephone interview with Elizabeth Wong, 8 July 1993.

36. Uno, *Unbroken Thread*, 265; Uno's emphasis.

37. Freida Lee Mock's and Terry Sanders's documentary film, *Maya Lin: A Strong Clear Vision* (1994), offers a fascinating portrayal of the artist and her work.

38. See Scruggs and Swerdlow, *To Heal a Nation*, for a complete history of the memorial, which also includes the directory of the names that are engraved on the wall. The highly charged emotional nature of the controversy is reflected in the narrative style of Scruggs and Swerdlow's book, sometimes disturbingly so, as one

paragraph on Lin's objections to the Frederick Hart sculpture bears the title "May Lin Attacks" (120).

39. Barroga's other plays include *Eye of the Coconut*, *Talk-Story*, *Rita's Resources*, and *The Bubblegum Killers*. In 1983 Barroga founded the Playwright Forum in Palo Alto, CA, and served as the literary manager of TheatreWorks (Palo Alto) from 1985 to 2003.
40. See, for example, Da Zheng, "'I Will Sing with You Our Song': Cultural Representations of Asian Americans," in M. J. Zaborowska, ed., *Other Americans, Other Americas: The Politics and Poetics of Multiculturalism*. Aarhus: Aarhus University Press, 2000. 163–77.
41. Scruggs and Swerdlow, *To Heal a Nation*, 59, 63.
42. For a recent example of the representation of the Vietnam War through the perspective of a nurse serving in Vietnam, see Sigrid Nunez's novel *For Rouenna*, 2001.
43. Scruggs and Swerdlow, *To Heal a Nation*, 178.
44. Norris, *Writing War*, 32.
45. Scruggs and Swerdlow, *To Heal a Nation*, 71.
46. Yogi, "Japanese American Literature," 147.
47. Telephone interview with Elizabeth Wong, 8 July 1993.

WORKS CITED

Barroga, Jeannie. *Walls*. *Unbroken Thread: An Anthology of Plays by Asian American Women*. Ed. Roberta Uno. Amherst: University of Massachusetts Press, 1993. 201–60.

Berson, Misha, ed. *Between Worlds: Contemporary Asian-American Plays*. New York: Theatre Communications Group, 1990.

Brockett, Oscar G. *History of the Theatre*. Boston: Allyn and Bacon, 1982.

Campbell, Joseph. *The Hero with a Thousand Faces*. Princeton, NJ: Princeton University Press, 1983.

Hamamoto, Darrell Y., and Sandra Liu, eds. *Countervisions: Asian American Film Criticism*. Philadelphia: Temple University Press, 2000.

Hennessy, Rosemary. *Materialist Feminism and the Politics of Discourse*. London: Routledge, 1993.

Houston, Velina Hasu. *Tea*. *Unbroken Thread: An Anthology of Plays by Asian American Women*. Ed. Roberta Uno. Amherst: University of Massachusetts Press, 1993. 155–200.

Hsu, Kai-yu, and Helen Palubinskas, eds. *Asian American Authors*. Boston: Houghton Mifflin, 1972.

Kingston, Maxine Hong. 1976. *The Woman Warrior: Memoirs of a Girlhood Among Ghosts*. New York: Vintage Books, 1989.

Kondo, D. "The Narrative Production of 'Home,' Community, and Political Identity in Asian American Theater." *Displacement, Diaspora, and Geographies of Identity*. Eds. S. Lavie and T. Swedenburg. Durham: Duke University Press, 1996. 97–117.

Moy, James S. *Marginal Sights: Staging the Chinese in America*. Iowa City: University of Iowa Press, 1993.

Nelson, Brian, ed. *Asian American Drama: Nine Plays from the Multiethnic Landscape.* New York: Applause Theatre Book Publishers, 1997.

Norris, Margot. *Writing War in the Twentieth Century.* Charlottesville: University Press of Virginia, 2000.

Park, You-Me. "Boundaries of Violence: Female Migratory Subjects, Political Agency and Postcoloniality." *Body Matters: Feminism, Textuality, Corporeality.* Ed. Avril Horner and Angela Keane. Manchester: Manchester University Press, 2000. 159–69.

Perkins, Kathy, and Roberta Uno, eds. *Contemporary Plays by Women of Color.* London: Routledge, 1995.

Schlote, Christiane. *Bridging Cultures: Latino- und asiatisch-amerikanisches Theater in New York.* Kassel: Reichenberger, 1997.

Schlote, Christiane. "Other Voices: Latino and Asian American Theater and Drama in New York." *Beyond the Mainstream.* Contemporary Drama in English, vol. 4. Ed. P. P. Schnierer. Trier: WVT, 1997. 107–16.

Scruggs, Jan, and Joel Swerdlow. *To Heal a Nation.* New York: Harper & Row, 1985.

Seller, Maxine Schwartz, ed. *Ethnic Theatre in the United States.* Westport, CT: Greenwood Press, 1983.

Stavans, Ilan. *The Hispanic Condition: Reflections on Culture and Identity in America.* New York: HarperCollins, 1995.

Trinh, Min-ha T. *When the Moon Waxes Red: Representation, Gender and Cultural Politics.* London: Routledge, 1991.

Uno, Roberta. Foreword. *But Still, Like Air, I'll Rise: New Asian American Plays.* Ed. Velina Hasu Houston. Philadelphia: Temple University Press, 1997. ix–xi.

Uno, Roberta, ed. *Unbroken Thread: An Anthology of Plays by Asian American Women.* Amherst: University of Massachusetts Press, 1993.

Wandor, Michelene. *Post-War British Drama: Looking Back in Gender.* London: Routledge, 2001.

Wong, Elizabeth. *Kimchee and Chitlins. But Still, Like Air, I'll Rise.* Ed. Velina Hasu Houston. Philadelphia: Temple University Press, 1997. 396–449.

Wong, Sau-ling Cynthia. *Reading Asian American Literature: From Necessity to Extravagance.* Princeton, NJ: Princeton University Press, 1993.

Yogi, Stan. "Japanese American Literature." *An Interethnic Companion to Asian American Literature.* Ed. King-Kok Cheung. Cambridge: Cambridge University Press, 1997. 125–55.

Notes on the Editor and Contributors

Cheng Lok Chua, a native of Singapore domiciled in the United States, is Professor of English at California State University, Fresno. Previously, he taught at the National University of Singapore, University of Michigan, and Moorhead State University (Minnesota). His articles have appeared in *Ethnic Groups* (London), *Massachusetts Review*, *MELUS*, *Revue des Lettres Modernes* (Paris), *Modern Language Quarterly*, and *Symposium*; he co-edited *Tilting the Continent: Southeast Asian American Writing* (2000).

Rocío G. Davis, Associate Professor of American and Postcolonial Literature at the University of Navarre, Spain, is the author of *Transcultural Reinventions: Asian American and Asian Canadian Short-Story Cycles* (2001) and coeditor (with Sämi Ludwig) of *Asian American Literature in the International Context* (2002).

Karen Fang, Assistant Professor of English at the University of Houston, has published numerous articles and reviews.

Guiyou Huang, Professor of English and Director of the University Honors College at Grand Valley State University, Michigan, is the author of *Whitmanism, Imagism, and Modernism in China and America* (1997) and *The Columbia Guide to Asian American Literature* (2005), and editor of *Asian American Autobiographers* (2001), *Asian American Poets* (2002), and *Asian American Short Story Writers* (2003), as well as author of numerous articles and reviews.

Wenxin Li, Assistant Professor of English at Suffolk Community College, SUNY, has published essays in *Paideuma*, *The Image of America in Literature, Media, and Society*, *Asian American Short Story Writers*, and *MELUS*. Currently, he is at work on a book entitled *Racial Maladies: Psychoanalysis, Diaspora, and the Asian American Literary Imagination*.

Vincent H. Melomo, Assistant Professor of Anthropology and Director of the Adventures Program at Peace College in Raleigh, North Carolina, wrote his dissertation on "Immigrant Dreams and Second Generation Realities: Indian Americans Negotiating Marriage, Culture and Identity in North Carolina in Late Modernity."

Amy N. Nishimura wrote her dissertation on "Talking in Pidgin and Silence: Local Writers of Hawai'i" at the University of Oregon. Her teaching and research interests include Asian Pacific American Literature, Native Hawaiian Literature, and Ethnic Literature of the United States. She teaches in the Writing and Rhetoric Program at Stony Brook University.

Gayle K. Sato, Professor of English at Meiji University, Tokyo, Japan, has published extensively on Asian American writers.

Christiane Schlote teaches English and American Studies at Humboldt-Universität zu Berlin, Germany. Her research interests include Postcolonial Studies, Latino and Asian American Studies, and Transnational Literatures. Her publications include *Bridging Cultures: Latino- und asiatisch-amerikanisches Theater und Drama in New York City* (1997), *Multifarious Resistances: Explorations of Space and Gender by South Asian British and South Asian American Women Artists* (in preparation), and *New Beginnings in 20th Century Theatre and Drama*, co-ed. with Peter Zenzinger.

Tamara Silvia Wagner, a Postdoctoral Fellow in the Department of English Language and Literature at the National University of Singapore, has published numerous articles.

Index